RAYNER HEPPENSTALL

The Intellectual Part

BARRIE AND ROCKLIFF

LONDON

First published 1963 by
Barrie & Rockliff (Barrie Books Ltd)
2 Clement's Inn, London WC2

Printed in Great Britain by
Robert Cunningham and Sons Ltd, Alva

I

THERE are two things to be said here about my schooling. One is that it was free and effortless, despite the fact that my father's income never rose much above five pounds a week. The other is that one of my headmasters was a man who is still remembered nationally and perhaps even internationally, though only in chess-playing circles.

A rich, Liberal-nonconformist town, Huddersfield ran its own little welfare state in the 'Twenties. At that time, it will be remembered, the school-leaving age was fourteen. From that age onward, the Huddersfield Education Committee paid my parents to keep me at school. I received, that is to say, a maintenance grant. There may have been a means test, though all the places at Huddersfield College were free. A headmaster's recommendation was also needed, but this was certainly made in cases of no outstanding brilliance.

The headmaster was H. E. Atkins, who, in two phases, had been British chess champion over a period of nine years. I have read at least one chess book in which he is described as having been one of the three greatest names in the history of British chess, and not long ago Harry Golombek was telling me a story about him in Poland as late as 1935. Golombek rates him as the 'strongest' player in all British chess history, putting him above even Staunton.

At school, Mr Atkins was known, inevitably, as Tommy. He was rather tall and extremely thin. His dark, lustrous eyes, often secretly smiling, seemed always averted from the world. He commonly held his left arm in such a position that he was able to tuck its long, narrow, brown hand into the armpit. The dark hair was brushed up in a quiff from a bony forehead of exceptional capacity, and a long moustache drooped over his hollow, dark-complexioned cheeks. His trousers were far too long, and so was the brown overcoat he wore out of doors, a huge and rather dirty grey trilby hat planted squarely upon his bony temples. Golombek remembers him as still dressed like that at the time of the Warsaw visit.

He was said to be a superlative pianist, though for his own pleasure alone. There were stories of parents calling at the school, mistaking him for the caretaker and asking him to show them to the headmaster. Shortly after I left school and went (equally without effort and for nothing) to university, Tommy married a mistress at one of the girls' schools in the town. It was said that he continued to address her as Miss Wilson.

During my last two years at school, I attended his lessons in differential calculus and conic sections. Until then, I had been aware of him mainly as a thin, abstracted voice at morning prayers and as a hush-compelling presence, flitting dreamily, hugging the wall, along the stone corridors or through the playground.

Caning at that school was purely upon the hand. Whatever might have been the attitude of middle-class parents, working and lower-middle-class parents in that area would not have tolerated the infliction upon their sons of those indignities considered normal at public schools. However, caning upon the hand can be very painful, and to maintain a smiling indifference after it may greatly tax one's stoicism and pride. Tommy caned rarely. His wraithlike physical presence and evident shrinking from human contact were understood not to prevent his stroke, when he did cane, from being of a merciless, crippling violence. It so happens that, although I really have a very good memory, I cannot remember whether I was once caned by him or not. I remember that three of us were together in his study in imminent danger of being caned for having cut gymnasium. Two of us did not much care, but the third, a Unitarian parson's son and now a Unitarian parson himself, showed signs of utter desperation. Tommy did not cane him, of that I am certain. I am not certain whether he let us all three off or whether he caned the other boy and myself because we did not mind.

That must have been when I was in IVA. That Tommy caned with vigour, I can believe. Later, when I was at net practice one summer evening, he joined us and, without removing either hat or long overcoat, picked up a bat, with which, his eyes twinkling and not a word spoken, he knocked the best of our bowling all over the place.

I don't think I ever discovered just where he lived, but he owned a smooth-haired fox terrier which sometimes found its way to school. We called this quiet animal Pythagoras. During a demonstration at the blackboard of some difficult theorem, Tommy would hear a faint scratching at the door. He would open the door, admit Pythagoras and return to the blackboard. The dog sat just in front of the first row of desks and, with head on one side, watched his master, right hand delicately holding the chalk, left hand tucked under left armpit, plotting one of those strange elliptical graphs.

The school had a chess club, which met on Monday evenings. I went only once and got no further than learning the moves. Tommy came in. Where a game of some interest was in progress, he stopped, and afterwards made detailed comments and moved the pieces back to where they had been. It is a minor but lasting regret in my life that I missed the free coaching I might have had from a true Master. I did not realise then how rarely in later life I should meet anyone who was really first-rate at anything.

It was a good school, and Huddersfield was a good town to be brought up in. The local boast was that everybody there could either sing or play cricket. A. Eaglefield Hull, a local musicologist with a national reputation (later blighted, alas, by a scandal which led him to suicide), said, at a lecture-recital on Beethoven's violin concerto which I attended (out of school) when I was fifteen, that our music library was the third largest in the world, after Leipzig and Chicago. Certainly it was large, and so were the other libraries.

II

ON the first day of the academic year, the Great Hall at Leeds was set out like a bazaar, the stalls being tables presided over by the heads of departments. One morning at the beginning of October in 1929, I made for a table under the joint presidency of the new Professor of Eng. Lit., F. P. Wilson (he had succeeded Lascelles Abercrombie), and the presently-to-move-on Professor of Eng. Lang., E.V. Gordon. Professor Wilson was a rather large man, with (I should presently discover) the kind of bad limp which requires a surgical boot. He was clean-shaven and plump-lipped and spoke with a beautifully modulated voice. He wore spectacles and a nobly fastidious expression. Professor Gordon was a short, dark Scot, with a closely trimmed moustache and a sarcastic expression. They turned up my Higher School Certificate (equivalent of to-day's A-level G.C.E.) results and shook their heads. I had not done really well in English. Why did I not take a degree in French, in which I had done much better? Or, if I insisted and if Professor Barbier agreed, perhaps I could do English as half of a combined Honours course, to be known as Modern Languages. So I also presented myself at Professor Barbier's stall.

I'd never really thought of anything but English. The order of my interests at the time would be Music, Philosophy, Eng. Lit. and Fr. Lit., with German as a kind of buried interest, since we hadn't had German at school but since the philosophy and the music I was most interested in were German, except when the philosophy was Greek (we also hadn't had Greek at school). I had no French cult, though my French experience to date had been uniformly happy, and my father's principal outlay on education had been in sending me twice to France. The family I had stayed with in Calais the previous year, that of a schoolmaster, had persuaded me that the French could be blissfully human (a conviction not easily ingrained in the

British psyche). I had enjoyed the set Balzac and Romantic poets. I had gone out of my way to procure, and had much liked, the other works of Prosper Mérimée (the set book had been *Colomba*). Yet I had never thought of doing French at the university. Music, I supposed, was out of the question. Philosophy, in this country, is not taught in schools, and it was understood that I should be a schoolmaster.

An advantage, I quickly discovered, of being compelled to do French would be that, in my second year, I should also be compelled to go to a French university. Moreover, one chose one's university. I chose Strasbourg, which gave me Germany as well.

Most of the Huddersfield men commuted. In the train we played cards, or we sang, having among us a fair gift for impromptu harmonisation. Two of my contemporaries sang tenor in a Methodist choir, and I had singing lessons, for which I paid by giving piano lessons to the two small children of a wool merchant. None of us, I fancy, had more than a few shillings pocket money a week. I had five shillings, which I sometimes eked out by skipping lunch in the refectory or by having only vegetable pie and no pudding.

Pushed up against the Pennines and built of local sandstone across the junction of two turbulent rivers, Huddersfield is rather a handsome town, at any rate towards the west and south-west. Emerging from the railway station in Leeds, one shivered on the sunniest morning. In the middle of City Square stood a sooty equestrian statue. There were also bronze nymphs (eight, I think), lifesize, each in one hand holding aloft a lamp, each with the other hand clutching sculptured drapery to her *bas-ventre*. They were big, splendid girls, much decorated in rag week, but it was more than they could do to make the neighbourhood look gay.

In its physical appearance, Leeds has improved over the past thirty years. It is not a beautiful city even now, but it is less depressing merely to look at. It has not grown smaller, however.

Towns up to a certain size continue to reflect the general *ethos* of the territory for miles around. There was not (and, so far as I can see, there still is not) any radical difference between the attitudes and the behaviour of people in a town like Huddersfield and those of people in the rural West Riding. Huddersfield was and is a Yorkshire town in some quite meaningful sense. Leeds, Sheffield, Middlesborough and, I fancy, Hull long ago ceased to be Yorkshire towns in that sense.

It is not specifically for Yorkshireness that I claim merit, but rather for any strong, long-established and widespread local *ethos*. In seaport towns, the destructive alien influences have long been clear. Middlesborough and Hull are in much the same case as Cardiff, Glasgow and Liverpool, or Marseilles. The destruction of local ways of life in a very large inland town has, I imagine, something to do with mere size, though also with a tendency for purely commercial interests to be centred on it. Huddersfield produced the finest cloth in mills that were rather small and paternal, the highly skilled weavers being true craftsmen. Leeds was merely a centre of the rag trade. In Huddersfield, there truly existed something in the nature of what recent theorists of the Left call 'a working-class culture'. This was predominantly musical, but there was also a thriving dialect drama, and there were dialect publications which people actually bought. By contrast, Leeds was cosmopolitan and nondescript. It showed even in the speech of the inhabitants. I suppose that to a southern ear it would seem that people spoke much the same all over the West Riding, but what struck us was an unpleasant flatness and sibilance, a *ts* for every *t*-sound, of much the same kind as one hears in Liverpool.

To see the university as it was then, the imagination must pull down all the currently visible off-white buildings. The Brotherton Library got itself built in my time. I remember the Duke of Kent opening it or perhaps merely laying the foundation stone. It was built round, an architectural feature now lost to view, since other buildings have been squared about it. The main university building (indeed, I think the only other building which had been designed in the first place for university purposes) was that which runs along the north side of University Road and which still contains the Great Hall, differently panelled inside and containing a white grand organ which is new. The porter's lodge was by the foot of those concrete steps, with their curious, Indian-patterned, orange-

and-green-tiled balusters, leading up to the Great Hall. A long row of houses on the south side of University Road was devoted to university purposes, as were a number of pleasanter houses nearby. From a plan, it looks as though what was then the refectory is now devoted to, or has been replaced by a building devoted to, the study of geography. Unlike many 'red-brick' universities (I never heard the expression while I was at one), the original university of Leeds really was built of red brick, which had turned a nasty purple in that atmosphere.

Including the Strasbourg interlude, I was four years at Leeds, three reading for my degree and a fourth in the Dept. of Education, taking Dip. Ed. I quickly got into the way of not working. I can think of several reasons why this was so. For a start, the daily commuting was no help. The train journeys were gregarious and largely given up to various forms of horse-play. If one had stayed up late, catching a train at six minutes to eight in the morning always seemed to leave one a bit short of sleep. If one stayed up in Leeds for a concert or to take a girl out, one got home very late indeed. In fact one stayed up rarely, and so one's life was divided into two parts, of which the Huddersfield part was the more important.

My subject itself set up a division in my mind. I could not take the same interest in its French and its English part at the same time. I was not at all keen on the idea of being a school-master. I wanted to be a poet and a composer. I composed music.[1] I wrote verse. At one point, I took to writing sonnets in French. I read a great deal outside my syllabus. In Huddersfield, I spent a good deal of time at amateur dramatic and operatic rehearsals, playing and singing an absurd variety of parts, Bassanio and Oberon in Shakespeare productions, Bob Acres in *The Rivals*, Dr Daly and Sergeant Merrill in Gilbert and Sullivan.

Much of the syllabus bored me. There was a fair amount of Old French and philology, but that was nothing to the Anglo-Saxon, which even those students who were slanted less to

[1] Indeed, I might claim that the first money I ever earned was for musical composition. At the end of my second year, I won a prize in the 'Mrs Sunderland' competition for a choral setting of 'For death is as deep as the sea' from Swinburne's *Atalanta in Calydon*.

Lang. and more to Lit. had to keep up for three years and take in their finals. In the end, I was *given* a Third. I had evidently got through all right in French, but at the Eng. Lang. oral I saw a gamma minus on one of my papers, and Lascelles Abercrombie, as external examiner in Eng. Lit., had had my prize-essay on Gerard Manley Hopkins thrust under his nose as if to prove to him that I was not a half-wit. He was a wizened little man in a bow-tie. Meeting me afterwards in English House, Bruce Dickins, who had replaced E. V. Gordon as professor of Eng. Lang., chuckled and spluttered and said he had never been able to make up his mind whether I was bone-headed or bone-idle.

He was a nice, plump man who lectured enthusiastically, but all his giggling and spitting had not been able to overcome the repugnance I had conceived for Anglo-Saxon under Gordon. Professor Dickins was married to a daughter of the great Edinburgh scholar, H. J. C. (later Sir Herbert) Grierson and is, I believe, still Elrington and Bosworth professor at Cambridge. Also in Eng. Lang. at the time was Alan S. C. Ross, a thin, spectral figure who meant little to me, since he dealt only with such matters as Old Norse and Old High German, which I was not expected to do. Now a professor at Birmingham, he made, some few years ago, a curious appearance in the *rôle* of *éminence grise* to Miss Nancy Mitford as inventor of the game of U and non-U.

But the Leeds English school at that time was clearly a very strong one altogether. It was not my teachers who bored me. Professor Wilson read poetry beautifully and was marvellously persuasive about Donne, Herbert and Vaughan (less so, to my taste, about Wordsworth). In my second year, there appeared J. I. M. Stewart, a small, pale young lecturer with a wispy moustache and a rocking gait, as though all his life till then he had been hurrying along polished corridors. He is, of course, none other than the fabulous 'Michael Innes', and we have long been friends.

In *Four Absentees*, I describe how, in the autumn of 1935, I wrote to Wilfred Rowland Childe, one of the few Catholics I knew. He was a lecturer in the English Dept., and as a lecturer *he was* boring. At one time, he had enjoyed a great reputation as a poet. He was a dear, kind man, but nobody listened to his lectures. He lectured on Wednesday mornings to a large audience composed of both Hons. and Ordinary students. He lectured sitting down. He read his lectures very quietly, with no gesticulation or other playing to the gallery. The gallery repaid him by getting along quietly with its other work or playing noughts and crosses. If you listened intently, you could make out part of what Childe was saying. It was evidently about Style, and perhaps it was very good. His mouth, when he lectured, was like that of a rabbit nibbling. His shirts were of soft material and brightly coloured, his ties broad and hairy. He wore spectacles. His hair was long. His poems were full of stained glass and, latterly (a modern influence), rows of dots. He was a convert from his university days, when, one understood, he had been a friend of Aldous Huxley's. He once presented me with a volume of his poems, called, I seem to remember, *The Happy Garden*. I liked one poem in it, 'The Lovers Come to the Rood', and it pleases me to remember that, when I was approached about poems of my own, I at least ensured that poem of Childe's a longer life by recommending it to the editor of an earlier '*Penguin*' *Book of Religious Verse*, which has since been replaced.

During our last degree year, those of us who were committed to the Diploma in Education had been made to attend two lectures a week on educational theory, a shocking practice which I hope has now ceased. For me, it was an unwelcome reminder of things to come, a disagreeable foretaste of a world I did not want. Not much at Leeds was snobbishly *chic*, but even there the Dept. of Education seemed a bit outside the pale. At a time when my own (as actors say) 'north-country' accent must have been still very marked, I even recall having snobbish feelings about the accent of one of the lecturers in Education. He turned out, the following year, to be a man of enlightened views and fine intelligence, but I thought his Reading variety of sub-Cockney-genteel low.

The long vacation, in 1932, was cut short by three weeks of school practice at an elementary school on the outskirts of Leeds. I had spent part of that vacation in London, where, during her absence, I was given the run of a flat near King's

Cross belonging to a Labour Party women's organiser with a Huddersfield connection. There was also a girl I had picked up in Hyde Park at Easter, sex having by then reared its delightful if also frequently torturing head. Among the periodicals lying about the Labour Party organiser's flat had been *The Adelphi*, beautifully printed, yellow-covered, whose founder, J. Middleton Murry, had just published a book called *The Necessity of Communism*. During that same vacation, at a bookshop in Charing Cross Road, I had also picked up a copy of a periodical called *The New English Weekly*. In the later part of the vacation, I got out of the Huddersfield public library a book called *Literature and Revolution* by the Trotsky whose photograph I had seen, bearded, bespectacled and gesticulating, in *The Sunday Pictorial* when I was no more than six or seven.

It was a magical book. Under the influence of Nietzsche (also out of the Huddersfield public library), my first Christianising visions had been destroyed, though that fact had not put an end to my attendance at a Wesleyan chapel, where one assorted oneself with the girls one took up on the moors after the service. This was a new vision. A writer in capitalist society, I was oppressed. As a writer, I was nevertheless involved in a historical process which in due course would bring about a new world.

I found it a very satisfactory view. I distinctly remember the afternoon in September when I thought how satisfactory it was. I was in Beaumont Park. The concrete paths were deserted. Gardeners were planting out dahlias, asters and chrysanthemums. The air was already acorn-smelling. I had to begin my school practice on Monday. I looked across the steep valley where the Holme ran. I saw Castle Hill, with the sun already westering to its right. I dedicated myself to the historical process.

Term began. I had school practice on Wednesday and Friday, at a different elementary school in Leeds. The teacher whose class I was then supposed to take over was a delightful fellow, who knew that I hated being there and was quite prepared to carry on and leave me to read in a corner. His class, moreover, contained one enchanting, serious-faced, literal-minded boy who would write you three or four Imagist poems at the drop of a hat, illustrating them, too, so that you should be unable to mistake his meaning. The trouble was that my supervisor looked in at unpredictable times. He was an extraordinarily depressing man, who winter and summer alike wore a drop on the end of his nose.

Meanwhile, I had taken to haunting a dingy basement in Leeds and there helping to duplicate a sheet designed to spread disaffection among the employees at Montague Burton's clothing factory. For some reason, the comrades decided that I had better be known by a pseudonym, and, for no reason that I can think of, the pseudonym I was known by was 'Comrade Shaw'. I conveyed messages to a mill-hand in Marsden, the only sign of a comrade for miles around Huddersfield. It never came out that the book which had impelled me to this course was Trotsky's *Literature and Revolution*. It would have surprised the comrades, and somehow I failed to discover that Trotsky was in disgrace.

I did not really enjoy myself in that basement, and very soon I retreated to the milder political climate of *The Adelphi*. I read *Leaves of Grass* and Edward Carpenter's *Towards Democracy*. I sent poems to *The Adelphi*. One or two were accepted. *The Adelphi* even sent me books for review. I wrote them an article on Carpenter's three stages of consciousness, a view of the historical process which, like some of Murry's own notions, largely anticipated what nowadays is found novel in the work of Teilhard de Chardin.

The New English Weekly also printed my poems, and its editor, A. R. Orage, sent me occasional books to review. *The New English Weekly* did not pay. *The Adelphi* paid a little. I had duty-writing to do, essays for my supervisor and even a thesis, as though the Dip. Ed. had been some kind of higher degree. My subject was *Language and the Development of Concepts*. The psychologist whose views we were expected to adopt was McDougall, but he had said little on this subject, which rather encouraged references to Piaget, whom I found a highly engaging writer, and permitted reference to the works of I. A. Richards, whose *Practical Criticism* (with C. K. Ogden) and *Principles of Literary Criticism* were then fashionable and who must have felt somewhat chagrined to see the American adoption of his ideas and practice described twenty years later as the New Criticism. I met Dr Richards at the *salon* Professor and Mrs Wilson held for him after a lecture in the course of which he had beautifully read Hopkins's *The Windhover* with circular planings of the hand and D. H. Lawrence's *The Donkey* with real brayings.

I received my Dip. Ed. in June 1933. That day, Herbert Read, who had been an undergraduate at Leeds for two years before the Kaiser's war, came for an honorary D.Litt. Apart from Childe, the only known poet I had seen till then was Walter de la Mare, who had lectured to the Literary and Historical Society in the Great Hall during my first term, almost four years before. He was short and quite unimpressive, with a red, bossy nose. I had decided that he looked like a barman, though at the time I had no wide experience of barmen. He had, I was told, made himself unpopular with the authorities, after the visit, with a letter about his expenses, though I did not gather whether he had demanded too much or was held not to be entitled to expenses at all.

Read was a more immediately attractive figure than either him or Childe. Rather tall, upright, neatly dressed in a navy-blue suit, dark hair yet waving romantically over one temple, he looked, I thought, every inch a *modern* poet. I nevertheless did not think that would be quite my style. At the dance in the Great Hall afterwards, Professor Dickins had him in tow. He introduced us just as I was dashing off to catch the last train to Huddersfield.

There was a scarcity of teaching jobs in those days. I was six months at home, filling in several application forms a week. Sir Richard Rees, the editor and financial backer of *The Adelphi*, put to J. Middleton Murry a suggestion I had made in a letter (I did not yet know Rees personally) that I should write a book on Murry. Murry fixed this with his own publisher, Jonathan Cape. I got a contract without so much as writing a synopsis, Murry having much liked my article on Edward Carpenter.

The Huddersfield public library shows up well here, as elsewhere. I did not know the librarians. I simply went and made my requirements known. Among other things, they got

16

me bound copies of *The Adelphi* back to its inception eleven years before, in 1923. By Christmas, I had written more than one chapter.

Also by Christmas, I had got a job. This was at a senior elementary school (equivalent of to-day's secondary modern) at Dagenham, in Essex. *Harmsworth's Universal Encyclopaedia* described Dagenham as a pleasant old-world market town of ten thousand inhabitants. On my visit there for an interview, I had discovered this to be no longer quite the case. I was to start in January, and to begin with it had been arranged that I should stay with a Huddersfield family which had moved to Hornchurch.

III

I TAUGHT at Dagenham for seven months, then was sacked for an ill-timed bit of absenteeism. It was (though the buildings themselves were first-rate) a tough school by the standards of those days. I dare say that working-class parents have since become more personally demoralised and more idiotic with their children, but the parents of those boys were uprooted people from the depressed areas of Clydeside, Lancashire, South Wales and the East End. That was the original blackboard jungle.

I went back to Huddersfield for three months, until my little book on Murry should be out. Orage had said that one could not hope to get paid reviewing until one had published at least one book of one's own. This seemed to me entirely reasonable. During the past ten or fifteen years, I have often recalled Orage's observation. The influential reviewers during that time have generally been people who either never thought of writing a book or, having once tried, then gave up the attempt. Frequently, one has been led to feel that those who write books are a kind of proletariat toiling on behalf of the far smarter people who review them.

As a matter of fact, I had already got some paid reviewing. This was of novels for *The Yorkshire Post*, whose London office sent me a bundle once every fortnight or so. I owed this to Geoffrey Grigson, then an important figure in my world as editor of *New Verse*.

During those three months back at home, I spent a fortnight with the Innes Stewarts in Leeds. I got the proofs of my little Murry book there.

Innes had begun to toy with the idea of writing a thriller, to be called, he already thought, *Death at the President's Lodging*. The name of his detective was to be John Appleby. This was the name of a younger contemporary of mine who had been editor of the university magazine, *The Gryphon*, during my post-graduate year. Appleby himself has since published detective stories, in which there occurs an Inspector Innes, to say nothing of a Sergeant Rayner. This was retaliation. When the first Innes thrillers appeared, Appleby was indignant at what he considered to be the misappropriation of his name.

At that time, Innes had written little, though he had edited the 'Nonesuch' Florio's Montaigne. To me, he was a somewhat older, and very much more sophisticated, man with whom, and with his wife, I got on and who seemed flatteringly well-disposed towards me. He was a marvellous conversationalist (later, I should discover him to be also a marvellous correspondent). He had spent some time in Vienna and made amusing use of the views of Freud and Jung.

I knew a little about both. I had had Freud's *Psychopathology of Everyday Life* out of the public library and read a popular exposition of his views by Ernest Jones, between school and university, in 1929, and certainly I had picked up the term 'inferiority complex' while at school. I do not think I had yet read any Jung, though I had read about him in *The Adelphi*, which preferred him because he placed less emphasis upon sex and seemed to lay the way open to religion of a vague, evolving, Bergsonian type, *his* Unconscious being larger and more diffuse, his Libido not necessarily libidinous. I am not sure, but I fancy I had not yet picked up, in London, the terms 'extravert' and 'introvert' or that I had not understood them to be Jung's. I saw him as a bit of a mystagogue.

It appeared that he, too, had his amusing side. There were, for instance, his delightful cases of split personality, notably that of the lady who knitted endless garments which her *alter ego* unravelled. I also understood 'fixations in the *flatus* type of anal erotism' to be a notion of Jung's, though in retrospect I am inclined to wonder if it can have been so. As an Eng. Lit. man, Innes used the notion to characterise those of his colleagues who were philologists and thus concerned rather with the sound of words than with their meaning. I do not remember him using it to characterise musicians, possibly because I was musical, but Innes himself was markedly non-musical, and the idea (of seeking gratification through breaking wind) fits musicians perhaps even better than philologists.

Certainly, Innes's conversation was eclectic. It must, for instance, have been rather with reference to Freud that he described Wilfred Rowland Childe as having a 'castration complex'. It appeared that Childe would always become agitated if blood or mutilation were mentioned. There was also his long hair, the idea being that, if you wore your hair long, people would think you were a woman and not attack you in that way.

It was at the Stewarts' that year that I read Yeats's thin prose volume, *Per Amica Silentia Lunae*. It is only more recently that I have seen how much of the later Jungianism there is *ante litteram* not only in that volume and in *The Vision* but in Yeats's verse. It was, I should discover, precisely 'like a great image out of *Spiritus Mundi*' that Jung's archetypes were said in dreams and some other states and experiences to present themselves to the individual consciousness. Both Innes and I were struck on Yeats at the time. Over the washing up, he and I recited together poems from Yeats's *Words for Music Perhaps*, which we both knew by heart. The 'mist and snow' one later provided him with the title and theme of a thriller, which I read some eight years later in the army.

My last sight of Leeds university buildings, inside or out, for twenty-seven years, was when T. S. Eliot lectured, that October, in the Great Hall. I do not recall the ostensible subject of Mr Eliot's lecture, but its argument seemed to be that, while social distractions might be all very well, when a man was alone he needed God. Quite early on in the lecture, the water in the radiators began to boil. By the end, Mr Eliot was talking gallantly but desperately against an uninterrupted barrage of bubblings and thumps.

I believe the boilerman was sacked afterwards, as he perhaps deserved to be, though at the time I should have taken his side. Within a month or so, I had met Mr Eliot at a *Criterion* party to which I was taken by Herbert Read on the evening of my return to London. I had installed myself in Chelsea, in what is now Chelsea Square. It was then called Trafalgar Square. However, during the years which followed, I was rarely to be found at the same address for more than a month or two.

IV

A. R. ORAGE died in November 1934, a few days after I had gone back to London definitively. I wrote often for *The New English Weekly*. It was foolish of me no doubt. Contributors were not paid, and, if anybody needed paying I did. However, one thought of one's writing as a vocation, and *The New English Weekly* allowed one to write much as one pleased. Its politics were Social Credit, about which I knew very little.

When Orage died, the paper was taken over by his former assistant, Philip Mairet, a man of great sweetness and no little intellectual distinction, but afflicted with a bad stammer. I first met him the day Orage's death was announced. He gulped, as I then imagined, from grief, for that day tears coursed freely down craggy cheeks. Later, I discovered that dear Philip gulped even when he was happy. In mid-speech, the muscles of his throat collapsed, and sometimes he emitted a distinct quack. After a few swallows, he would abandon the sentence on which he had come to grief and begin a new one. Physically, he was not impressive. Orage had been a big, dark, shambling bear of a man, with a hypnotic eye. Mairet was small, and the lenses of his spectacles were thick.

Later, Philip Mairet turned Anglo-Catholic. In early 1935, he was still an Adlerian. I heard him lecture to an Adler[1] group. He had also studied and commented on that other exponent of

[1] Alfred Adler, 1870-1937. I ought perhaps to say here that, even in those days, he seemed a bit less smart than either Freud or Jung. For him, primacy lay with the power urge, and I fancy that 'inferiority complex' was in the first place his term, not Freud's. I suppose that the term 'masculine protest' (sometimes more crudely known as 'penis envy') must have been one of Jung's, since it ties in with his view that we all have our feminine side, our *anima*, and that the ladies of our acquaintance may be expected to display more or less of a masculine *animus*. However, I first heard the expression used by Mairet in his lecture and so assumed it was Adler's.

the positive attitude, Nietzsche. More recently, he has translated Sartre.

Under the new editorship, *New English Weekly* contributors met on Monday evenings at the Silver Buffet, a long bar in the famous Holborn Restaurant, since pulled down. I commonly went along with a friend of my own generation, Michael Sayers, who had been made drama critic. Invariably there with Mairet was the chief political columnist, a Yorkshireman with a broken nose and a tear always glistening wet in his eye-corner. There were at first only the four of us on a date which must have been February 11th, 1935.

Mairet and the political columnist were perched on tall, padded, red-rexine-covered, chromium-plated-tubing-legged stools. The two stools between them bore their brief-cases. In the political columnist's hand were galley proofs. Mairet was dealing with the white-coated barman at the black-glass counter.

When he had paid for the half-pints of bitter ale in pewter tankards, he rooted in his brief-case for theatre tickets.

'There's not much this week, I'm afraid,' he said. 'There's something at the Embassy on Thursday and *Major Barbara* at the Old Vic next week. Oh, yes, and at . . .'

His speech-mechanism failed him, and, swallowing as though a large and lively fish had slipped down whole, he thrust at Michael Sayers a slip of paper admitting two persons to the Duchess Theatre for a performance by the Marie Rambert ballet company, which normally confined its activities to a little theatre of its own at Notting Hill Gate, the Mercury, which in the winter months is visible from the windows of the fourth-floor flat I live in nowadays.

'They're having a West End season for three weeks,' Mairet, now recovering, explained. 'I don't know whether it's quite in your line, Michael.'

And that is how I came to take up ballet criticism. For it was not in Michael's line, and indeed he refused to go to the Duchess that evening until I had said that I would do a short note.

Michael and I at that time still had rooms in Trafalgar Square, Chelsea. Shortly afterwards, we moved to Kilburn. Michael

22

was usually not there. He normally slept at the house of his parents, a Dublin-Jewish family of some wealth who lived not far away. I sometimes had no food. On the other hand, I possessed a dinner jacket and in due course was commonly to be observed drinking whisky in press representatives' rooms on ballet first nights and familiarly greeting leading *balletomanes* and the dancers themselves.

Whatever else I may have to reproach myself with, I have always been thorough about what I did. In those days, I commonly spent my mornings watching classes at ballet schools. More often than anywhere else, I went to Legat's near Baron's Court tube station. Round the corner at St Paul's, cricket practice would be going on at the nets. The clicking of bats and thin cries faded as you entered the house and walked up to the *piano nobile* past the portrait of the late H.I.M. Nicholas II, Tsar of all the Russias.

The advanced class began at eleven o'clock. Usually, when I arrived, Nicholas Legat, with his neat, shaved, ruddy-brown head and his ramrod-straight back inclined at an angle of fifteen degrees to the vertical, would be sprinkling the floor with water from a pale-blue watering can. His feet, as he walked, were turned out with a turning-outward-from-the-hips which few of these young dancers would ever achieve, though with him it was rigid.

In this man, a world ended. The last of the masters of the Russian Imperial Ballet, his own family's connection with that glorious institution had begun a hundred years ago, under the first Petipa, when Ivan and Samuel Legat were rooted out of their private theatres in St Isaac's Square and the Field of Mars. Pavlova, Karsavina, Fokine and Nijinsky had all been his pupils. When the de Basil company came to London in June, some of its stars would come here for lessons. There would be, for instance, André Eglevsky, with his wonderful slow pirouettes.

At one end of the big studio, rows of red-plush tipping chairs had been disposed to either side of the huge, dingily gilt-framed, damp-spotted mirror, which reflected the star pupil, a Jugo-Slav, Anna Roje, at a depth of a yard and a half, and, behind her, others and parts of others in practice dress of black or pink tights and various tops, their heads diversely bound. I always tried to get the seat nearest the long-tailed piano. The others would be occupied by ballet mothers, a distinct family of the human species, or by favoured visitors, one famous *grande dame* among whom[1] was familiar enough with this world to expect that all the men in sight would be White Russians and that, at her departure, they would therefore rise to their feet, click their heels and kiss her hand, an expectation I did my best not to disappoint.

Legat himself played the piano. As he gave out the instructions for a new *enchaînement*, his fingers would dance it on the piano top. Every now and then, he left the piano and walked across the floor to correct by touch the line of an arm, the tension of a knee, a hip-bone insufficiently pulled in.

There was some use of the voice. To a Russian pupil fluent instructions might be called, but for the most part there were merely the names of steps in a crude and guttural French. English was reserved for one or two favourite jokes.

Legat would call out, with mock ferocity:

'Strong back! Not spaghetti!'

Each time, he drew himself up like an offended beauty at the piano, then winked at me.

The bar once vacated, the order in which the young women disposed themselves over the available floor-space was subject to protocol. Normally, Anna Roje stood in advance of the front row proper. If, however, there were visiting pupils of a certain public eminence or notorious proficiency, they flanked her, and one or two of the most advanced regular pupils would then feel impelled to move forward and complete the row. The men were always at the back. Sometimes, Kyra Nijinsky would join them, preferring their *enchaînements* to the women's.

The *prima* at the Ballet Club was then Pearl Argyle. She was not quite a first-rate dancer, but she was, I think, the most beautiful woman I have seen. I also went to Mme Rambert's classes, but Pearl Argyle was never there. When she took classes (and she was, I gathered, lazy by that world's standards), she went to Legat's. It was there I got myself introduced and from there I took her out to lunch (she ate, I seem to remember, a lettuce leaf). It cannot have been more than two years later

[1] Margot Asquith.

when Pearl Argyle died in childbirth, having married a Hungarian millionaire. Before that, she had given up serious dancing. She appeared in the film of H. G. Wells's *Things To Come*, dressed in diaphanous plastic garments as chief female representative of a physically perfected younger generation of the future. I was in love with her for a while, though it did not get me anywhere.

I wrote a number of poems about, as it were, the metaphysical significance of Pearl Argyle. The essential point was that the human body, unlike words, sounds, pure form and colour, does not lend itself to the purposes of art. My argument in favour of dancing, as against all other arts, would have been precisely that its material was more recalcitrant to those purposes. This I thought particularly the case with Pearl Argyle, who, unlike most women dancers, seemed to me exceptionally perfect and desirable as a woman. For instance, most good women dancers are rather flat-chested. Though elegantly slender elsewhere, Pearl Argyle, rather markedly, and indeed quite marvellously, was not. Given the importance of the body's centre of gravity in dancing, this fact itself may have impeded the development of her technique. It may also have made her apparently lazy. In dancing, fine breasts might, I imagined, constitute a positive affliction.

There were three poems in thirteen-line *terza rima*, which seemed to me a better form than either of the traditional sonnet forms, the break occurring half way through the eighth line. One of them goes as follows:

> So pure a form had not been stressed in stone, ever,
> Nor shook itself out from pipes and strings, but only
> Filmed an eye once, tapped on the ear then, and left
>
> Some blown equation, a blister of thought.
>
> Yet
>
> *look now:*
> *So intricate a substance as her body is*
> *Has made itself a calculus of such purities*
>
> *And they are fluid, they have tension, bright shiftings of poise*
> *So devised that the air must lean to and lock them.*
>
> *This lady*
>
> *Cancels the clotted history of bodies:*

So intricate and pure she is. She makes known
That final request of the flesh, to be made word, being
So intricate and pure in her device

That no words or deeds are able to gloss her first seeming.

This, which appears in my volume *Sebastian*, was reprinted some years later in *The 'Penguin' Anthology of Religious Verse* as a poem in praise of the Blessed Virgin Mary.

By August 1935, I had written about half of the book, *Apology for Dancing*. One Friday morning in that month, I went to Legat's and, in the afternoon, to Covent Garden with a photographer, Howard Coster. At Covent Garden, that afternoon, the de Basil company, with Toumanova, Baronova, Danilova, Riabouchinska, were doing *Firebird*, *Sylphides* and *Les Cent Baisers*. At Legat's in the morning, there was a new pupil, a dark slender girl of fourteen or fifteen in a plum-coloured cardigan and black tights, her hair tied with a scarf also plum-coloured or near it. Those poultry-fanciers, the *balletomanes*, had already noted this child for her Sadler's Wells performance as the young son of the house in *The Haunted Ballroom*. Her name was Margot Fonteyn, her family recently back from China. Fairness compels me to state that, utterly charming as she seemed to me, just how up-and-coming she was had at once become more quickly apparent to Coster, though he was unfamiliar with the ballet world. With him in the afternoon, at Covent Garden, I lurked in the wings, climbed about the balcony, invaded dressing-rooms. Three of the photographs eventually found their way into the book.

V

IN the autumn of 1935, I decided I would become a Catholic and was for some months under instruction to the dazzling and wholly delightful Fr. M. C. D'Arcy, s.j. There is some account of all this both in *Four Absentees* and in a monograph I was to do on Léon Bloy, the writer who during that period exercised most direct influence on me. I can see that 'I decided I would become' must seem to give an inadequate account of the matter, particularly to those who like their human impulses nicely determined. Yet a decision is just what it was. No doubt I was feeling a bit chaotic, and certainly I was attracted by the unambiguous system of Catholic practice and belief.

At the beginning of these proceedings, I was sharing a flat in Kentish Town with Eric Blair ('George Orwell'). By the end of the year, I had moved to an address off Tottenham Court Road. By April of the following year, it had become pretty clear that the intended conversion would not take place. For some time thereafter, I remained much stirred by Christian imagery, and my state of mind was frequently characterised by metaphysical anguish. However, I could not surmount those barriers to literal belief which more agile converts apparently take in their stride.

Since the Newman-Kingsley controversy a hundred years ago, there has persisted in this country a notion that Catholic belief has about it something very subtle and that you are likely to make a fool of yourself if you question its validity. It is a notion which has led, and which still leads, to displays of charming but misguided politeness on the part of Protestants and agnostics, to imperturbable complacency on the part of born Catholics and, I suggest, to a great deal of shiftiness and equivocation on the part of converts. Indeed, I am afraid I must go further than that. A quarter of a century ago, very anxious to believe what I was supposed to believe in order to be a Catholic with a good conscience, it seems to me that I examined every possible means of honourably liquidating doubt. The result is that I cannot believe in the good faith of any adult, educated and intelligent convert from an agnostic position.

An adult, educated and intelligent born Catholic, who has lapsed briefly into agnosticism, may reassert his childhood faith in order to give continuity and identity to his life. That kind of *pietas* I can accept. If it is not logically, it may be psychologically, temperamentally, existentially, sound. It is perhaps much the same with a man who, up to the moment of 'going over', has gone on believing literally in the main Christian doctrines as understood and propounded by some other church. A convert of many years standing may begin to behave, inwardly as well as outwardly, like a born Catholic. He may truly have forgotten the intellectual sleight of hand he had to perform in order to make his profession of faith. But I do not believe that any well-informed man of high intelligence in our time ever first made that profession of faith without some kind of intellectual trickery and for motives which weakened his self-respect at least for some years, unless that self-respect had previously got to a very low ebb.

The differences between Newman and Kingsley were only those between the special claims of Roman Catholicism and a nineteenth-century Anglicanism which, however shaky its definitions, yet did not then question what we may describe as the basic doctrines of all organised Christianity. We may be sure that Kingsley enunciated the Apostles' Creed without the slightest element of doubt. This Creed is simply a translation of the Catholic *Credo*, differing from it only by the *filioque* which concerns only a very minor article of faith, the procession of the Holy Ghost. Kingsley believed we may be sure, in the Creation, the Fall and Original Sin, the Incarnation by Virgin Birth, the immortality of the soul, the Resurrection of the Body, the omniscience and omnipotence of God.

I could not really manage any of these, except the immortality of the soul and perhaps the Fall and Original Sin understood symbolically, perhaps also in some sense the Resurrection of the Body. If you can accept, as, I imagine, any nineteenth-century Anglican did, all the basic doctrines in essence, the rest is mere trimmings. If, for instance, you accept both Original Sin and the Virgin Birth, the Immaculate Conception becomes almost obligatory. It should not have worried Kingsley. I could not manage the omniscience and the omnipotence of God, which are pretty basic. I could not manage the Incarnation. That is to say, I could not admit what it is supposed to have done to the world.

The picture is this. God creates a world, and He gives men free will, punishing them if they exercise it wrongly. He does it at a particular date, about which there is some disagreement. The first people, Adam and Eve, almost at once exercise free will wrongly, and that throws everything out, though, of course, God, being omniscient, knew it would happen and, being omnipotent, could have stopped it. After enjoying His little joke for some thousands of years, He decides it has gone far enough. He therefore splits Himself into three parts (it is uncertain whether He was so split beforehand or whether the arrangement was made *ad hoc*). One of the parts (it was rather like Jove's dealings with Danaë) impregnated a Jewish virgin who had married an old or otherwise impotent or sterile man at a point in historical time when Palestine was occupied by the Romans. The baby which the young Jewess in due course produced turns out to be really the third part of God incarnated, as though it had been a human soul, in a human body. This gives rise to a new joke. For almost two thousand years, it is enjoyed exclusively by God Himself. Indeed, its early stages were not very enjoyable even to that part of God which had been incarnated. His sublunary career was at once edifying and productive of the most charming anecdotes, but it was terminated by one of the most unpleasant forms of death human beings have ever devised for each other, though its torments did not last as long as they tended to do with less intellectual persons of more robust frame. The awkwardness thus created between the three parts of God was no doubt laughed off in due course.

In any case, that was not the essence of the new joke. The new joke essentially was that human beings could now be rewarded or punished on a new scale. The Incarnation was also, though in a rather limited sense, a Redemption. This meant that rewards never envisaged before could be made to persons who, on the one hand, believed in the Incarnation and, on the other, carried out the moral precepts which God's third part had enunciated during His (or Its) edifying career in Roman-occupied Palestine. Anyone who had spotted Jesus's divine nature and done what Jesus told him went, of course, at his death straight up to Heaven, where he was given a whale of a time, though (of course) there was nothing unrefined. By their subsequent behaviour, lots of others, who kept the rules, were elected to this new club.

For the club was certainly new. Between the Fall and the Incarnation, nobody went to Heaven, not even Moses, Virgil or Isaiah. A long time after their death, efforts were made to get them in, but for at least a thousand years they were left, no doubt feeling rather frustrated, in the company of such very nice if unprophetic pagans as Socrates and of the first thirty generations of post-Christian but unbaptised infants, in a region eventually known as Limbo, which seems to have been not too unpleasant. The other new thing was Hell, with its *annexe* Purgatory. These were part of the new club system. It was a bit like a public school. After a year as a fag in Purgatory, you might get moved up. On the other hand, if you utterly failed as a fag, or if you had utterly failed to get into the school at all, there was Hell, equally new and of a frightfulness never before imagined. That was really the essence of the new joke.

Being still omniscient, God knew very well who would land up in Hell. Being omnipotent, He could have stopped anyone landing up there. A rule He made for Himself was that, once in Hell, nobody could get out. They could linger for more than a year in Purgatory, then still get out into Heaven. Once in Hell, you were there for good. It was no good even praying for you then.

In tone, this is all very flippant no doubt. I should like to know at what point it unfairly paraphrases Catholic doctrine. I know what the doctrine is. I know it better than many Catholics, perhaps better than most Catholics. But this is autobiography, and I am not concerned with what I know now but with what I knew a quarter of a century ago. I did not see the whole thing so sharply drawn, but that is the picture I saw. I was rather particularly concerned with the good pagans. Except in so far as a Virgil or an Isaiah might be thought to have intuited Christ, the whole of time between the Fall and the Incarnation was reduced to meaninglessness.

So was the whole of the non-Christian world (by far the greater part of the world) up to our own time. One might view all the Mahometans, Hindus and Chinese Buddhists, all the Jews, polytheists and primitive animists, with kindly indulgence, banishing them to no Hell (since they knew no better) but letting them congregate with Socrates and the unbaptised children in Limbo, in 'a state of natural bliss'. But, really, that would not do. It made their lives meaningless, and I could not stand it. Fifteen years later, I should find this same 'love for what is outside the visible Church' made an objection to faith by Simone Weil. To what she also describes as 'idolatry of the Church as an institution' (making it just another version of Plato's Great Beast) I might have been subject enough if I could have managed the doctrine, the eschatology, the world picture.

I had another objection to the eschatology. The Church, I understood, proclaimed the uniqueness of the individual soul. Yet, in the end, the soul had only three alternative destinations, Heaven, Hell and Limbo, surely too few, surely too indiscriminate a regimentation, too much an averaging out. A unique soul might need something in the nature of a unique destination.

And I still had a hankering after some meaningful historical process, a cosmic process, a total evolution. This same hankering, I should find twenty years later, then already dominated the thought of a French Jesuit priest, Pierre Teilhard de Chardin, his name and the awkwardness of his thinking perhaps already known to Fr. D'Arcy, though it seems that the two did not meet until 1954, the year before Teilhard's death, in New York.

I do not to-day find Teilhard's vision credible, nor does it seem to me that that kind of evolutionary optimism can be reconciled with Christian doctrine. In his lifetime, Fr. Teilhard's books were not allowed, by his Jesuit superiors, to be published. Since his death, a number of Jesuits, including Fr. D'Arcy and the late Fr. Martindale, have seemed to give them a partial endorsement, which, I fear, despite my respect for both men and the affection in which I still hold one of them, strikes me as unconvincing, opportunist and, if you look at it closely, very cagey indeed. Twenty-five years ago, I should have been enormously taken with Teilhard's speculations. I was wracking my own mind for terms in which to describe some kind of total pull of the world towards God.

Pull, not push. Moreover, pull without push. Not, that is to say, a Creation way back in time and a Dissolution and Judgment in the remote future, with provisional arrangements in force meanwhile. To create a world, give it a run for its money and then take it back seemed absurd, indeed seemed wantonly cruel if some who had not asked to be created were to be left in Hell for eternity. If one could somehow place Creation in the future and see it as God slowly drawing a world into existence through chaos towards Himself, that would make better sense.

I tried quite hard to work this out in detail. I can no longer remember just where I got stuck. Perhaps it was merely that I tired myself out and put the problem aside for another time. Chronologically, my abortive conversion to Roman Catholicism post-dates, but also to some extent overlaps with later stages of, my ballet phase. A further preoccupation had thus at one point been the attempt to reconcile my sacred and profane interests. St Thomas Aquinas had been a help there, with his statement that the soul is 'the form of the body'. Pursued too far, the notion would no doubt have landed me up in some form of gnostic heresy. I argued (with myself) that, the more perfectly formed a body, the better it was for the soul, that, indeed, perhaps only the perfectly trained, the more highly articulated, the more, as it were, explicit, body of a dancer could free the soul from hideous physical encumberment, could leave it uncrippled.

In works of theology since, I have seen this same notion of the soul as 'the form of the body' used as an argument against reincarnation, with which a few years later I was to toy for a while. It, of course, serves the purpose of no such argument.

32

It serves against the more popular Greek and Hindu ideas of a transmigration of souls even into the bodies of lower animals, but the reincarnation envisaged by a higher Buddhism or by, say, the disciples of Rudolf Steiner could well be a periodical resumption of the same body. I understand that, in fact, the doctrine of reincarnation has never been formally condemned by the Church, though Origen got into trouble for one specific gloss upon it. The doctrine is, in several ways, more reasonable than the usual Christian view of immortality, which is unilateral. If souls created unceasingly *ab nihilo* then stay immortal, one is faced in the end with a terrible problem of overcrowding in the afterworld. The doctrine of *karma* further introduces an element of pragmatical fair play into human life, since the soul born to affliction may at once be regarded as having in some way chosen it or brought it upon itself and as being likely to have the opportunity of further life-times in which it can be compensated or can get everything right, certainly risking no final damnation for a failure under conditions abnormally difficult.

What I now find impossibly difficult is to conceive of an entity, the soul, susceptible of any kind of immortality. In 1936, I was still able to imagine a soul. But I gave up theology without having worked all this out to a firm conclusion. No doubt it was simply that my preoccupations had changed. I had my practical concerns, one of them leading to marriage. It also happens that, on the day I met my wife, there broke out in Spain a civil war, its quasi-official attitude towards which did not, as I thought then, present the Church in any too pretty a light.

VI

FOR a period of about two years, from the summer of 1936 onwards, I should have described myself as a pacifist, though I never did much about it. In fact I am rather inclined to suppose that my attitude to the obvious threats of war was much the same as that of the high-minded young at the time of the abortive re-occupation of the Suez canal zone twenty years later. The sense of moral outrage then widely expressed seemed to me in 1956 to indicate mainly a fear, among the cosily uninvolved, of suddenly being caught up in something they would have to take seriously, perhaps even to the point of conscription. Twenty years before, I didn't want to take sides. I had other concerns.

My own life was decidedly *mouvementé*, partly as a result of hardly ever being able to pay the rent. Sometimes I was in Cornwall, sometimes in the red-brick back-end of Hampstead, once briefly in Huddersfield and Manchester, once near Borough Green in Kent, then, after a spring without her in Cornwall, for the early summer of 1938 at Newport (Mon.) which was my wife's home town, though I had met her a long way from there, in Essex.

Just before leaving Cornwall, I had written one or two paragraphs of a novel, to be told in the first person as by a blind man. I wrote about half of the book in Newport. I had previously tried my hand at a novel and at an occasional short story, but my friend Michael Sayers had not thought well of so much of the results as he had seen and had assured me that I could never write a novel. In addition to his drama criticism, he had written many admirable short stories and had for long been at work on a novel, set (it need hardly be said) in Ireland at the time of the Troubles. He, it was understood, was the novelist, I the poet.

Michael was now in America, where he had gone as English play editor to Norman bel Geddes. It was, nevertheless, with the idea of specifically meeting his challenge that I began my novel. Indeed, it was he who (unknowingly) had provided me with my subject. While I was living in Kilburn, he had told me about a blind *masseur* who was in attendance on his mother. It was through the other senses of such a man that (as I have phrased it elsewhere, and it was the way I put it to myself at the time) I tried to re-apprehend my world. I laid the scene in Cornwall.

Other matters went into the book. I read Helen Keller's remarkable autobiography and was led by it, thinking of her even deeper affliction, to introduce the blind-deaf-mute Amity Nance. While I was still in Cornwall, my wife had described to me in a letter the birth of a calf at the farm of one of her family outside Newport. I put this in almost *verbatim*, glad in that way to make her participate in the creation of my novel. In the evening, I later got her to lead me about the streets of Newport with my eyes closed. Presumably as a result of all this concentration on blindness, my own eyesight was markedly affected, though neither too badly nor irreparably.

I finished the book in London during the Munich crisis, while some people filled sandbags in the street and some got into their cars and tooted off westward and yet others went round fitting each other with gasmasks. I found all these activities rather disgusting. Afterwards, I felt that the war had really taken place and that some of my friends were among the casualties. At the same time, my pacifism was shaken. Its purpose was to avert war. If war broke out, I clearly saw that one would to some extent have to take sides. One must inevitably prefer the victory of one side or the other, and so one would have to exert oneself however feebly to that end.

A first publisher turned my novel down. It went to a second, who in due course took it. I had no title for it, and it had gone out without a title. The eventual publisher gave it one, *The Blaze of Noon*. In the meantime, I wrote for the BBC a dramatic script on the Gunpowder Plot, to be broadcast on November 5th. During the past two years, I had written a number of scripts on such subjects as frozen meat, unicorns, the lost continent of Atlantis, explorers (Sir John Franklin and Ludwig Leichhardt), Malta, the industrial North a hundred years ago.

They were easy to do, and one got tremendous sums of as much as twenty pounds for doing them.

By way of research on the Gunpowder Plot, I read a book by a Fr. Garnett who proved that it was a frame-up. The parallel with the Reichstag Fire Trial was obvious. I adopted this view. My little play showed the machinations of the horrible Cecil, and at one point Guy Fawkes under torture was heard (as it were) off-stage, like the tenor in *Tosca*.

In 1938, November 5th fell on a Saturday. The following week, there were letters in *The Times*. One of these came from the Earl of Powis.

> Sir, – I wish to protest against the disgusting broadcast by the BBC last night, when we were treated to a description, which must have been mostly imaginary, of the Gunpowder Plot and the subsequent torturing of Guy Fawkes and his confederates, and we had to listen to their groans and also to the conversation between the King and his officers of State, which were both unedifying and fictitious.
>
> When I heard that we were to have an account of the Gunpowder Plot I imagined that we should hear something to which we could listen with pleasure and enlightenment, but instead of that we had to listen to a lurid description which must have disgusted everybody.
>
> Yours faithfully,
POWIS.
>
> Powis Castle, Welshpool, Nov. 6.

It was *The Daily Herald* which avidly took the old creature up and on Wednesday produced an amusing little piece under the headline:

EARL LETS OFF FIREWORKS AT BBC

Guy Fawkes has produced another crop of fireworks – this time for the BBC. . .

Powis was represented as telling a reporter on Tuesday night that

> The broadcast was just too horrible . . . The BBC actually represented the King and his chief officers witnessing the sufferings and gloating over them . . . It is the horribleness of the whole thing that I object to, as much as the complete travesty of history

. . . It is extremely horrible that a King should be represented as enjoying such a horrible spectacle.

The BBC made no statement (I, at the time, was not on the telephone). Noticing, however, that already scheduled was a programme on astrology with a script by me, various senior BBC officials, deciding that this was a controversial subject, apparently briefed the producer to require me to make a number of alterations in the script. These struck me as either foolish or mutually contradictory, and so I refused.

That was the end of my pre-war dealings with the BBC, except that, early in the New Year, I wrote the dramatic inserts for a television programme on sea-serpents, based on the researches of a Commander Gould of whom I had not heard till then. I did not see this presented. I set off towards Alexandra Palace, but got caught up on the way.

VII

THREE disadvantages of extreme pen-
ury are that you are unlikely to travel abroad, that you do not
own a piano and that you are dependent on other people for
new books. In 1939, I lived in rather more style than hereto-
fore, though without security. I had travelled abroad only once
since my second year at Leeds. I did not travel abroad in 1939,
and, as it happens, I was not to see more than the coastline of
France again until 1947, but in 1939 new books and a piano
were always to hand. The piano (not my own) was a Blüthner.
Many of the books were in French.

My reading has been predominantly in French at four separate and distinct points in my life. This was the second. Till
then, I had read very little in French since graduation. During
my abortive conversion, I had read Léon Bloy *in extenso*. A bit
later, I had read, in translation, *The Diary of a Country Priest*
by Georges Bernanos, as well as his book on the Spanish war.
And the principal literary influence on *The Blaze of Noon* had
been Henry de Montherlant's Costals novels, also in English,
and his *Paradis à l'Ombre des Epées*. But that had been all. Even
in 1939, I did not read only in French. For instance, I read
and was affected by the anti-stories of William Saroyan and the
anti-novels of Henry Miller. I briefly met both Miller and
Lawrence Durrell that year in London.

All the same, I read a great deal in French. Rather along
Miller lines, I read Louis-Ferdinand Céline's *Voyage au Bout de
la Nuit*, and I suppose that Marcel Jouhandeau was also an
anti-novelist in his way. I developed a particular fondness for
him and for C. F. Ramuz. My interest in Jouhandeau has persisted. My interest in Ramuz belongs quite specifically to the
period just before and during the first months of Hitler's war.

Ramuz was Swiss, and his novels are placed in remote villages in the French-speaking canton of Vaud. In each novel,
some disturbance of the course of nature brings the sparse

population (mainly of wine-growers) to the brink of catastrophe, and indeed one novel, *La Présence de la Mort*, of which an English translation exists, verges on science fiction, since it presents us with an earth cataclysmically approaching the sun. A Frenchman who in those days dealt with much the same kind of subject in severely regional (in his case, Provençal) terms was Jean Giono. Since the war, he has written in a quite different, Stendhalian vein. He was a coarser, more emotionally overcharged writer than Ramuz, and, in translation, his more-than-Laurentian *Chant de la Terre* was the kind of thing one read aloud to other people for laughs. However, I very much liked the shorter and simpler *Colline*, and I read with some interest and respect a first-world-war book of pacifist tendency, which got Giono put in gaol when Hitler's war began.

One's happiest association with anything of Giono's was the marvellous film, *La Femme du Boulanger*, with Raimu. The bones of this come from the autobiographical volume, *Jean le Bleu*, though Giono also made a stage-play on the story. In the same way, I suppose that what most people know by C. F. Ramuz, without, perhaps, ever having taken in the name, is the libretto of Stravinsky's *Histoire du Soldat*.

Jouhandeau was a very different kind of writer, sophisticated and feline. At the time, his amusingly shameless account of his own family, *Les Miens*, was running serially in the *Nouvelle Revue Française*. The *NRF* was also printing instalments of *Rêveuse Bourgeoisie* by Pierre Drieu la Rochelle, and from time to time it contained critical articles by a name new to me, that of Jean-Paul Sartre, who discussed Husserl and possibly Heidegger, besides demolishing Mauriac and Giraudoux and taking, as I thought, too seriously William Faulkner and John dos Passos, who had just been translated into French. I myself, without much understanding, glanced at Husserl's *Ideas* and the volume of Henry Corbin's gallant attempts to translate Heidegger into French.

At the time, I took little interest in Drieu la Rochelle. He was, I understood, one of those (as we said then) 'crypto-Fascist' writers, milder than Maurras and Léon Daudet, perhaps a bit like the Massis and Brasillach once so close to the

39

heart of Mr Eliot and *The Criterion*. I doubt whether I had so much as heard of the PPF (Parti Populaire Français) or its leader, Jacques Doriot, popular mayor of the working-class suburb of St Denis. If I had known more about these, I dare say I should have found their variety of French crypto-Fascism less unattractive than the varieties I knew something about.

If I had taken more interest in Drieu, I should no doubt have discovered that both he and Doriot had been and, in a sense, still were socialists and that Drieu had formerly pinned his faith on the League of Nations. He disliked the *côté soldatesque* of the Nazis (the uniforms and the marching and parading) but conceived that the Germans must expand in some direction and that it had better be eastward, the only alternative being to let them have their colonies back. Drieu was not anti-British in the least, though he thought that we paid too little attention to French needs. He wanted a strong Franco-British alliance which should deal firmly with the Germans, while giving them a free hand against Russia.

I should not, I fancy, have responded at all favourably to these views. Encouraging the Germans to attack Russia had, till that April, seemed to be the policy of the Chamberlain government, against which everybody I knew railed. Though myself less-than-average political-minded at that time, I never-theless automatically hated and despised anything which our own Tories stood for. That *côté soldatesque* was not perhaps even the worst thing about the Nazis. The news reels at the cinema showed us Germans goose-stepping and the grotesque, yelling heads of Hitler and Mussolini, but they also showed us pathetic little Jews being trundled about in hand-carts and otherwise ill-treated and humiliated by gangs of young oafs.

By contrast, perhaps even Russia seemed tolerable. It was farther away and not so much photographed. Certainly, no rational being had grounds any longer for thinking well of Russia. Three years before, I myself had been properly in-formed about the purges of which Arthur Koestler wrote in *Darkness at Noon*. Within a year of the outbreak of the Spanish war, I had been told by 'George Orwell' just what kinds of bloodiness the communists had been getting up to in Spain. It was not only on the Right that one learned something of the truth about communism in practice. From a very close friend who was a Labour Party official, I knew that British socialists by and large now feared and hated communists more than Tories. And yet the sentimental myth of 'the great Russian experiment' persisted. Just why and how, it really is very difficult to recapture. The whole thing was, certainly, near-schizophrenic. Perhaps this means little more than that, not having thought very hard and not being very well-informed, our sense of reality was undeveloped.

I claim no special immunity. For instance, when the American Col. Lindbergh, justly a folk-hero for his solo Atlantic crossing by aeroplane, came back from Russia and said that its air force was rotten and the country no use as a possible ally, I was shocked. To the extent to which I believed what he said, it simply made me sorry for the Russians and the more inclined to feel that it would be wrong to leave them unprotected against the deadly force of the Germans.

This was our *côté chevaleresque*. We had beautiful moral attitudes. As time went on, these produced new varieties of schizophrenia. Take, for instance, the Evelyn Waugh variety. The eventual Russian alliance was, for Mr Waugh, national dishonour. And yet he rejoiced in 'the Churchillian *renaissance*', which benefited nobody but Russia, at any rate on this side of the Atlantic, and could only lead to the Russian alliance. We all ought to have been able to see this. We all ought to have seen that any war between ourselves and France on the one hand and Germany on the other could only be to the advantage of Russia.

We must have known that the battle would be a stiff one and that, whatever the outcome, Germany, France and Britain would all three be damaged. Perhaps we could not foresee the extent of the damage or just how great an advantage it would be to Russia. For my own part, I could have imagined a great deal of physical damage, but I could not, I think, have conceived what it would mean in economic and political terms, especially to ourselves. I could not have imagined a world in which only the physically unscathed America and a Russia itself badly damaged would have any real say. I could not have imagined those largely barbaric countries wholly displacing

Britain and France in the world, with France and a part of Germany lamely combining and ourselves muttering apologies this way and that, all of us sick for years with the fear of Russia.

I do not suppose that Neville Chamberlain or any of our 'men of Munich' saw quite so far, but up to a point their instinct had been right. The fatal moment came when, in the spring of 1939, France and Britain gave Poland guarantees which it seemed likely both countries really would implement at need. Even on the Right, many people had felt dishonoured by the non-implementation of guarantees to Czechoslovakia. The guarantees to Poland, with a determination to meet them at need, appeared to be simply what honour required. Again, it was our *côté chevaleresque*.

In retrospect, how foolish it seems. Over Danzig and the Polish corridor, the Germans had a real grievance by any standards. To implement those guarantees would involve us in declaring war on Germany, but could not directly help Poland. True, we had not yet seen the new *Blitzkrieg* technique at work. We did not know just how fast a German invasion could move. But a mere look at the map makes it plain that troops from Britain or France can only reach Poland through Germany. A further look at the map makes it equally plain that German troops can only get into Russia through Czechoslovakia, Poland and Roumania.

And there, in our high-mindedness, we all were, our steps firmly planted on the road to ruin. For myself, all I can claim is that I took no part in any Leftish demonstrations or other political agitation. I was at least harmless. My attitude was one of pure and, in an odd way, blissful fatalism. I waited for *The Blaze of Noon* to come out. The publishers had got for it an extremely flattering Foreword by Elizabeth Bowen, a novelist I greatly admired. I had then not met Miss Bowen. I was not to meet her, or even to correspond with her, for some four or five years more.

That was a wonderful summer. Then, on a Friday, the 1st of September, the Germans invaded Poland. Two days later, on a Sunday morning, a tearful Chamberlain came on the wireless, to say that we were at war. The sirens went. I was alone in the house, and I felt a bit frightened, expecting that the bombing would start at once. Poland collapsed very quickly. Life went on as before. There seemed no reason why now the war should not be called off. Just before the invasion of Poland, the Russians had signed with the Germans a pact clearly intended to be a go-ahead in the west. The Russians did not mind about us. We continued to behave as if we minded about them. We all knew that Russia was the Germans' ultimate objective. If we had made peace with the Germans that autumn, we could just have sat back and left the two dreadful opponents to fight it out. However, the ridiculous *Sitzkrieg* was kept up.

The Blaze of Noon came out on November 10th. I had not expected any critical attention that day. At about noon, my wife rang me up from somewhere in the neighbourhood of Baker Street. A gentle-mannered young woman, she sounded angry.

'Darling,' she said, 'have you seen what some awful little pimp has written about you in *The Evening Standard*?'

I hadn't. I went out and got a paper. A headline stretched right across the page.

'FRANKEST' NOVEL IS CHALLENGE TO THE CENSOR

AN AFFRONT TO DECENCY

Story of Poultry-yard Morals

Since the late D. H. Lawrence's banned book, 'Lady Chatterley's Lover', no novel has been published in this country so boldly challenging the censor by its frank dealing with sex matters as 'The Blaze of Noon' by Mr Rayner Heppenstall . . .

There followed a summary of the plot, which did indeed sound a little like that of my novel. The book (admitted the editorial voice) was rather well written and contained much delightful matter, but that, if anything only made matters worse.

. . . The problem for the censor remains – has public toleration of what used to be considered indecent literature so far advanced that a book like this . . .?

The telephone rang again. It was my publisher. The book was sold out. Outside their offices, in Essex Street off the Strand, at present stood a queue of old ladies and of gentlemen in riding boots, offering three or four guineas for a copy. I was to keep my end up. My telephone number would not be given to anyone. This would go on all week until it was stopped (whatever that meant). They would presently begin to reprint. Alas, it would take a fortnight.

Other reviews appeared. None of them agreed with *The Evening Standard*. Several explicitly disagreed. The book was distinguished and austere. So I had a *succès d'estime* as well as a *succès de scandale*. There were (there always are) the knowing people who wanted to know how much we had paid *The Evening Standard*.

VIII

THE winter was severe, and snow lay over London for weeks. Further north, the Russians invaded Finland. The small Finnish army battled superbly. At the cinema, one saw them in news reels, white-cloaked figures on skis. The Finns were greatly admired, and a volunteer force was mustered here to go to their aid.

At that point, nobody loved the Russians, not even the members of the Left Book Club. At any time within the next three months, the Chamberlain government would, I fancy, have carried the public with it if it had made peace, stating clearly that this would allow the Germans to march into Russia instead of turning west. The military operation itself could hardly at that point have taken long. When, almost two years later, the Germans in fact attacked Russia, they had lost a good deal of their air force and had to keep very considerable forces on guard in the west, while the Russians were better prepared and were supplied with *matériel* and political encouragement by ourselves. An invasion in the late spring of 1940 must have defeated Russia very quickly. Occupying and reorganising that vast country and thereafter standing on guard against the Chinese would have kept the Germans busy, to our enormous advantage and that of all Europe, for several generations if not for ever.

Alas, that course of events, to hindsight so obviously desirable, was not to be realised or even widely desired, though, again I fancy, public opinion would have accepted a peace made with Germany after the withdrawal from Norway, after Dunkirk or after the fall of France if the Germans had not then been so foolish as to attack us directly from the air. However, by that time, the war party at Westminster had brought the bellicose Churchill into office.

From December of that year onward, I was in the Army. For a year and a half, I remained torpid. Then, in the summer of 1942, I took up a novel I had started two years before. In the early autumn, I finished it. This time, it was, very conveniently, a *picaresque* novel. The essence of a *picaresque* novel is, on the one hand, that it is told in the first person by a social parasite, rogue, picaroon or (as we say now) anti-hero and, in the second place, that it has no formal plot but that the episodes simply follow each other serially. It is thus a very suitable kind of novel to be written by a man in the Army, since he can post off the separate episodes to a friend, wife or typist as he writes them and need not, in any important way, bear the whole thing in his head. The other influences were Henry Miller, Céline and *Fabian*, a book by Erich Kastner.

The title of my book was *Saturnine* (later, modified and extended, it became *The Greater Infortune*). It came out in the autumn of 1943. It came out in a small edition at (for those days) a high price, the publisher being very nervous of it (the understanding being that, if it did not 'run into trouble', there would in due course be a normal edition, an agreement which after the war he refused to honour). It did not get much of a press, though once more a voice was raised demanding that it should be suppressed. This was the voice of James Agate, again in a Beaverbrook publication, *The Daily Express*. The heading was: A BOOK MORE DANGEROUS THAN BOSH. Agate's sexual peculiarities were, I have always understood, much the same as those which Proust ascribed to M. de Charlus in wartime. He was, that is to say, a masochist in the full clinical sense, who used to pick up sailors and other young thugs and get them to tie him up and flog him. I am inclined to believe this, because the only old friend of Agate's I have met (I was to meet him about six months later) was a sadist, whose boast was that he had once 'killed a nigger in Jamaica' (a Jew from Hamburg, he was also a Maupassant addict and chairman of his local Conservative Association). I had fallen foul of Agate (in print) before. He had attacked my *Apology for Dancing* in five or six different papers under as many pseudonyms.

Saturnine, he felt, should never have been printed 'at the height of the greatest war in history'. He was particularly appalled by one 'passage of the most revolting connotation in which the highest in the land are mentioned by name'. Years later, after Agate's death, that delightful man and fine actor, Esmé Percy, told me that at the time Agate was to be seen in the bar at the Savage, clutching a copy of *Saturnine* and, with purple, congested face, reading aloud that passage of revolting connotation to all the old soaks who came in. I may say that the passage in question does not occur in quite the same form in *The Greater Infortune*.

For us, the greatest war in history had passed its worst stages. The North African campaign was over. The Italian campaign was just beginning. It was already clear that we should be on the winning side. We ourselves had done much to ensure this, but the decisive factor would be the sheer weight of American *matériel*. The German feat of arms would clearly go down in history as the greatest the world had ever seen. Meanwhile, the dreadful business had to go on for another year and a half. Nothing less than 'unconditional surrender' was demanded of the Germans. Their cities were to be largely obliterated. For at least a generation, the whole of Germany would be garrisoned by the troops of other nations, a preponderance of them not even Europeans. As to ourselves, we should come out of the war as a nation of valiant imbeciles, pitied and derided by everyone. How the French would appear began to transpire when, in August 1944, Paris was liberated.

Before that, newspaper items had made it clear that, while no great mass of national courage had been required of the French, whole groups had suffered worse things than anyone here, while of those who were heroes a harder, more desperate courage was required, because it was lonely and because it might well lead to unspeakable penalties. There had been a formidable *maquis* or Resistance. There had also been collaborationists or collaborators. Among the latter, some had behaved very badly indeed, others more or less venially. The bulk of the population had perhaps rather little to reproach themselves with. Many had gone underfed, and there was a great deal of tuberculosis among the young. There had been a fair amount of black marketeering, not necessarily linked with collaboration.

During the four years of our otherwise total separation from France, one or two books had sneaked over and been printed here. We had especially been warmed by Aragon's two volumes of nostalgically patriotic verse and by Vercors's *Le Silence de la Mer*. The chief of the new names seemed to be Camus and Sartre, the former to most of us quite new, the latter perhaps just noted in the *Nouvelle Revue Française* before the war. They were described as *existentialistes*, and they had all resisted in one way or another. Indeed, *existentialisme* was so much linked with the Resistance that before long its exponents began to be rather irritatedly known as *résistantialistes*.

Under the Occupation, the *NRF* had been edited by Drieu la Rochelle. That meant he was now in serious trouble. As in due course appeared, none of the French writers I had been particularly interested in at the beginning of the war had resisted conspicuously. Céline was in very bad odour. Montherlant was a bit *mal vu* for a time and Jouhandeau rather longer.

The various armies pressed on into Germany. It was known even at the time that the idiot Roosevelt had procured that the Russians should get to Berlin first. In March 1945, Drieu committed suicide. In April, I was invalided out of the Army. Within a month, Hitler, Roosevelt and Mussolini were dead. The full horror of the German concentration camps was revealed, and we learned that six million Jews had been systematically exterminated.

That made us feel better about the war. If anything, we had underestimated the bestial wickedness of the Nazis. At least that horror had been stopped. Yet we had not saved all those Jews, any more than we had saved Poland. We had closed all the western and southern escape routes, and it might well be argued that, by our policy of *guerre a l'outrance*, we had forced their 'final solution' upon the Germans. Even thereafter, under Ernest Bevin, we were to go on for years denying the Jews proper access to Palestine and, once they were there, conspiring at their murder by Arab bands.

Neither in 1945 nor until more than fifteen years later did I seriously question the myth about the war, *viz.*, that it had been necessary. In retrospect, I do not much blame Churchill, who was no doubt carried away by some kind of emotion and who could not have been expected to refuse the *rôle* which seemed thrust upon him, since clearly he had desired it all his life. Roosevelt may, I think, be blamed for his sly anti-Europeanism. We have lived ever since in the fear of some apparently inevitable conflagration between the Russians and the Americans, from which it was clear we should suffer more than either, and, eighteen years afterwards, the soil of Europe is still littered with American military equipment and *personnel*. It is a pity that from, say, 1936 onwards we did not sufficiently appreciate the fact that the Germans stood between us and the Russians. Still, in the end, I imagine that Americans, Europeans and those remoter Europeans, the Russians, will find themselves in alliance on the ground that they are all 'white' and speak languages of the kind known as 'Indo-European'. We shall, I hope, then feel sufficiently thankful that the Russians stand between us and the Chinese.

IX

THE lights came on in the streets, and the various black-out materials and structures were removed. That was very pleasant. For me, it was also pleasant not to be in the Army. I was a little demoralised. During a period of four years and four months, I had obeyed countless orders in which I saw no point, so that the continuity of my will had been interrupted (until late 1940, I had obeyed nobody's order since I left school). There is an element of luxury in obeying orders. I now had to decide for myself at what time I would get up, how I should spend my day, when I would eat, even (within rather narrow limits) what I should wear. During the next year or two, one observed a good deal of behaviour on the part of discharged soldiers which had roots like these.

As I had been invalided out of the Army, I was not subject to the regulations governing employment still in force. I need not do anything 'of national importance'. In theory, I could once more have lived as a free-lance writer. In practice, I quickly discovered that it was no longer possible.

Before the war, it had been possible, though it had not been easy, to be a serious, full-time professional, free-lance writer. If I had been able to go straight on from *The Blaze of Noon*, I should have had no serious difficulty. The species was now extinct. To all intents and purposes, in this country, the species has been extinct these twenty years.

The number even of those who could live by actually writing literary journalism is extraordinarily small. There are two prestigious top spaces in *The Sunday Times* and two in *The Observer*. The incumbents of these four spaces have not (it being at the present moment early autumn, 1962) changed for many years. Some years ago, I was given to understand that those livings yielded a stipend of not less than two thousand pounds a year. None of the incumbents, so I am told, began life as a poor man. Unless I have been misinformed, three of them were, in the first place, pin-money columnists, though since then the price of pins has gone up. A similar post to theirs has more recently been created on *The Sunday Telegraph* for Mr Nigel Dennis. For some years, in the late 'Forties and early 'Fifties, Mr V. S. Pritchett, I fancy, could have lived wholly on *New Statesman* 'Books in General' articles. Latterly, Mr Kenneth Allsop seems actually to write the whole of the *Daily Mail* book page. That makes a total of five or six people at a given moment earning what could be lived on by actually writing literary journalism. I do not think that there can be any others. There are no doubt also one or two film and drama critics the bulk of whose work might be described as actual writing.

Poets have not been expected to live by their work for a long time, even under garret conditions, but until 1940 a novelist could get by comfortably on a novel a year, if it brought him in, say, three hundred pounds. The equivalent of that now is two thousand pounds, and very few novels bring in that amount. I have no doubt that it continues to happen to one or two novelists whose names we all admiringly know. It also happens to some who are described as 'popular' and whose names, by and large, we do not know, since nobody writes about them. Occasionally, a new writer suddenly and unaccountably hits the jackpot with a first or second book. It may drive him out of his mind, or he may begin to organise himself. Mr Kingsley Amis, for instance, for eight years kept up the second job. With perhaps less immediate temptation to throw caution to the winds, Miss Iris Murdoch and Mr William Golding have, for the moment, gone on doing so.

Apart from those who live on inherited income, the rest of us have two jobs at least. Women novelists, in general kept by their husbands, also function as housewives, hostesses and perhaps even mothers. A certain number of men writers are kept, either by women or by other men (their second job, therefore, is that of gigolo). Among good writers, Miss Murdoch and Mr Golding are not alone in being university teachers or schoolmasters. Some are in other honourable professions. One or two are in business or advertising. There are nonwriting jobs in the literary world itself. There are literary editorships and assistant literary editorships, full-time or part-time jobs in publishing houses. A man may combine one or more of these activities with some book-reviewing. He may reasonably then claim to be a professional man of letters, and his income may be further increased if he can also contrive to become popular on radio and television. Great figures are cut by versatile operators of this kind. They are not serious, full-time professional, free-lance writers.

Writing books has become almost entirely an amateur province. A writer of books may be a very hard-working person in some other field. With very few exceptions, a man can only afford to write books if, at least temporarily and in part, he pensions himself off with money from some other source, which may be more or less respectable.

In 1945, I was certainly not so far-sighted as to see just how all that kind of thing would develop. Nor were all the circumstances then yet the same. For instance, the cost of living had not yet gone up very much. The great circumstance then, and for several years to come, was the continuing shortage of paper and of labour in the printing and book-binding trades. Once you had got a book written, it would still take a year and a half to get it out, and, though books continued to sell and the competition was comparatively light, editions were small and reprinting slow. I had not yet got a book written.

I had, moreover, a family to keep now, and my total capital was a sum of twenty-seven pounds and a few shillings, the amount of my Army gratuity. During what I fancy were the eight weeks of 'leave pending final discharge' (at any rate, my 'date of effective discharge' was June 3rd), there would also be continuing Army pay of two pounds or perhaps two pounds ten a week. But for a quite remarkable series of coincidences, I might have been very rich indeed by my standards, but, at the beginning of the year, the money intended for me had gone elsewhere, under circumstances not unlike those I was to describe in *The Lesser Infortune*, a notable difference being that the real-life 'Richard St Hilda' was not mistaken about his sister's condition at the time of his last departure overseas.

It looked as though I should have to take a job. I went to the British Council. The European plums had been picked already.

The only jobs left were in more remote parts, and the salaries attached to them were smaller than was thought suitable for any but single men (they seemed quite big to me, but clearly one could not have kept up much style). I went to the Ministry of Information, where Cecil Day Lewis worked on publications. I knew him, though not intimately. I also had a tenuous acquaintance with his boss, the Robert Fraser who nowadays rules Independent Television, whom I had first met when he worked on *The Daily Herald* and for whom I had done a little reviewing when he briefly took over *Clarion* as an Odham's newspaper. A kind of reader's digest in French had been put out jointly by the British and American information services. It had recently been arranged that there should henceforward be separate British and American reader's digests. I could edit the British one. That would be very nice. For instance, it would probably mean a monthly trip to Paris, to see the thing through the press. However, the job had to be created, and the Civil Service does not hurry such matters.

I was living in Hampstead. A near neighbour was Edgell Rickword, who edited the fellow-travelling periodical *Our Time*. I did a little reviewing for him and for *Time and Tide*, whose literary editor then was C. V. Wedgwood. Also in Hampstead lived William Empson, who worked in the BBC's Chinese section at 200 Oxford Street, pending a long-desiderated return to Peking. He was the only man I knew any longer at the BBC. I wrote two little pieces for him, on Virginia Woolf and the philosopher R. G. Collingwood, to be translated and read in Chinese, and he put me in touch with a man at Broadcasting House, for whom I might be able to write the kind of dramatised script I had done for other producers before the war. That might tide me over until the M of I job was created and until I was installed in it.

An appointment was made, and I went to see the man. I was shown not into his office, but into that of his departmental head. It became apparent to me that the two of them were interviewing me as though for a job on the staff. I had intended no such thing. I had merely wanted to write an occasional script. However, my twenty-seven pounds were giving out. I might have preferred to edit the French reader's digest, but I must clearly sign on whichever dotted line first appeared under my nose. It turned out to be the BBC one. I was offered a six months' contract at twelve pounds a week, with some likelihood of thereafter being taken on to the staff at much the same rate of pay. I had liked the two men who interviewed me. I signed on the BBC's dotted line.

The explanation of the interview lay with Empson, who was later reported to me as having gone about saying (he writes Basic English and speaks shorthand):

'Heppenstall. Fellow's miserable. Find him a job.'

Upon being asked who I was, it appears that he said:

'Heppenstall? Oh, elderly thinker from the North.'

I was, of course, thirty-three at the time and somewhat younger than Empson. I started at the BBC in late July, a few days before my thirty-fourth birthday. I had not been there long before a General Election took place and not much longer when atomic bombs were dropped on Hiroshima and Nagasaki, putting a decisive end to the war.

That should not be forgotten. At the news of the dropping of those two bombs, most of us felt a degree of superstitious horror, but they did stop the war and thus probably saved as many lives as they took. Moreover, they kept the Russians out of Japan.

The Attlee government was already in office. No doubt because of my ambiguous position, neither quite in nor quite out of the Armed Forces, no voting papers had reached me. If I had voted, I should have voted Labour, and the landslide victory pleased me, though I did not expect much to come of it. In his next *Horizon* editorial, Cyril Connolly described the British people as slow to change, but said that, once in a while, they gave a great shrug of impatience and something was done with for ever. Well, of course, it wasn't to turn out like that. The something was not done with for ever. Within the next year or two, it began to creep back. I don't know whether Connolly is sorry. I don't know what the British people really meant by their vote or what they had meant, a few days before, by pelting Churchill with rotten tomatoes. Perhaps, obscurely, they knew what fools had been made of them by the war they had fought with so much valour.

After having been in opposition all one's life to date, it was a bit uncomfortable to find oneself suddenly a government supporter. As I say, I did not expect much. I had never considered that the Labour Party as a whole was socialist. I was rather surprised when, almost at once, they began to nationalise coal and railways, though, alas, paying ruinous compensation. Their determined voting at the General Election had inclined me to feel sentimental about my countrymen, especially the workmen. I was dismayed and, indeed, even disgusted when they quickly began to go out on strike against what, after all, was supposed to be their government, striking all the more readily because it *was* their government and would therefore presumably give way more easily. This I thought low. We all ought, I felt, to be rallying round.

X

THE public arts seemed in great shape. The inspiriting thing towards the end of the war had been Benjamin Britten's opera, *Peter Grimes* (first heard, I suppose, over the wireless, the previous winter, on leave). That really seemed to put us on the map, operatically speaking. Almost as hopeful a portent was the Olivier film of *Henry V*, to which also music, William Walton's fine score, contributed largely. From BBC diary entries and old programmes, I see that by the end of 1945 I had sat through an admirable *Lady Windermere's Fan* at the Haymarket and Olivier's electrifying *Oedipus Rex*. In March 1946, I watched the two parts of Olivier's *Henry IV* at the New, a full-scale *Sleeping Princess* at Covent Garden and Cocteau's film, *L'Éternel Retour*, politically suspect because of its Wagnerian theme and the Germanically blond hair.

In April, there was a new Sean O'Casey play, *Red Roses For Me*. At the New, Olivier was playing *Uncle Vanya*. In May, we had a French ballet company at the Adelphi (Chauviré, Jean-maire, Roland Petit, Babilée, I seem to remember, and certainly I remember wondering how people who must have been terribly undernourished could possibly dance so energetically). At the tiny Mercury (visible from the windows of the room in which I write), there were plays by contemporary poets. War-time themes were beginning to find their way on to the stage, *Friede* at the Westminster and, the following month, *No Room at the Inn* at the Winter Garden.

Although I had finished a book, I stayed on at the BBC. The book was rather slender and *ad hoc*. It was called *The Double Image*, and it dealt with four French Catholic writers, Léon Bloy, Georges Bernanos, François Mauriac and Paul Claudel. Writing it had been decidedly somewhat less than a creative act. A more ambitious book on the same lines had been a war-time commitment in my pre-Army days. I had written most of the Bernanos stuff towards the end of the war, on leave.

The Bloy was essentially pre-war. Though I read for the first time most of the Mauriac and Claudel, all but a few of their books had lain to my hand before and at the beginning of the war, as had the issues of the *Nouvelle Revue Française* from which I quoted reviews done at the time.

Three other publications were in hand. A reprint of *The Blaze of Noon* was being set up, for the English publisher, in Holland. Preceded by no more than two short pieces written later, the bulk of the contents of my two pre-war and one early-war-time volumes of verse were to be done as a kind of selected-collected *Poems 1933-45*. I had revised, and was to publish with an Introduction, a translation, made by my closest friend just before his death, of Guido de Ruggiero's essay on *Existentialism*. In addition, a French translation of *The Blaze of Noon* was under way. I saw it in typescript and was able to make helpful suggestions about it. I was reviewing novels for *The New Statesman*, whose literary editor at that time was Raymond Mortimer, with V. S. Pritchett as his assistant.

All this gave me the illusion of being creatively active, as sometimes did my work at the BBC, even before (in October 1946) the Third Programme started. I think I saw the danger. Indeed, I remember saying, quite early on, that the trouble with broadcasting was that it so very nearly satisfied the creative appetite. By way of a second job, one might, I felt, have done better, like Spinoza, polishing lenses. With something purely routine, something essentially boring, one could have let impulses stir vaguely in one's mind during the day, then clarify as, at a fixed hour, one snapped out of it, giving the job never a thought at the week-end. As things were, whenever my mind was empty, it began to fill up with programme ideas, refinements of production method, new uses of music and so on.

It was rather nice at the BBC. In varying degrees, I liked all my colleagues. I had not expected to find them either so intelligent or so pleasant. Here I had better insist on the extent to which the BBC is large and departmentalised. I knew very few people outside my own department, which was Features. There was some variety of departmental *ethos*. Producers in Drama Dept. were more interested in the theatre, while those

57

in Features generally had some literary or journalistic background. They dressed less smartly and drank more. In the course of seventeen years, I have met few Talks producers and even fewer Music and Variety producers. One had much to do with highly skilled and admirable people (several of the most brilliant were young women) who saw to the technical side of one's programmes. At first they were known as P.E.s (programme engineers), later as S.M.s (studio managers). A group of these was attached to each production department, and one stood on terms of easy friendship with them, as one did with the secretaries in one's own department. But, of course, the BBC was like the Army in at least one respect. In the Army, for each (even potentially) combatant soldier, it was reckoned that there were between eight and twelve men at base. At the BBC, those directly concerned with broadcasting were a minority, and those personally familiar with microphones a small *corps d'élite*. On the one hand, there were messengers, liftmen, studio attendants, canteen girls, telephone switchboard operators, pool typists, commissionaires and so on, together with their supervisors and manageresses. On the other hand, there were administrators at all levels and with all functions, from those with heavily carpeted office suites, huge desks in fumed oak and (it was said) white telephones down to harassed-looking, white-haired ladies in Welfare. One knew a little of some on the legal side, in Copyright or Programme Contracts. On first joining the Corporation, one had seen the Medical Officer, and one might have called on the Matron with a headache or a trapped finger. But one knew very little of those legions of administrators or, indeed, of the bulk of engineering staff. Of the more elevated Controllers and such, after a first D.G.'s lunch, one merely from time to time heard the names spoken, usually with jocularity.

My colleagues, then, were, in effect, other Features producers, the one or two Drama producers who spent their money in public houses, the P.E.s and those enchanting girls, our secretaries. The two most prestigious of my immediate colleagues were Louis MacNeice and Stephen Potter. Though he had some little distance to come, Empson would sometimes appear in the Stag's Head at midday. And there was a floating population of outside writers, musicians, actors, war heroes, distinguished foreigners and gardening experts, who added colour and diversity to those middays and early evenings during which it was agreeably easy to drink oneself silly on weak beer, day after day and from one quarter's end to another.

For one had to think in terms of quarterly schedules, cut across by those periods of a month or eight weeks during which casts and studios had to be booked, scripts and music finished and duplicated, for each individual programme. This may have accelerated the passage of time, real or apparent. In fact, one lived according to two markedly different time-scales. On the one hand, quarterly schedules, programme budgets eight weeks in advance. On the other hand, split-second timing, the tyranny of that 'ghost in galoshes,' the red second hand of the studio clock, striding relentlessly, unnervingly round, threatening fade-out or a delayed beginning.

Nowadays, most programmes are pre-recorded. In those days, everything went out 'live' in the first place, a recording being made off transmission. The change was gradual. Long after Third Programme had accepted a general practice of pre-recording, Home Service and Light Programme continued to insist on live transmissions. It was felt that the listener responded more keenly to what he knew was going on at that moment in the studio, that there was some kind of active *rapport* between him and the actor. At the production end, it was frequently said that, under conditions of greater tension, better performances were given. It may well be so. During a live transmission, if an actor 'fluffs' he must quick-mindedly cover up, and anyone else in the scene must go along with him. Once tape-recording became universal (a later phase), actors began to fluff very frequently, knowing that everything could be put right subsequently.

For producer and P.E.s, especially for the senior P.E. at the panel, the tension of a live transmission could be very great indeed. There might be five or six microphones in use, each under separate control. There might be a choir, soloists, a sizeable orchestra, a large cast, many recorded sounds to bring in, as well as spot effects in the studio. With a score still new to him and an orchestra with which he had not had more than three hours' rehearsal, the conductor might well have twenty cues to take on headphones. The spot P.E. would also wear headphones and, apart from firing off his blank cartridges, ringing bells, smashing up matchwood, doing footsteps on wood, stone, gravel, would have to keep his eye on the cubicle window in case we wanted him to move some actor a bit further back from a microphone or warn another who seemed to have lost his place. The programme might last an hour and a half, and there might have been three days' rehearsals altogether. There might or might not have been a complete run-through with the noisy and indifferent musicians.

After a last break, as everyone reassembled, the senior P.E. would send up 'tone' and 'level' to the Control Room. Any discrepancy in the synchronisation of their clock and ours would have been noted. Perhaps an announcer had appeared and been taken through his announcements, or perhaps the opening announcement would be coming through from Continuity. We listened to the last few minutes of the preceding programme on our wavelength. One minute to go. Their concluding announcement, ours perhaps from Continuity, a last pressing of the identification buzzer, the red light intermittent, then steady, and we were on the air, with, you would have thought, no statistical likelihood of getting through the next ninety minutes without a breakdown of some kind. One always made it. Often enough, there was a *contretemps* of some kind, but the resourcefulness of one or other of the P.E.s or occasionally one's own rapid decision covered it, even if, once the transmission was over, one had to stay with the recording channel and do one passage again. Then, invariably, all round to the nearest public house, at any rate producer and P.E.s and secretary and several of the cast.

All this was at once nerve-racking and exhilarating. It worked like a drug, with distinct withdrawal symptoms over the next day or two. In the end, one knew how good or otherwise the programme had been. There were some very good programmes. The texts of a few have found their way into print. A few have been revived more than once. In general, one's best work had been forgotten within a fortnight. Perhaps that did not make it less creative. Public interest in a book will be spread over a longer period, but that does not mean that more people have read it than may have listened to a programme transmitted only once. Subjectively, the human satisfaction of the programme might well be greater.

Still, it was not quite the same thing. In some way, it was all sub-creative activity, and one knew it. I even found it temperamentally hard. This had little to do with the programme tension described above. One might have an occasional bad dream about cue-lights not working or microphones going dead, but temperamentally (as, I think, in terms of sheer skill and capacity) I was soon able to cope with all that kind of thing pretty well. But I am only intermittently gregarious, and perhaps I am not by nature co-operative. I was a fair mixer, but quite often I wanted not to mix. In the Army, I had not much cared for obeying orders. I did not much care for issuing them. At times, even a secretary, even a P.E., might need to be bullied, though rarely. As a rule, one's immediate colleagues were always very easy on the nerves. What there did seem to be rather a lot of was people at the other end of telephone lines who were either trying to browbeat oneself or whom, worse still, one had to browbeat. This I found utterly hateful and ulcerating

Similarly, among the members of the acting profession, there were angels, some of them brilliant angels, but there were also ninnies, awkward customers and persons of incredibly poor intelligence. Occasionally, insuperable boredom or a strange mood of corporate resistance would infect a whole cast. One's own mood might also be tainted, and rehearsals, planned weeks beforehand, could never be put off to another day, nor could a script which unaccountably failed to come to life be abandoned.

However, I shall begin to look as though I were inviting sympathy, and I know very well that such difficulties as I had were nothing to what people in other occupations may have to put up with daily. My lot was a pleasant one. I spent my days among people I liked. Not everything seemed equally worth doing, but (and this was peculiarly the case with almost all that was done in Features Dept.) it was extremely rare for me to find myself doing a programme which I had not, in some way, initiated myself. What I did might occasionally be worthless, but it was never, like a great deal of what is done by, say, business men, lawyers or men in advertising and journalism, directly harmful to the community. During the whole course of eighteen years, I have never once had occasion to pause and wonder if what I was doing was faintly dishonourable.

It was simply that I was doing something other than writing or that, when I was writing, it might well be something I should not otherwise have written. I was under constraint. I would have preferred it otherwise. I very frequently thought, and sometimes said, that, if I had been able to pay outright for however small a cottage with an acre of garden, I would have given up London and the BBC and lived entirely on my writing. I have never been in a position to do that (to be free, that is to say, of rent or mortgage and always certain of at least vegetables). That being so, it appeared to me that my behaviour was morally praiseworthy. I had a family. From month to month, I kept it housed and fed.

After being trapped in Australia by the war, the Innes Stewarts returned to the United Kingdom in 1946. After a year or so in Belfast, Innes went as a fellow or (as they quaintly say there) a student to Christ Church, Oxford. By post, he had long continued to be in some things my mentor. Upon my presenting my position to him in something like these terms, he said a hard thing, not, I am sure, with any complacency.

He said:

'Ah, yes. Sheltering behind one's children.'

I went on doing it. The problem is an existential one. That is no doubt why, having earlier been much taken with Kierkegaard and with the little I knew of Heidegger and Jaspers, I was now much attracted by the French existentialists. This kind of philosophy clearly means different things to different people. To me, what it meant above all was taking decisions and sticking to them, knowing that some discomfort was inevitable. It was the end of recourse to the comfort of Freudian, Marxist or Christian alibis. The reasons for a decision might be what they would, but there could not be any going back. I resigned myself to a high degree of uncreativeness.

XI

THAT I specifically gave up writing verse or, at any rate, direct, lyrical verse was due to other considerations, for, after all, short poems are the most convenient things for a busy man to fit in between spells of other work. They may be worked out in the head on top of a 'bus or in a tube-train or an ordinary train or while walking along the street. They may be set down on scraps of paper at a pub counter or in bed or while, the table being already laid for dinner, one's guests are awaited.

Prose is more difficult, for, as a tycoon of the cinema once observed:

'You gotta sit down to write a book.'

I have in fact taken almost no interest in contemporary verse for ten years, very little for seventeen or eighteen and not very much for twenty-three. Yet, for eight or nine years, the longest years of all, those of early manhood, I had regarded myself as primarily, almost exclusively, a poet. This is a case-history of sorts, and I had better try to explain it.

The mere writing (in 1938) and publishing (in 1939) of a novel I still quite approved of and which had been successful may account for something, though I had written a good deal of verse between the writing and publication of *The Blaze of Noon*. Moreover, after its publication, I remember being asked by an older novelist (Louis Golding, at the time a neighbour in St John's Wood) whether I now thought of myself as, mainly, a novelist or as a poet. After thinking hard for some minutes (for I had not till then considered the problem), I said I still thought of myself as mainly a poet. Yet, by the summer of 1946, I was in the position of having subsequently written only five poems during the war and one after, and since then I have written verse only by way of translation or for special purposes in work otherwise of a didactic-narrative or dramatic nature.

T. S. Eliot once wrote, in some essay, of a kind of youthful

63

poetic impulse which gives out at the age of twenty-five. According to Herbert Read, mine gave out when I was twenty-nine. While I was in the Army, he sent me a poem which contains (I quote from memory) the lines:

> Hands apt for love and poetry
> finger the hostile gun-metal. Your impulse
> died in the second winter of the war.

He didn't inscribe the published version to me, but in the accompanying letter he said that it had been me he had in mind. In fact my impulse had not then quite utterly died, but it was weak.

In his essay, I fancy that Mr Eliot, with his usual caution, had avoided using any such word as 'real' or 'genuine' or even 'authentic' of the more persistent impulse or any derogatory adjective of that which does not persist. Otherwise, he might have found himself committed to the opinion that all kinds of elderly persons are more truly poets than was, say, Rimbaud. Still, that is the implication, more or less.

It can hardly, I think, be argued, and, certainly, to argue it would not be at all in Mr Eliot's line, that the poetic impulse is as specific as the sexual urge or that the capacity needed to fulfil it is as organically determined or, indeed, that the two things are directly related to each other, except perhaps at the moment of their first awakening. The age of twenty-five may also be that at which most people, as they adopt a regular sexual habit, abandon that auto-erotism of the imagination which may be thought quite normal in civilised youth. If that is so, then we might regard the one urge as having been a surrogate for the other. It is true that what I say can hardly be argued has in fact been used to explain the longevity *qua* poet, as well as the late marriage, of W. B. Yeats. He is said to have been rejuvenated by the Steinach operation, which, it is said, left him in a state of almost permanent tumescence, genital and poetic. So far as I know, Mr Eliot's own late marital activity has not been attributed to any such cause. Certainly, he would, one still feels, be the last to argue from it to any persistence of the poetic impulse. He has never dealt in such analogies.

64

It had, as a matter of fact, been on starting to read a poem by T. S. Eliot that I first questioned the good sense of writing poems at all. That had been in the autumn of 1940, just before I was called up into the Army. I was living in the country, while London burned. A copy of *The New English Weekly* had come in the post. It contained a long new poem, *East Coker*, by T. S. Eliot. I turned to the poem with some eagerness. It began:

In my beginning is my end . . .

I flung the paper across the room. It was like a signature tune. The poem might just as well have begun:

This is T. S. Eliot speaking . . .

In due course, I picked up the paper and read the rest and no doubt liked some of it, as I do now. It is not, after all, in that poem that Mr Eliot bids us so oddly to pray for fishmongers.

I wrote, as I say, a few poems during the war, the two best of them very short and 'occasional'. Towards the end of the war, I nodded with agreement when, in *The Unquiet Grave*, Cyril Connolly (whom I then admired only with the very greatest reluctance) described modern poets arguing about poetry as jackals snarling around an empty well and elsewhere said that the new poets reminded him of people who had discovered a billiard table and were trying to play on it, not knowing what the cues and pockets were for.

In 1946, Robert Graves's *The White Goddess* came out. Mr Graves's white goddess is the Muse, but she is also womanhood contemplated with a sacred horror under three aspects, as mother, as bride and as the crone who lays us out at death. Mr Graves lived, we might say, under an imaginary matriarchy, and his religion was a cult of *das Ewig-Weibliche* conceived in dark, primitive and sacrificial terms.

We may, I think, truly call it a religion. It was trinitarian, and the triune nature of womanhood was somehow conceived as ultimate reality, to be worshipped and invoked, as three male persons in one masculine God are in the Christian religion.

Mr Graves's religion had its obvious attractions. Certainly, I had no opposite belief in the truth of a Christian or other religion centred upon *das Ewig-Mannliche*. I rather liked worshipping women, especially if a touch of sacred horror was allowed.

I was quite prepared to say:

'I adore women, though sometimes they give me the creeps.'

For one thing, it is expected that goddesses shall reward their worshippers and that, even if it is their nature to be terrible, they will be less terrible to those who offer them sacrifice. If the goddess was also the Muse, then poetry might be considered the only proper magical and effective invocation of some kind of ultimate reality. Thus the eternal need for writing and publishing poems was guaranteed. The poet was a special and at the same time a necessary person. There was an esoteric poetic tradition, infallible if frequently obscured historically.

That was the essence of Mr Graves's appeal to those who were abandoning verse in 1946. The central argument had been surrounded with much weird and delightful pseudo-scholarship, much of it connected with early Welsh poetry. I liked this. I quite liked the central argument and even the strong suggestion that it would be better if a matrilineal form of social organisation could be restored.

It wouldn't do, of course. Or it would do only for those who like Mr Graves (in Majorca) lived outside the modern world. In that world, it seemed to me that everything needed carefully saying again from the beginning, in prose and preferably in words of not more than two syllables. Lyrical verse was not explanatory. It celebrated deep and wide agreements among men and women, and after Hitler's war there was a notable lack of agreement or understanding. To arrange words in little patterns, so that they went *ti-tum ti-tum*, seemed pointless and affected.

The poetry of the past retained its point, by and large. Something awful had taken place in the late nineteenth century, especially in France with Mallarmé, but here too with Hopkins, though his influence was delayed. Words had begun to be regarded as concrete, substantial things, quite apart from the meanings they could be used to convey. This accounted for the clotted obscurity of much of the verse of the 'Thirties and

'Forties. It spoiled Dylan Thomas for me, though I had known him quite well and though I enjoyed the lighter word-play of his prose excursions. Still, the symbolist trend had not ruined Yeats in the end, and in much of his work Mr Eliot had surmounted it. I could still see the point of most of what W. H. Auden had done and was doing. I had very much liked early Betjeman, and, among the poets who had first appeared in war-time, I thought well of Henry Reed and Laurie Lee.

I had, as it happened, been responsible for switching both of these last two to their first essays in dramatic verse, Reed with his *Pytheas*, Lee with *The Voyage of Magellan*. Neither has written much lyrical verse since. I hope that is not my fault. I don't think it is. Lee's kind of gaily coloured song could not have been endlessly repeated, and Reed's most-acclaimed pieces (his 'Naming of Parts,' for instance, and his Eliot parody, 'Chard Whitlow') had been a kind of anti-poetry. So had Mr Betjeman's early poems, and so had much of the best Auden. I felt I knew what all these had been up to, and I felt that it was all by way of being an epilogue to something. I saw, as I felt, the point. Apart from Louis MacNeice's dramatic verse, I could not see the point of what their contemporaries might have thought they had recently been up to, while about most of their successors I felt sure they were persons writing verse in part because they were incapable of writing so much as a paragraph of lucid prose.

To verse, also, there was attached a traditional prestige, which made untalented people take to it. To set up as a poet required very little effort, and, once set up, you became a deserving cause. Already in the 'Thirties, Herbert Read had put about the debilitating notion that poetry should be subsidised, like farming or inshore fishing or decayed gentlewomen. Nobody was interested in poetry, but all literate people felt that they ought to support it. Other writers felt guilty about poets, because it had been so overwhelmingly demonstrated that to live by writing poems was impossible. The payment by number of words was in fact higher for verse than for any other kind of respectable writing, and, what with the charitable perks, so, I had begun to suspect, was the payment by output in terms of talent or effort. It might have been better not to

67

subsidise verse, but to penalise it. There ought perhaps to have been a moratorium on writing verse at all. Writing verse ought perhaps to have been made illegal, with very severe penalties for any transgression. Then only the most utterly genuine impulse would have survived.

I was thinking that kind of thing in 1946. I still think much the same. Poetry now is even more *supported*. In 1946, a sensible and welcome characteristic of, for instance, *The New Statesman* was that it printed no verse, apart from the political jingles of 'Sagittarius' and four-to-eight-line column fill-ups in the form of epigrams by Frances Cornford. Now *The New Statesman* prints pages of the most tedious new verse. So does *The Times Literary Supplement*, which, indeed, specifically employs a poetry-chooser. Luckily, verse is easily recognised on the page, so we don't need to read it. Very few people read it, I fancy. I glance occasionally, if the name at the bottom of the poem is that of someone I know or of someone I have recently heard praised. It was by pure accident or instinct that, in *The Spectator* some ten years ago, I thus glanced at a poem called 'Churchgoing' by Philip Larkin, a name I had not even heard. In, say, fifteen years, that is the only time I have not regretted letting my eyes so wander. Perhaps, unknown to Mr Larkin, that poem was a true swan-song, its underlying theme, and the source of its extraordinary pathos, regretful *adieu* not only to churches but also to poetry as it had been understood throughout the Christian era and in late classical times.

I don't even care now. In 1946, I was a bit worried. I felt a bit as though I might have lost something. I certainly couldn't altogether explain the sudden ineffectiveness of verse. For painting and for music, distinct traumas could be discovered. Painting had lost some of its functions when photography was invented and would clearly lose more when colour photography became less primitive. Our music had developed on the basis of a diatonic system, the entirety of whose permutations and combinations might well have been exhausted by 1946, as the atonalists thought, while their own projects were based on the idea, surely fallacious, that the trained ear could from moment to moment shed one set of listening habits and adopt another, the alternative system certainly not being grounded in nature, as the diatonic system was. It was difficult to see what equally specific trauma had been suffered by poetry, at any rate in recent times, the blow against the purely mnemonic function of verse having been struck five hundred years before with the invention of printing.

The music I had to do with was in fact incidental music, and perhaps all the most effective music of our time has been incidental. Music in opera, as well as in ballet, films and radio, *is* incidental to some extent. Perhaps all vocal music, since it involves some degree of subservience to words, is incidental. Certainly, our most talented composers were not writing symphonies. As to painting, in its dominant abstract form it was clearly no more than a branch of interior decoration, which would attain its apogee ten years later in the *espresso* bar. Its main development since, which I take to be action painting, itself abstract in the result, is art without an artist, which I suppose is what the art theorists have always wanted. So perhaps lyrical verse was in no worse plight than the other pure, *i.e.*, simple, unentangled, non-incidental, non-occasional arts. On the other hand, verse drama also seemed to be having a last fling at the time, in the work, *e.g.*, of Christopher Fry and in one or two curious pieces that were being performed at the Mercury, along the road from here.

XII

BETWEEN July 1946 and June 1947, I saw a good many plays, some French films and two or three operas, and went to a fair number of ballet performances. There was another French company, with one or two of the same dancers as the previous year. The Covent Garden ballet itself was in excellent form, and there also came to Covent Garden a New York company whose principal choregrapher was Anthony Tudor. In America, Tudor had become famous. Only I had rooted for him while he still worked in London before and during the first year of the war.

We met again, and in fact, during the winter of 1946-7, I had rather a lot to do with ballet people, but very much as an outsider, very much as a BBC man doing a programme, with perhaps readier *entrée* because some of them remembered my name. A Home Service rubric then in use was 'Professional Portrait'. I proposed and was encouraged to do 'Professional Portrait: a Ballerina'. I centred it on not-yet-Dame Margot Fonteyn and on rehearsals, then in progress, for a full-length *Swan Lake*. The assignment also involved me with Robert Helpmann, then still principal male dancer at Covent Garden, with the choreographer Frederick Ashton, with the formidable Dame Ninette de Valois, with Vera Volkova who was at the time Fonteyn's teacher and with the former Diaghilev star, Tamara Karsavina.

I remember the programme itself with nostalgic pleasure. But much of the pleasure I took in it at the time was already nostalgic. I had effectively given up the ballet eleven years before.

Those of my readers who never took an interest in ballet may yet care to be told a little about *Swan Lake*. It was first danced at Moscow in 1877. The music is by Tchaikovsky, the choreography by Marius Petipa. The story concerns a young person called Odette who, with her companions, has been turned into a swan by a wicked magician. A prince, who has been ordered by his mother to find a wife, goes swan-hunting. He aims his bow, a cross-bow, at one of the swans, who turns into a young woman. This is Odette. The wicked magician is about, however, in the guise of an owl, and the girls must go away and become swans again. In Act III, the magician brings his daughter Odile to court. She resembles Odette, but is dressed in black. One and the same dancer plays both parts, though at one point another dancer temporarily representing Odette appears in great agitation, spot-lighted behind a gauze curtain, when the prince is bamboozled into plighting his troth to Odile.

The climax of this act, choreographically, is the performance by Odile of the fabulous thirty-two *fouettés*. Using the blocked toe of her left foot as a peg, the dancer, with her right leg, whips herself round like a top thirty-two times to the music. There have been many *Swan Lake* recordings under various conductors, but, of those available in 1947, none included the tune to which this feat is performed. It is in fact a dreadful tune, thumped out like a circus march, with plenty of bass drum and trombones. I wanted it for my programme, and Sir Adrian Boult, with the BBC Symphony Orchestra, recorded it for me in the course of a rehearsal otherwise devoted to works of more gravity. As this unaccustomed noise blared and thumped out from the enormous main studio at Maida Vale, people from offices and canteens all over the building crowded about the entrance to see what was going on.

I began my programme on this tune, to which supposed fans in the audience were gradually to be heard counting up to thirty-two and then vociferating. In the interval, an elderly *balletomane* was heard saying to his younger neighbour that it was extraordinary how all the young women could do thirty-two *fouettés* nowadays, whereas in his youth they'd done only eight or nine. It had been started by an Italian, Legnani, and the first of the Russians to do it was Kchessinskaya. The younger man, bent on knowing what goes on behind all this, is next heard talking to Margot Fonteyn over luncheon. He was an actor. So was the elderly *balletomane*. Fonteyn played the part of herself, from a script put together by me from notes made at the luncheon table and elsewhere, in one case, Miss Fonteyn being laid up with 'flu, at the bedside.

The script is before me as I write, and I see from my office diary that the lunch took place on November 26th, 1946. It was not at the Ivy but at a restaurant just across the way, this being close to the hall in which Mme Volkova's classes were held. Fonteyn normally put in two or two and a half hours there every day. The information conveyed in the luncheon scene was of the elementary biographical kind with which the readers of books on dancing are familiar but with which I could not assume familiarity on the part of my listeners. It transpired, for instance, that Miss Fonteyn had been born at Reigate in Surrey on May 18th, 1919, that she took up dancing at five, went up on points at seven or eight, was first taught by a lady in Ealing, went to China, living for six years mostly in Shanghai, her father being an engineer, had Goncharov there for a teacher and at fourteen, back in England, went to Sadler's Wells.

The next scene was at Volkova's. I had engineers at a class, with their recording gear. In the programme, with the evocative sound of the class going on, the actor (in effect myself) commented upon the proceedings. It was, he noted, like a church hall, with pointed ecclesiastical windows. The distemper was pink. The upright piano stood on a platform. At that moment, in another room in the building, the Tiller girls were practising for a Christmas pantomime. Here, in white blouse, black trunks, pink tights and shoes, a striped orange belt and a blue band round her hair, Fonteyn limbered up at the bar, next to a young man in new, bright-blue tights and scarlet shoes.

Volkova says:

'I think we do stretch now, yes?'

Each dancer's right foot goes up on to the bar. The torso wanders forward, backward, sideways, towards the floor, on an impossible pilgrimage. Volkova goes to each pupil in turn, adjusting positions, touching some muscle that is wrongly tensed.

Vera Volkova was quite a young woman. She had trained and danced in Leningrad after the Revolution. She left the company on a Chinese tour and made her way to England, where she began teaching during Hitler's war. I seem to remember hearing later that she had gone to Sweden.

Next came a scene at a drill-hall off Tottenham Court Road. Fonteyn was not there. Ninette de Valois was rehearsing the festivities in Act III of *Swan Lake*. There was a Czardas and a Mazurka.

Then the dress rehearsal, Constant Lambert conducting. The huge red theatre was dimly lighted. At the back of the stalls, there was a table fitted with a lamp for Miss de Valois. Twenty or thirty privileged people were sitting in the stalls circle. I got into conversation with two girls who were not yet in the company, though one of their chums was on stage. In the programme, I called these three Bee, Georgie and Gwen. They were played by young actresses. Bee had a Scotch accent.

It was a bitterly cold morning. The frilled muslin billowed out from beneath cardigans and sweaters. One girl had brown woollen stockings over her tights.

Another lunch scene, with de Valois. Conversation with Frederick Ashton about his new ballet and about working with and writing for Fonteyn. More conversation with Fonteyn herself, on diet, number of pairs of shoes worn out each week, liability to sprains, other interests.

And then the performance itself. I hung about backstage. Georgie was in the wings. Bee *had* got a part, as a black swan in the last act. Only Georgie was left out. She was furious. She kept trying to unnerve Bee by telling her that her mascara was running, telling her that her eyes were made up wrong. All the lines went downward. It made her look half-witted. One up, one down. That opened the eyes wide. Poor Georgie.

Helpmann's dressing room in the first interval. He doesn't like classical rôles, except *Giselle*. The prince in *Swan Lake* is a cardboard figure. In the most literal sense, it's a supporting rôle, hard work. Talk with the still-enchanting Karsavina, who recalls the Marinsky at the turn of the century.

There was a Field-Marshal in the audience (Montgomery, I suppose, but the script doesn't tell me). He was going to Moscow in a day or two, and it was thought that he'd come to a ballet performance at Covent Garden in order to give himself a subject of conversation there. In the second interval, the two stars had to visit him in the Royal Box. He was affable, said he would tell the Russians the ballet was better at Covent Garden.

I took the performance up to the end of Act III, fading out on the *fouettés* tune, but there was an epilogue in Fonteyn's dressing room after the show. I may say that one thing work on the programme left me with was a fanatical admiration for the character of Margot Fonteyn, stubborn and essentially modest. My interest in the art did not revive. Or, perhaps I should rather say, I no longer saw any point in watching actual performances of ballet.

XIII

THE various books came out. All got fair reviews (apart from the *Blaze of Noon* reprint, which got none at that time, though a later reprint was seriously considered). Even my verse, which had never found much favour in the past, was treated with respect. Fancy (was the general line) Mr H. being such a good poet, and we never knew. It was, however, also darkly wondered, as well it might be, what, as a poet, Mr H. had been up to of recent years. *The Double Image* got one really well-informed review, and it was by 'Donat O'Donnell', the Conor Cruise O'Brien who more recently was much photographed rampaging around the Congo in a striped shirt, egging the black men on. Dr O'Brien very truly pointed out how bad I was on Mauriac. He was so obviously right about this, I felt no ill will towards him but resolved to do better in future. I did later think him a bit mean to give me not even bibliographical credit in his own admirable book, *Maria Cross*, on the same group of French Catholic writers, and of his field career with the U.N. I take a very dark view indeed.

In the summer of 1947, I got to France for the first time since the war. It was, in its own way, *la vraie France*. That is to say, the people I stayed with were rich, but they were not intellectuals. They were not quite Nancy Mitford French, but a sort of *haute bourgeoisie*, conventional in politics and religion. They lived outside Paris, but at no greater distance than allowed me to go in most days and explore a city which, before the war, I had visited only briefly and in winter. I did not fail to respond in the usual ways. I found, on the whole, the mood of French people pleasanter than that which had developed in London since the war, though, of course, there were still currency touts outside places like Notre Dame, and certainly there were things which could only be got on the black market, dairy produce mainly. The bread, made largely of maize, was very unpleasant, and good coffee was not easily come by.

One took coffee abroad as a gift to one's friends. One brought back scent, lipsticks and anything which could be managed in the way of small articles of clothing. At this distance in time, it is perhaps difficult for us to remember just how long rationing went on after the war. It was certainly to be five more years, for instance, before we in England could freely buy meat or butter. In those days, raising all the foreign currency they could find pretext for, business men went abroad just to eat steaks. As a matter of fact, so did many quite respectable members of the community, who, often enough, also went to Ireland purely in order to acquire suit-lengths of tweed.

In the Paris underground were to be seen posters advertising a play called *La Putain Respectueuse*, by Jean-Paul Sartre, only the noun was heavily blacked out, so that one read *La* ▆▆▆▆▆ *Respectueuse*. Some kind of wave of puritanism had washed over France after the war. A Mme Richard had introduced a bill to abolish the State brothel service, and it had been passed without serious opposition, a traditional and important feature of French life thus collapsing at a touch, on Leftish grounds one supposes, the idea being that only poverty drove girls to prostitution, a notion we have since seen massively disproved in our own country and one which, in France, has certainly deprived many elderly men of much innocent pleasure with good-natured girls of low intelligence. In London, a mistranslation of M. Sartre's play, *The* Respectable *Prostitute*, showing at the Lyric in Hammersmith, had been advertised without police interference.

At the Lyric, M. Sartre's play about racial prejudice in America had been shown together with *Men Without Shadows*, a play in which members of the Resistance are tortured on stage by uniformed members of the Vichy Militia. The English version was cut. The original, *Morts Sans Sépulture*, had been reported in our newspapers as causing mass exhibitions of fainting among the audience in Paris. I had seen the plays at the Lyric. I did not see either in Paris.

London was pretty well aware of Sartre. The Arts had done *Huis Clos*. Third Programme had done both that and *The Flies*. The paperbacked *New Writing* had printed several of the stories from *Le Mur*, and the first two of the *Chemins de la Liberté* sequence of novels had appeared in translation, as *The Age of Reason* and *The Reprieve*. M. Sartre had appeared in London, and a *Picture Post* article, with photographs, had described him as a 'dumpy little man with a twitching right arm' and as a 'sandy-haired forceful little Frenchman who looks out on the world from behind pebble glasses'. I was not myself to set eyes on M. Sartre until the following year, but I had read him comprehensively and admired a good deal in his work. At least in terms of brute calories, he seemed the most vital of our contemporaries, the literary airs and graces and the personal charm being provided by Albert Camus, a name at that time still always linked with Sartre's.

The term '*littérature engagée*', the idea that a writer should be fully committed to the life of his own time, including notably its political life, had been promulgated two years before, in 1945, in *Les Temps Modernes*, which, under M. Sartre's editorship, had taken the place of the *Nouvelle Revue Française* as the monthly house organ of Gallimard's, the *NRF* being then considered to have been too deeply compromised under the Occupation to be started up again. But M. Sartre was not yet a communist. He had argued against communism both in public debate and in *The Age of Reason*, and his most damaging anti-communist tract, the play *Les Mains Sâles* (known here as *Crime Passionel*), was not to appear until the following year. The trend might, I suppose, have been perceived. As it happens, in the summer of 1947, I did meet in Paris one pupil of Sartre's, a Corsican banker's son, who had himself become a communist.

As to the war-time Resistance, M. Sartre's weight had certainly lain behind that. I myself saw it as a matter of black and white, sheep and goats. In respect of their war-time activities, I thought of Frenchmen as having been divided into virtuous *résistants*, wicked collaborationists and the mass of the timid who, one supposed, had mildly inclined this way or that, most having behaved well in a negative kind of way. I could not imagine anyone collaborating actively except for base reasons of personal self-advancement. On the other hand, one readily imagined that as much personal spite had been satisfied during the past three years by persons denouncing their neighbours for collaboration as during the four years before that by persons denouncing their neighbours to Vichy or the Germans, and certainly I did not care for the excessive zeal with which certain members of the communist-dominated *Comité National des Écrivains* (operating, oddly, under the chairmanship of Paul Claudel, himself not uncompromised) bayed after the blood of writers of whom the worst that could be said was that they had been a bit foolish. To me, the most conspicuous of these was Marcel Jouhandeau. A particularly noisy bloodhound was the aged Julien Benda, whose *La Trahison des Clercs* had been well-known even in England before the war and who in the summer of 1947 also published a book against the existentialists.

In this book, *La Tradition de l'Existentialisme*, Benda found in M. Sartre's doctrine of *engagement* a new form of *la trahison des clercs*, a current phase in the perpetual war of life against thought. From the point of view of philosophers, perhaps this was true enough. From the point of view of the general reading public, the opposite, surely, was true, for they were now getting philosophy with their literature, whether they liked it or not. The nature of old Benda's resentments was complex to the point of contradictoriness. A Jew, he particularly deplored the influence of the Jewish philosopher, Henri Bergson. To him, all young writers were existentialists, and Bergson was the father of them all. And, surely, he was himself guilty of a *trahison de clerc*. He had been pursuing Jouhandeau, the least political of writers, on political grounds.

If I myself deplored Sartre in any way, it was for his lack of devotion to purely literary and contemplative values. I was not sure that a point of rest was not what the age found it most difficult to achieve and that the 'inwardness' of Kierkegaard, the 'creative repose' of Jaspers, the 'fidelity' and the sense of irreducible mystery in Gabriel Marcel, were not existential studies as worthy of application as the detonation of consciousness Sartre had discovered pre-war in Husserl. In a talk by Étienne Gilson, which I had had the pleasure of translating so that Professor Gilson might have the pleasure of himself broadcasting it in English from Paris, it had been stated that in such-and-such a century M. Sartre would have been a monk of this-or-that order. I, on the other hand, thought it a weakness of M. Sartre's thought that he allowed too little value to the monkish virtues of contemplation. His was a philosophy of hard living, a modern cure for 'the monk's disease,' *accidie*, which had latterly got too much hold of the laity. Before the war, M. Sartre had denounced Jean Giraudoux's Aristotelian world of intelligible forms. In *L'Imaginaire*, he had, at the beginning of the war, made a very distinct contribution to aesthetics, but now his philosophy seemed to preclude aesthetic judgments. In his world, there was clearly such a thing as admirable action. It seemed doubtful whether there was in that world any admirable state of rest.

I did not object to the idea of commitment. In my own way, I felt sufficiently committed. Not that I was in any way politically active. My work gave me the sensation of leading an active life, but politically all that seemed required of me was a patient loyalty to our government of the day, which, despite its aberrations in Palestine and its timidity in dealing with commercial interests, I thought right in the main. I should have liked more display of European imagination. I should have liked to see what I should have been very willing to call a 'Christian socialist' Europe, thumbing its nose both at the Russians and at America. On that point, M. Sartre was unhelpful. In his *Temps Modernes* articles, he overtly excluded the United Kingdom from Europe, culturally and politically, anticipating General de Gaulle's more practical exclusion by sixteen years. Yet M. Sartre is no Gaulliste, nor indeed has the General ever been thought an existentialist.

The unreality of British life was nicely revealed in the first play I saw on returning to London. This was Noel Coward's *Peace In Our Time*. In this play, Mr Coward showed us a London imaginarily occupied by the Germans. He showed us a sturdy, Tory-minded publican's family and their Right-wing customers resisting nobly (at the end, the publican's daughter dies after torture), while the wicked collaborators are Left-wing types, principally a leading journalist. In other words, we were to suppose that, if we had lost the war, Mr Coward and his friends would have behaved with exemplary patriotism, what time, say, Mr Kingsley Martin betrayed them to the occupying forces. This, of course, was an exact reversal of what the French analogy might have led us to expect. In France, by and large, the Right had collaborated, the Left resisted, and Mr Coward's French equivalent, Sacha Guitry, had been gravely compromised. I saw *Peace In Our Time* in the company of a visiting French writer of Russian extraction, who had lived in Paris all through the war. He viewed the matter calmly, but I was appalled by the complicated (and, I fancied, guilt-voiding) nastiness of Mr Coward's intention, so that for years thereafter I felt some inclination to spit whenever I heard or saw his name. I was not much less appalled by the fact that the audience seemed willing to swallow this nonsense.

The most interesting event in the London theatre that autumn was the visit of the Vienna State Opera. I saw *Fidelio*, and I saw Richard Strauss's *Salome*, with that finest of post-war dramatic sopranos, the unfortunate Ljuba Welitsch. The only original play I have any note of was Donagh MacDonagh's *Happy As Larry*, at the Mercury. There was still quite a lot of Shakespeare to be seen, including two productions of *Richard II*, one from Stratford, one by the Old Vic Company, who also did a *Taming of the Shrew*, at the New. As, at that moment, *The New Statesman* lacked a drama critic, I wrote these productions up for them. I might have continued, but it quickly became apparent to me that either I should have to pull my punches unduly or I should find that I had offended actors I wanted to use in broadcasting. As it was, years went by before I felt I could book Robert Harris, the Shakespeare Memorial Company's Richard.

The other Richard was Alec Guinness. I had seen two Richards before, that of John Gielgud and, before the war, that of Maurice Evans, *at* the Old Vic, where in those days Sir Alec was a bit-player. He had made his post-war mark with the Fool in *Lear*. Both the new Richards were, I may say, admirable, though I noted in poor Mr Harris a tendency to roll his eyes frequently to heaven like an El Greco saint and though, in the dungeon at Pontefract, his wig and make-up, the agitation of his shoulders and the lighting, had conspired to make him look (as I fear I said) like a mad theosophist who suddenly finds herself figuring as the heroine in a play by Sartre.

Shakespeare on the London stage had not yet become so absurd as, during the next few years, it was to become. The two productions which finally sickened me were a *Much Ado About Nothing* in comic hats (the Benedick was Sir John Gielgud) and an *All's Well That Ends Well* in which Lafeu's daughter was actually brought on the stage to have her ugliness unveiled and during the course of which there was much audible Latin not in the text. Already, in the autumn of 1947, however, the supposedly bad old days of the actor-manager were all too far behind us, and Shakespeare had fallen into the hands of the producers.

The histories are perhaps a hopeless proposition, anyway. The ceremonious blackguards who made England certainly bore no resemblance to the smooth juveniles of London's West End. The Stratford producer had used a great deal of real armour, which his cast were unable to carry without sagging at the knees. He had contrived some good scenic moments, especially for the tournament at Coventry, with the passing of the tall lances. But what I chiefly recall is the vision of all those young men staggering about under all that iron. Then there were all the challenges, the flinging down of gloves on a dusty stage. Each glove, petulantly flung down, raised a puff of dust and made the audience laugh. At the New, the designer seemed to be having a practical joke on his colleagues. It was odd how the drops swayed and the small pavilion rocked at the most impressive moments and, in general, how bits of this and that kept going up and down on pulleys. The reader will no doubt be able to imagine for himself what opportunities *The Taming of the Shrew* offered to a producer bent on the invention of comic business.

At the BBC, I was presenting Plato dialogues, with actors playing Socrates and the rest. I was much affected by that passage in the *Crito* in which Socrates explains why he will not flee.[1] He has, he explains, till then explicitly subscribed to the laws of Athens, by which he is condemned. He imagines the laws personified and addressing him.

'Any Athenian, on attaining manhood and seeing for himself the political organisation of the state and us its Laws, is permitted,

[1] The translation is that which was used in the programme. It is by Hugh Tredennick and later appeared in a Penguin volume.

if he is not satisfied with us, to take his property and go away wherever he likes. If any of you chooses to go to one of our colonies, or to emigrate to any other country, not one of us Laws hinders or prevents him from going away wherever he likes, without any loss of property. On the other hand, if any of you stands his ground when he can see how we administer justice and the rest, we hold that by so doing he has in fact undertaken to do anything that we tell him.' They would point out, with perfect justice, that there are very few people in Athens who have entered into this agreement with them as explicitly as I have.

I applied the argument to all the conveniently Tory-minded business men and others who were at the time so eagerly sabotaging the measures of the Labour government. But I also applied it privately to myself. I am no longer sure what the logic was, but I very distinctly recall the emotional colour of the moment. There was some element of consolation in it, but it was not a happy moment. It was a contracted, not an expansive moment. It contained a suggestion of wrung withers. The colouring was dark, at best nobly dark. Perhaps it had something to do with the fact that, at that time, going away to live in another country was precisely not possible for us, on account of currency restrictions.

XIV

FROM early 1947 till now, I have press-cutting books kept regularly in good order. They contain articles, book-reviews and so on written by me, as well as reviews of my books. A single press-cutting book was more than enough to hold everything of both kinds over a period of more than eight years. I wrote nothing for any periodical between November 1947 and late October of the following year. For 1949-50, there was an inconsiderable amount of reviewing for *The New Statesman*, but then from the beginning of 1951 the gap for more than four years is almost total. If I was not writing verse, neither was I writing the amount of expository prose which my view of contemporary needs might have been thought to require.

A crisis of some kind might no doubt be diagnosed. I cannot diagnose it, though I have a good memory and know what the pressures were at particular moments. Any more general trouble must have been well-established by 1948. That year, I published hardly a word even in *The New Statesman*. In a number of other ways, it was a good year, at any rate from May onwards. The previous seven or eight months had been made tiresome by circumstances quite outside the range of this book.

Among the wireless programmes I produced that year, three were among the seven or eight I recall with most satisfaction, among them *The Hawk and the Handsaw* by Innes Stewart, just then established in Oxford. It had music by William Wordsworth, a composer I had first known in 1936 at the Middleton Murry centre in Essex. I went less often to plays and, apparently, only twice to ballet, but the films included Sartre's *Les Jeux Sont Faits*, while at the opera the *Tristan und Isolde* must have been Flagstad's and the *Traviata* Schwarzkopf's. The Vienna Philharmonic was in London for some weeks. In the summer of 1948, moreover, I spent more time (very happily) abroad than in any year since 1931, unless war-time Ulster is abroad.

In Paris, I met a fair number of French writers. A visit I recall with quite disproportionate pleasure took place on the afternoon of May (I think) 26th, a Saturday. With my translator, I called on Marcel Jouhandeau. There had been some war-time question of a sponsored trip to Germany, and the year before Jouhandeau had still been in the position of not being allowed to publish in France (the *Essai sur Moi-même* I bought then had been published in Switzerland). He remained a bit *mal vu*, with old Julien Benda and the communists still after his blood.

Beyond the larger of Napoleon's triumphal arches, you cross the impossibly wide Avenue de la Grande Armée and, after a brief glance at your street map, turn down the Avenue Raymond Poincaré. The Rue du Commandant Marchand is already much narrower and shorter. Each of those houses might well be inhabited by a single family, which seems odd in Paris. You find the number shown in your address book and gaze briefly at the modest façade. So this is the home of the Master? But you are wrong. You have not yet reached the heart of this system of Chinese boxes. After enquiries made in the hall, you pass through into the back garden, where, among trees, a smaller, very narrow house has been built.

Pressure upon a button presently brings to the door a woman in middle age, stocky and robust, with dyed hair about her shoulders, her eyes heavily ringed with mascara. She is wearing pale-blue, rumpled beach pyjamas. Her manner could be described as one of defiant resignation. The physical presence is aggressive, the voice retiring. It must be Élise, the wife about whom you have read so much and will read more.

You are encouraged to precede her to the top of the house and find, as you hesitate before an open door, that she has left you. Inside the room are two extremely well-dressed women of forty and a very young Frenchman in an English sports jacket and grey flannel trousers. He scowls. Jouhandeau greets you with ostentatious cordiality. His hand is soft, his features sensitive rather than fine, his head bald but well-tanned, his shirt deep blue, his well-pressed lounge suit fawn with a faint

chequered pattern, his spectacles gold-rimmed. He is lightly
hare-lipped. The ladies smile volubly. Their daintily gloved
hands leave their furs to seek you.

The very young man goes, scowling. He is clearly not in a
good mood, is in any case a rather disagreeable type of young
Frenchman. You wonder about him. Jouhandeau has never
made any secret of his homosexual tastes, though he always
returns to Élise. Presently, the ladies also go, in clouds of
expensive scent.

The walls of this room are painted a dark, ecclesiastical
green. It contains a harmonium, a number of embroidered
fire-screens and a Spanish four-poster bed of which the tester
has been sawn off because the ceiling was too low. Over the
harmonium stands a crucifix. The fire-screens have something
to do with Marie Laurencin, who also painted a portrait on the
wall.

You are told a story about Marie Laurencin's powers of
divination, which you do not quite follow. The next book will
be called Élise Architecte. Latterly, Élise has been on an interior
decoration and structural alteration rampage. She is going to
make changes even in this room. The prospect is understood
to be a source of dismay to the Master, but this you take with
a pinch of salt. You feel that you understand his method of
work. He begins each day with a literary idea of which his
actions throughout the day, together with the actions and
utterances he elicits from other people, will provide experimental verification and all the detail for a final draft. Élise is
the guinea-pig-in-chief. Formerly a dancer, she has boundless
energy, but is, you feel, a bit simple-minded and highly
suggestible. The Master himself will have put it into her mind
to devise new fittings and decorations, in order to provide the
material for a book to be called Élise Architecte. A recent English
visitor was Francis Burdett, described as a priest or something.
You don't know him, though you have heard his name.

The autographed book you eventually depart with is Animaux
Familiers, which you have not read. On the cover are several
faint pink stains. Apologising for these, as he inscribes the book
to you as to one whom he is bien heureux de connaître, Jouhandeau
gratifies you by inventing a legend to account for their presence.

They are, he says, the cock's blood. As you will discover, the reference is to a story in the book, 'La Vie et la Mort d'un Coq'. Élise had been induced to kill this favourite bird out of jealousy and as an act of defiance.

You go away, totally captivated. You will renew the efforts you first made ten years ago to find Jouhandeau an English publisher. For once, a writer whom you admired has failed to disappoint you. Not since you took tea with Miss Compton-Burnett had you imagined such perfect identity between an author's personality and his work.

But this continuing present will not do. That was fifteen years ago. On no subsequent Paris trip have I been seriously tempted to repeat the experience, perhaps feeling, with a favourite cracker motto by William Blake, that

> He who bends to himself a Joy
> Doth the wingèd life destroy;
> But he who kisses the Joy as it flies
> Lives in Eternity's sunrise.

Besides, in 1948, Marcel Jouhandeau was sixty. He must now be seventy-five, which is not young even by French standards for the well-preserved man of letters. Élise cannot be much less. I understand they still live in the same house in the Rue du Commandant Marchand, Passy. I understand this from Martin Turnell, who has been there more recently and who did, some years ago, translate selections from Jouhandeau in, I fear, a pitch-queering kind of way. Turnell tells me that my visit is not remembered, a fact which I find sad, though it all-too-evidently delighted Turnell.

The books have continued to appear. From those on my shelves, I can tell which appeared later, or which I acquired later, than Animaux Familiers, the last of those I had bound. Still paper-backed are Nouveau Bestiaire, the correspondence with Gide, Dernières Années et Mort de Véronique, Contes d'Enfer, Ménagerie Domestique, Jaunisse, Journaliers 1957-9 and a book on Jouhandeau by Henri Rode. Two others have disappeared, one of them Carnets de l'Écrivain, the other, I fancy, Notes sur la Magie et le Vol. Élise herself has now, it seems, taken up writing.

For several years before 1946, Jouhandeau had represented,

and for some ten years more was to represent, the kind of writer I should have liked to be. What I mean is that I should have liked to write, from day to day, simply about the moment and its concerns and any past matters which pressed on the memory, the prose being merely careful, transparent, exact, easy on eye and ear, varied only by the variety of the mind's approach to what it scrupulously dealt with, utterly shameless, wholly personal. That it was quite impossible is due to the rigid formality of British literary customs. The novel and the diary-without-dates cannot flow into each other here, and I had long been sickened by the contrivances expected of a novelist.

XV

FREUD'S *Wit and the Unconscious* appeared in German as long ago as 1905, and an English translation was published in 1917. I first read the book only recently, when a new translation appeared. Among the many jokes it analyses, two were familiar from the 'Thirties. One was the story of a young Jew, unhappy in the artillery, to whom his commanding officer said: 'Itzig, you seem out of place here. Why don't you buy a gun and set up on your own?' The other concerned a man who, at the dinner table, on being served with fish, dipped his hands in the sauce and ran them through his hair and who, observing his neighbour's astonishment, said, 'Oh, dear, I'm sorry! I thought it was spinach!' If my built-in chronometer is keeping time, I heard the first of these two jokes, quoted as in Freud by Herbert Read, in 1935. The second I had not realised was in Freud. I had taken it simply as an early example of what later became known as the 'shaggy dog' story. I heard it from Dylan Thomas in, I fancy, 1936. I don't know whether Dylan knew of its provenance.

I suppose that, in those days, most of us had read a little psychology, but its main purpose was to provide us with small talk. This had been true even of Innes Stewart, who knew a great deal more than average about the subject, as, indeed, I suppose, did Herbert Read. Case-histories were interesting or amusing in themselves, wherever they came from. In drawing-room, public-house, bed-sitter and shared-flat conversation in the mid-'Thirties, two words of jargon had become habitual terms of abuse. Just as, in the late 'Fifties, people were afraid of being caught out using words like 'mantelpiece' or 'mirror' or (worst of all) 'serviette,' so in those days they were mortally afraid of being thought 'repressed'. To be repressed was, as it were, to be sexually or, more broadly, emotionally non-U. But so also it was, in Bohemian and sub-intellectual circles, to be 'an extravert'. Extraverts were noisy and insensitive, with a probable disposition to some form of crypto-Fascism. Extravert/introvert was understood to be a Jungian game, while repressions were understood to be Freudian. So, by and large, were complexes. Freud was, on the whole, more amusing than Jung, but more amusing still (almost as good as Krafft-Ebing) was the Freudian extremist Groddeck. He had been discovered by W. H. Auden. On the other hand, Henry Miller had proclaimed as 'the greatest healer since Paracelsus' E. Graham Howe, whose gay and stimulating volumes, aimed at showing the general reader how he could avoid becoming neurotic, I read with pleasure just before and during the war and whom, in 1948, I should discover to be an heretical Jungian.

Just before the war, I became acquainted with a gifted and charming Freudian, D. W. Winnicott, who specialised in children. I had previously met, among Freudians, only the sinister Eric Strauss, Jewish Catholic convert and homosexual. I had met, I fancy, no Jungians at all, but only one or two Adlerians. During the war, I met behaviourists, but during the war some knowledge of psychiatry became very widespread. All the working-class boys in the Army knew about 'the trick-cyclist' and had discovered ways of playing him up which would come in handy when, after the war, they appeared before progressive magistrates, the plea, 'I come from a broken home,' being almost the first words on the lips of any young criminal nowadays.

At least in the writings of Winnicott himself, the Freudian emphasis had shifted off repression during the war. In those years, he had been concerned with homeless and other deprived children at hostels in Oxfordshire and Berkshire. His conclusions had been the very reverse of those on which pre-war progressive education had been founded. The child, Dr Winnicott had decided, *wanted* discipline, required its original feeling of infinity to be closely delimited and its life confined within a circle. If the laws established by a child's parents proved unreliable, if the child could break them with impunity, the feeling of infinity became an abyss of nothingness and set up acute distress and indeed despair in the child. He then looked elsewhere for his circle of authority and tested the law personified by his teachers and later by the police.

The young delinquent values and loves the policeman.

And again:

The thief's inability to keep and enjoy what is stolen is well known. The boy who steals apples from an orchard and who eats the apples himself is not ill, is not a delinquent. He is just greedy, and his greed is relatively conscious. The anti-social child steals apples and either wastes them or gives them away. Intermediate is the boy who eats them and is sick, the sickness being a bodily form of feeling guilty.

Within the collectivity:

Each child, according to the degree of his distrust, and according to the degree of his hopelessness about the loss of his own home (and sometimes his recognition of the inadequacy of that home while it lasted), is all the time testing the hostel staff as he would test his own parents. Sometimes he does this directly, but most of the time he is content to let another child do the testing for him. An important thing about this testing is that it is not something that can be achieved and done with. Always somebody has to be a nuisance. Often one of the staff will say: 'We'd be all right if it weren't for Tommy . . .,' but in point of fact the others can only afford to be 'all right' because Tommy is being a nuisance, and is proving to them that the home can stand up to Tommy's testing, and could therefore presumably stand up to their own.

This perception of Winnicott's is one of the most searching I have ever encountered. I used it in *The Double Image*, dealing with the 'scapegoat' *rôle* of priests in the novels of Georges Bernanos, but its application is boundless. It seems astonishing now, eighteen years later, that the idea is not commonplace, that, so far as I know, not one book offered to the general public has used it to illuminate the depths of our social behaviour in all spheres. It explains the *rôle* of the communist shop steward in a 'home' which clearly cannot 'stand up to his testing', so that he seriously damages us all. It explains the yobboes of the district in which I live. It explains a great deal of black, Arab, Russian and nuclear-disarmament behaviour. Nearer home, as I found myself repeatedly noting between 1945 and 1948, it explains those married couples of one's acquaintance, one of whom is generally liked and the other not so, the one who is not well thought of (usually, as it happens, the wife) clearly performing her bits of wickedness and her social *gaffes* on behalf of the other, so that he may be free to bask in the glow of public esteem.

That was one, as I then thought, trend in psychology. Alas, it has not become a trend. Magistrates, progressive education- ists and so on still behave as though Dr Winnicott's discoveries had never been made. A more popular trend in the post-war years had been set when, towards the end of the war, the University of Cambridge foolishly conferred the degree of Doctor of Medicine on the author of a thesis published under the title *Paranormal Cognition*. Telepathy and other phenomena of extra-sensory perception (familiarly known as E.S.P.) be- came respectable and even fashionable. We all had a *psi*-faculty. The Society for Psychical Research thrived. There were books and plays on *Poltergeister* and witches.

All this was so much power to the Jungian elbow, though in fact the collective unconsciousness of C. G. Jung differed markedly from the one apparently revealed by experiments in telepathy and so on. It was to our next-of-kin that the death-apparitions came, by them that the cards were recognised. The messages transmitted through that psychic ether were personal. But Jung's collective unconscious was more in the nature of a racial memory. He had indeed described it (as I did not know in 1948) as the objective or autonomous psyche. Those 'arche- types' of his went quite unstudied by the learned gentlemen at the Society for Psychical Research. At least one of them, an autonomous *anima* quite different from the *anima* of the *anima/ animus* dichotomy of the 'Thirties, was (as, again, I did not yet know in 1948) closer to Mr Graves's white goddess, and, dur- ing the next few years, this later development of Jung's thought was to exercise a similar attraction on poets.

A poet much affected was Herbert Read. During the war, he had been an anarchist. Then he had briefly turned existentialist. At any rate, when his autobiography, *Annals of Innocence and Experience*, appeared in 1940, his philosophy was described as, 'in the proper sense of the word, materialist'. When the volume was reissued towards the end of 1946, that sentence had been altered, and the same philosophy, no less 'in the proper sense of the word', had become 'existential'. The explanatory gloss was the same: 'It is made actual in deeds.'[1] The Jung association must have been formed towards the end of the war, for there had already been two PQ conferences, held at provincial university colleges, the lectures having subsequently appeared as printed volumes and the name of Herbert Read being prominent among the lecturers. It was through Herbert that I had met Heinz Westmann and been engaged to lecture, in August 1948, at a PQ conference in Oxford.

The initials stood for 'Present Question'. PQ was essentially a conference-holding organisation, devoted to the idea of synthesis. Among its founding members had been the E. Graham Howe whom I mentioned earlier and another Jungian of some originality, R. Channing Pearce. By 1948, some kind of disagreement and split having taken place, the organisation was in the hands of Westmann, a German-Jewish psychologist who had once been a farmer, with, as his second-in-command, a Scot, Brigadier Torrie, a leading psychiatrist at the War Office, still in uniform. The other lecturers were all persons of the very greatest distinction in their own fields, which might be almost anything but psychology. The 1948 conference, for instance, was dominated by D. M. MacKinnon, professor of moral philosophy at Aberdeen. Other lecturers, during the next four years, included Sir John Cockroft and Sir John Wolfenden, Professors Michael Polanyi, C. D. Darlington and Christopher Dawson, Dr Bronowski, Dr J. H. Oldham, Canon V. A. Demant and Mr Ritchie Calder, the Christians, I seem to remember, being especially prominent at an Easter conference the following year, when also the delightful Fr Thomas Gilbey, O.P., was much on the scene, though he did not, I think, lecture.

Apart from Herbert Read, the persons of purely literary distinction most in evidence at various times were L. A. G. Strong, the poets Kathleen Raine and John Heath-Stubbs,

---

[1] Sir Herbert has remained prone to self-modification. In 1950, at my instigation, he wrote for broadcasting a dialogue for three voices called *Moon's Farm*. It was in prose. In the volume of 1955, it was printed as verse.

Montgomery Belgion and the 'French writer of Russian extraction' whom I have already mentioned as over from Paris when I saw a nasty play by Noel Coward, my friend Wladimir Weidlé. On occasion, we were entertained by pianists like Harriet Cohen, Natalia Karp and Paul Hamburger or by the musicologist Paul Hedley, who lectured to us on Chopin while wearing a silk waistcoat which had been Chopin's and with Chopin's rose-bowl on the table in front of him (Natalia Karp illustrating the lecture by playing *inédits* from actual manuscript). A certain amount of verse-speaking was done, for the most part by Leonard Strong, Mr Heath-Stubbs, myself and a lady from the Central School of Speech and Drama, then functioning in the corridors of the Albert Hall and lectured to or adjudicated by Strong. I also remember Olaf Stapledon, though I hardly know whether to list him as a person of purely literary or of wider intellectual distinction. So far as I know, everyone lectured or performed otherwise for nothing, though one's train fare was paid and one might stay a whole week in Oxford, putting away quite a lot of Westmann's liquor in the evening with the lecturers and other stars.

In August 1948, I lectured. At Easter the following year, I was chairman for two other speakers, one of them Miss Raine. Thereafter, until 1951, I was always invited along in a capacity never explicitly defined, but in effect as a concert organiser who, at need, could be called on to silence bores, a kind of intellectual strong-arm man. What I lectured on in 1948 was education, which seems odd. The lectures were arranged in pairs. Two lecturers, of differing if not opposed views, would speak on the same day, both in the morning, I fancy, taking two aspects of the same general subject. After dinner, the two speakers appeared on the same platform, where they were both faced with questions prepared at discussion groups before dinner. As a result, our old friend synthesis was expected to appear or, in the expression more frequently used by Westmann, the opposites to be reconciled. For the 1948 conference, we were billeted at Magdalen College, the lectures being held in the Examination Schools. Most of the later conferences were held at Lady Margaret Hall, which had an adequate lecture room of its own, though in fact when, the following Easter, we first stayed at Lady Margaret Hall, the lectures were at the Taylorian Institute.

Those weeks in Oxford were an amenity. For one thing, the Innes Stewarts lived accessibly nearby. For another, I had always delighted in Herbert Read's company. Latterly, some of his views had begun (and have continued) to strike me as odd, but I have never ceased to find him a man of the utmost charm. In 1937, he had been one of the witnesses at my wedding. Latterly, I had seen too little of him. Since, in 1951-2, the PQ organisation broke up, I have seen too little of him again. There were other charmers, notably Donald MacKinnon and the Dominican Fr Gilbey, the latter of whom first properly showed me Oxford. Heinz Westmann himself I liked very much. I did not respect him intellectually. To me, what he said was just so much Central European jargon, though of a perfectly inoffensive kind. But, at conferences, he effaced himself intellectually, and even in matters of organisation his handsome and agreeable wife was more prominent. For a number of years, I was friends with them outside conference time. There were many pleasant shared dinners in London.

The Westmanns, I gather are now in America. There was, I remember, talk in 1951 of getting money for PQ from one of the great American foundations. Earlier, there had been an influx of scientists, politicians, industrialists and Moral Rearmament tycoons, and one had begun to hear the weird language of *personnel* managers and the exponents of time-and-motion study. They and the industrialists themselves were inclined to be condescending. They, we were given to understand, were the practical men, concerned with real facts and with productivity, which was the nation's and indeed the world's life-blood, without which the rest of us would not be able to indulge in our fanciful talk. True, there were problems of industrial *morale*, about which the psychologists might have something useful to say. In dealing with the workers, Moral Rearmament was sometimes a help, but did not invariably provide a solution. So I began to think that perhaps my Jungian friends were hoping to muscle in on the field of industrial management.

Even before that, one heard very little psychology talked.

The distinguished lecturers were not themselves psychologists. They had their own terminologies, historical, anthropological, religious, scientific, literary, artistic, political. Their views were the opposites to be reconciled. I don't remember hearing archetypes mentioned. It would have been '*the* archetypes'. It was always '*the* opposites' (I took this to be an idiomatic mistranslation of German). Then there was 'wholeness' and 'becoming a person', but otherwise not much Jungian undertow, certainly not enough to bother me. With the whole idea of the thing, I was intellectually uninvolved. It was simply that every now and then I would get on a train to Oxford and spend a week gassing with distinguished chaps, many of them amusing. Most of the time, my interests lay decidedly elsewhere. Only later did I begin to think of Jung as perhaps the most pernicious brain-softener of our time.

XVI

IT is generally understood that the story of Shakespeare's *Hamlet* goes back, *via* a French writer, Belleforest, to the Danish history of Saxo Grammaticus, a twelfth-century monk. Fired by my admiration for *The Hawk and the Handsaw*, in which Innes Stewart had marvellously presented a psycho-analyst's view of Shakespeare's sweet prince, I proposed to do a saga Hamlet,[1] under the title of *The Fool's Saga*. I therefore read Saxo in the Elton-Powell volume of 1894, together with a contemporary translation of Belleforest, Sir Israel Gollancz's version of the later (later, that is to say, than Saxo) Icelandic *Ambales Saga* and a fascinating study by Kemp Malone which reaches back to pre-Christian sources. That was in the autumn of 1948. At much the same time, I got hold of the two volumes (1868) of William Frederick Skene's *The Four Ancient Books of Wales*.

The relevance of these was as follows. Unlike Shakespeare's Hamlet, Saxo's Amleth had in fact reached the island of Britain with the equivalents of Shakespeare's Rosencrantz and Guildenstern (in *Ambales Saga* known as Cimbal and Carvel). There had been, that is to say, no conveniently plot-shortening encounter with a pirate ship. In Britain, he married a British princess and, bigamously, a Pictish queen, thereafter taking both his wives back to Jutland, where he was slain in battle by an uncle, his mother's brother. The likeliest date would be about A.D. 500. At that date, British and Pictish kingdoms and queendoms would be in contact only in what is now lowland Scotland, across the Clyde-Forth neck, the earliest Welsh poetry, according to Skene, having come from the area south of this line, the line broadly of the Antonine north wall, in Lothian and Strathclyde.

[1] As Goethe had once thought of doing. I cannot be certain whether I already knew this, but a Goethe centenary fell due the following year, and plans to celebrate it were already in hand.

The two volumes included, with translations, the contents of *The Black Book of Carmarthen*, *The Book of Aneirin*, *The Book of Taliesin* and *The Red Book of Hergest*, manuscripts dating from the twelfth to the fifteenth centuries but containing verse believed to go back as far as the sixth century A.D., at which time the Welsh-speaking kingdom of Strathclyde flourished (and was to remain independent for three or four hundred years more), though by then at least some of the Cymric princes of Lothian, 'the sons of Cunedda,' had taken themselves off to Wales, where they founded new kingdoms. But a great deal which later Welsh legend places in our south-west counties appears to have taken place in what is now lowland Scotland, the battles of the *condottiere* known as King Arthur, for instance. Like St Patrick earlier, the poet Taliesin certainly belongs to the northern kingdom, centred on Dumbarton and extending down into Cumberland.

A side of the Hamlet saga which might have been expected to appeal to Mr Graves was its evidence regarding the matriarchal system of the Picts, which gets a reference in *The Golden Bough*. This had some historical importance, which in a curious way persists. When succession to a throne is through the mother and when the selection of fathers for her children by a queen is exogamic and purely temporary, a neighbouring tribe whose king has begotten a son upon that queen might well then try to impose the principle of patrilineal succession upon her people. This is what seems to have happened as between the Scots and the Picts, doubtless with the help of a palace massacre, in the ninth century, when a Scot (*i.e.*, a colonising Irishman from Argyll) installed himself on the Pictish throne of Scone as Kenneth I of a kingdom which then began to be known as Scottish. Two hundred years later, the problem was still being fought out, for the Pict Macbeth's claim to the throne was by matrilineal succession through his wife. The kingdom of Scone still did not reach south of the Clyde-Forth neck, but what had already happened long before largely accounts for the fact that nowadays the inhabitants of a large part of this island all think of themselves as Scots, with odd effects upon their attitude to the rest of us and at the cost of much confusion in their own minds.

The present site of Edinburgh castle, with, quite possibly, an auxiliary hill fort on what in due course (and perhaps quite properly) became known as Arthur's Seat, might well have been the headquarters of Hamlet's Pictish queen (and so I meant to make it). It was something like a hundred and twenty years later when the Christian city (Christianised by St Cuthbert) was founded by and named after the Northumbrian king Edwin, whose capital was York. At that time, the rule of Northumbria was powerful and widespread, generally extending a long way north of the Forth and at moments as far as Anglesey and into Ireland. From the time of Malcolm Canmore (Macbeth's slayer) and during the centuries which followed, when there was an independent kingdom over the whole of what is now understood to be Scotland, the Scottish kings had gone on referring to the people of Lothian as their English subjects, while the poets of the great period had never thought their language other than English.

Beyond embarking several times from or landing at Stranraer and spending one night in Dumfries during the war, I did not know Scotland at all. Even before the war, I had heard of Scottish nationalism, among the many intellectual dottinesses of the time. I had once met 'Hugh MacDiarmid' (C. M. Grieve) at some Leftish gathering as long ago as 1934. I had read some of his admirable verse, not supposing for a moment that he considered the language in which it was written to be other than a Scottish dialect like that of Burns. I should probably have described him, in all innocence, as 'the best English dialect poet since William Barnes'. Not till late in the war did I hear of 'Lallans' and gather that it was understood to be a language quite distinct from English. It was a kind of dialect Esperanto. I had never thought highly of Esperanto (my father had once tried to make me learn it, but when I found that the word for a bird was 'birdo' I could no longer take it seriously). Still, Esperanto had had the worthy object of facilitating understanding between nations, whereas the object of Lallans seemed to be quite the reverse, viz., to diminish understanding between people north and south of the Tweed and to create a difference where none had existed.

In matters of this kind, I was less easily imposed on than

would be most southern English people or, indeed, northerners who might have been brought up in circumstances more genteel than those which had attended my early life. As a boy in the West Riding, I had called a bridge a brig. I had not called a church a kirk, but I had grown up surrounded by villages like Kirkburton, Kirkheaton, Kirklees, Kirkstall and Kirkleatham. A throat to me, too, had been a thropple or a weazen, according to whether you swallowed down it or slit it. My mother had not been busy, she had been *throng*. There had been people and things she could not *thole* (pronounced 'thoil' in Huddersfield, where also, for instance, the coal-cellar was 't' coil-'oil'). In connection with *The Fool's Saga* (wondering what sort of dialogue to write for my demotic Picts), I read Burns comprehensively in the winter of 1948-9 and was myself astonished to discover how many of the words I had used in my boyhood were shown and explained in glossaries as peculiarly Scottish.

I had been immunised learnedly, too. At Leeds, I had gathered from the lessons of Professor Dickins just how far north 'northern English' had extended in early times, and I knew that, while the language of Henryson, Dunbar, Gavin Douglas and Sir David Lindsay (the later poets among those who were known as 'the Scottish Chaucerians') had begun to develop in the direction of separateness, the language of John Barbour, who lived near Aberdeen, had been indistinguishable from that of Richard Rolle, who lived at Hampole, a village near Doncaster, some way south of Huddersfield. I knew that a 'Lykewake Dirge' recently set to music by Benjamin Britten had been set in a deliberately Scotticised version, from Scott's *Border Minstrelsy*, of a poem located by John Aubrey, in the seventeenth century, in Yorkshire and always known as 'The Cleveland Lykewake Dirge'. I knew that various well-known Tyneside ditties were often included in Scottish song-books, that even nursery-rhymes like 'Sticks and stones will break my bones' might be differently spelt as 'Sticks and stanes will brak ma banes' and shown as distinctively Scottish in respectable folklore anthologies and that the source of many fine late-medieval ballads got shoved a hundred miles north because they contained forms not in current use south of the Trent.

A yet more homely instance of the same linguistic imperialism was provided, in the autumn of 1949, by a gifted and wholly pleasing woman who proposed to put me up for a few days near Glasgow and to take me sailing 'down the water' in November. I had asked her what the weather could be expected to be like at the time, and she said it ought still to be quite mild, adding:

'As daylight lengthens, cauld strengthens' – as we say in Scotland.

As it turned out, that trip down the water from Gourock was to be memorable, partly because of the extremely cold weather and the fact that I faced it with a painful stye on one eyelid, but also because, on the deck of a MacBrayne's steamer that Saturday morning, I read in a newspaper of the death in an air-crash of the glorious young French violinist, Ginette Neveu.

I was spending almost a whole month in Edinburgh, from late October to late November. I was still interested in the saga Hamlet, though *The Fool's Saga* had gone out months before and was already in proof, together with *The Hawk and the Handsaw* and another Innes piece and my displays of prefatory learning.[1] My reading in related topics continued. But the trip had perhaps more to do, accidentally, with 'George Orwell'. Orwell himself had by then gone into University College Hospital, London, from which he was not to depart alive. Sir Richard Rees, former editor of *The Adelphi*, had gone into partnership with the man who was to marry Orwell's sister to farm the land on Jura which Orwell had taken three years before. At the end of 1947, Orwell had gone into a hospital near Glasgow, from which he temporarily emerged the following year. Rees, who had taken up painting before the war, then bought a flat in Edinburgh, where the light, he understood, was good for painting, rather like Mediterranean light. The flat was in Douglas Crescent, in what is still (somewhat oddly) the New Town. I stayed with him there for some four weeks.

At that time, a document simply known as the Covenant was being passed round for signature all over Scotland. It was a political document, calling for a measure of Home Rule.

[1] The volume is called *Three Tales of Hamlet*. No doubt it is still available at some libraries.

According to Rees, the young men who went round collecting signatures for the Covenant would ask nice, simple workmen whether they thought it fair that nine out of ten carcasses of prime Angus beef should go to Smithfield and be devoured by the English. If the person questioned scratched his head and said he supposed not, then he was asked to sign on a dotted line which made him in favour of Home Rule. In fact, nine out of ten was the right proportion, the population of Scotland (about the same as that of Lancashire) being one tenth of the population of Britain. However, meat was very strictly rationed in those days, and many people in Scotland probably imagined that people elsewhere ate more of it than they did. My impression was that one ate better in Edinburgh than in London. A further argument advanced in favour of a separate parliament for Scotland was, apparently, that, from outlying parts of the Hebrides, it might take a man three and a half days to travel to Whitehall, the centre from which he was governed. Since it takes only half a day to reach Whitehall from Glasgow or Edinburgh, it seemed to me he would gain little by being governed from either, particularly from Edinburgh.

It seemed, too, that the kinds of remarks which, in London, middle-class persons would make about the Labour government tended in Scotland to be made about 'the English', on whom even the weather could be blamed, as, further south, it was blamed on Mr Attlee and his colleagues.

'No wonder there's an outbreak of crime in Glasgow,' a rich Edinburgh woman was quoted as saying. 'No sooner do we get a policeman trained than he's dragged off to London.'

Rees had begun to find all this kind of thing rather worrying. As he pointed out, many of the most vehement nationalists were intellectuals of a kind, journalists and so on who had tried to make their way in London and failed and gone back home, tail between legs. As things stood, they were at best provincial worthies. Their calculation must be that, if Edinburgh were a capital city, they would be national figures. As Rees said:

> Sma' frogs in ane sma' pond maun greater seem.

And, indeed, I thought I detected some of this mood among the people I met at the Abbotsford and elsewhere, in a *milieu* which Rees did not frequent.

With Rees, I met such figures of an older world as Sir Herbert Grierson and his friend Dr Menzies, whose beautifully modulated English was, I suppose, rather an Aberdeen than an Edinburgh product. Also in Edinburgh was Professor John Macmurray, whom I had not seen for ten years. During the war, he had been at Aberystwyth. After the war, he had gone back to Edinburgh, where in 1949 he was still Professor of Moral Philosophy. Before the war, he had been the first serious academic to take up Marxism as a philosophy (but also the first to see that the Russian revolution had been betrayed and to insist that, according to Marx's predictions, Russia should have been the last country to have that kind of revolution). By 1949, his thought had moved in the direction of primitive Christianity, and he was much involved with the Iona community.[1] His appearance also had changed. At one time it had seemed that he rather cultivated than discouraged a natural resemblance to D. H. Lawrence. Now, although he must have seemed a youngster to Menzies and Grierson, his hair was white, and he wore it longer. He found the nationalist climate even at the university suffocating. He, certainly, had not returned to Scotland as the result of any previous failure in London. He had gone back at a mature age because that was what he wanted to do. Fond Scots and 'true' Scots, both he and his wife now thought of nothing but how to get out of Scotland again.

I got to know Edinburgh moderately well. I found it an attractive city, though perhaps the Victorian-Gothic skyline of the castle and so on from Prince's Street was a bit theatrical and a bit inclined to make untrained minds brood stupidly on history. With St Andrews I fell quite in love, though I was only there for a matter of hours. It was, I discovered, a town of about the size Oxford must have been in the eighteenth century. Unlike Oxford, it was still a true university town.

[1] About which I learned something, but perhaps not enough to attempt to go into the matter here. One thing I remember Macmurray saying that autumn was that he thought our only hope was to adopt a deliberate frugality of life.

Against the pale-grey, beautifully weathered stone of the buildings, the undergraduates passed in gowns of bright red nap cloth, blowing in a sharp wind off the sea. That day, fourteen years ago, I thought that it would be pleasant to have my daughter go to St Andrews in nine or ten years' time, as in due course she was to do.

That afternoon, I crossed the Tay to Dundee and took a 'bus eastward along the coast road to Broughty Ferry. My host was a poet whom I had first met in London fifteen years before, with Dylan Thomas (and through Rees at *The Adelphi*). That evening, he was rung up by Douglas Young, whose name I knew as that of the leader of one wing of the nationalist movement. Young lectures in Greek at St Andrews. In those days, his lecturing was done on the Dundee side (it is the same university). Next morning, my host and I met him in the senior common room at Dundee. The Principal at that time was General Wimberley, who, during the war, had commanded the 51st (Highland) Division. He had evidently met my host before. Young introduced me as another poet.

'Another Lallans poet?' Wimberley gently enquired.

There might, I fancied, sometimes be constraint in that common room. During the war, I understood that Young had in some way taken up his stand as a conscientious objector against what he regarded as English wars, no concern of Scotland's. It would have been difficult to imagine two men differing more in physical appearance than Young and 'Hugh MacDiarmid'. MacDiarmid was a small man of indeterminate colouring, with a large, round head and with small features printed on his broad face. Young was enormously tall, with black hair and beard, spectacles and sharp, pink, eager nose. If a race is constituted of people who share a majority of physical characteristics, the two were certainly not of the same race.

That morning, over the coffee and biscuits, Young was amusing about 'Hugh MacDiarmid' (who, among those who know him or wish to be understood to know him, is referred to as 'Chris'). Had we, Young asked my host and myself, noticed how little Lallans verse Chris had written for some years past? Alas, we said, yes. And had we noticed, asked Young, that latterly Chris had begun to do a little and that his new verse was highly alliterative? No, we said, we had failed to notice this, but were delighted to hear it. The explanation, said Young, was as follows. Chris's eyesight had been deteriorating, so that he could no longer read the small print in Jamieson's dictionary (Dr John Jamieson's *Etymological Dictionary of the Scottish Language*, a curiosity published in 1808). Latterly, however, he had been given a pair of spectacles on the National Health, and with these he was able to make out a page at a time.

Young himself had been reported to me as having, at the Abbotsford in Rose Street, Edinburgh, wished to order a round of drinks and as having called to the barman:

'Some mair!'

Whereupon, it had been said, the barman opened a window. I can well believe this. But, indeed, the reason why he had telephoned my host the previous evening was that he had been asked to give a reading of his own Lallans poems and wanted my host (who himself did not write in Lallans) to go over the poems with him beforehand, in order to get the pronunciation and inflexions right. And, indeed, Young frankly acknowledges his source, for in a poem he writes:

Frae Jamieson's muckle buik the words tak wing.

Not long afterwards, in London, I'm afraid I passed on Young's story about the new spectacles to a friend of Mac-Diarmid's who would, I knew, pass the story on to MacDiarmid. The effect was amusing. The friend presently reported back to me that MacDiarmid had growled and said *I* was a Jacobite (I knew that those Scottish nationalists who were also communist or at least *communisants* regarded the Douglas Young variety as romantic Jacobites). I did not see MacDiarmid on that first visit to Edinburgh. I have met him there since, and we got on very nicely. Clearly, he is a divided man. Even in 1949, I thought it odd that he should be able to accommodate both Scots nationalism and Marxism in his mind. Certainly, Russia would encourage any movement whatever that would act disruptively in any capitalist society, and presumably a Scots nationalist might welcome the policy of any nation bent on harming England, but I did not see how a gifted man could at one and the same time sincerely hold two sets of views which, in any positive way, were so manifestly incompatible. It is only more recently that I have been given occasion to wonder how a man so committed to hating 'the English' can be so gratifyingly amiable with individual Englishmen. But, indeed, Douglas Young, too, is privately the kindest and most engaging of men, as I have since had numerous occasions of finding out.

Last year, at the extraordinary writers' conference which formed part of the Edinburgh International Festival, both were on the platform for the session devoted to writing in Scotland. Young was mild, but MacDiarmid, kilted, thunderingly from the platform still described England as 'the old and only enemy'. In the autumn of 1949, he had begun to publish a series of articles on what he called 'the Scottish renaissance movement'. After quoting some figures to show how advantageous Scotland's financial position was in those post-war years, he concluded:

> In other words, there is clearly no question of Scotland not being able to afford to cut adrift from England. She cannot afford not to, or must inevitably be dragged down in England's well-deserved and unavoidable ruin.

Those articles also quaintly spoke of 'getting back' to Gaelic as the task of the renaissance movement in its second phase, so that Lallans, we must presume, a language invented by himself, would eventually wither away like the Marxist state. I dare say 'Chris' is not the only Scotsman to imagine that Gaelic was formerly spoken all over what is now Scotland, whereas in fact it can rarely have been heard much beyond the areas in which it still lingers.

XVII

THE manuscripts composing *The Four Ancient Books of Wales* contain all that had provided a basis for Robert Graves's most elaborate magifications in *The White Goddess*. Most of it should, however, be treated as medieval interpolation. The original Taliesin must have been a court bard whose duty was to sing the praises of his king or tribal chieftain, Urien Rheged, and to describe battles. Although legend later placed him, as it placed King Arthur, further south, all respectable Welsh scholars agree that he must have flourished somewhere in Strathclyde or Cumberland. At some point in 1950, with the help of cribs, I made versions of two of the poems which Sir Ifor Williams considers may be truly ascribed to a sixth-century Taliesin. I may as well print these here, to give some idea of the kind of thing they were. The first is a *marwnad* or heroic elegy on Urien's son.

TALIESIN'S
PRAISE-IN-DEATH OF
OWAIN VAB URIEN RHEGED

Now the Lord have mercy on
The soul of Owen, Urien's son,
Prince of Rheged, and him reward
Whose body lies in the green sward.

Mettle high, lofty brow,
Low the cell that contains him now:
Lance's ash and roof-tree split,
Where are the bards to find a seat?

He was the paragon, he was the pick:
Incendiary Theodoric
Bore down this prince of the glittering west,
And all are losers, him at rest.

Like father like son, so it had been
With Cynfarch and with Urien:
The English in whole companies
Went to sleep with the light in their eyes.

Those who turned at the first attack
He, like a wolf leading the pack,
In his gay trappings hunted down:
The sheep of Catterick's grey-walled town.

Model hero, horses he gave
To any but a tonsured slave
Who to the harp would set his hand
And sing what all might understand.

What he amassed in hard coin
He likewise turned to his soul's account:
God see to it now in its need —
Owen's soul and Ceneu's seed.

At this point, he passed the hat round. I had better say that the
precise designation of 'Catterick', though in keeping with Sir
Ifor's point of view (Skene's 'Catraeth' was further north), is
my interpolation, as are various proper names in the second of
these poems.

TO URIEN

It will happen with speed
To him of Coel's breed
Out of whose long hand we feed
On wine, meal and mead,
A conqueror without greed
Memorable in his every deed,
To lead
Those of our creed
Anew,
Under his broad thigh his steed,
Flags and captains, a crowd
Of tall spears, all Rheged's retinue,
To battle in Lothian.
Back will come
Familiar long-haired cattle of the Pict,
Cow, heifer and milch-cow, the ox
Loaded both sides with liquor furnace-distilled,
Eight score beasts of a colour in line,
Barns filled,
Frisian grain to be milled
All winter, everything else we need.

What should we do
If luck deserted Urien,
The darling of his countrymen,
Dread
Of the Saxon, who
With his white hair wet and a cracked head
On a red bier rides home?
The ill-defended bleed:
Insolent once, now they plead.
Lloegr lacks wherewithal to impede
A widower of her wives,
And I have wine.
Wine is what I like:
It builds up the brain, gives
To the heel pace
And a twist to the wrist when it comes to rearing
                                    a pike
And lunging face to face.

Ah, but listen! –
You at the door,
What do you hear?
Is it an earthquake,
And does the whole land shake;
Or is it blowing up a gale?
Does the sea glisten,
And do its white crowns borne upon the swell
Tumble about your feet pell-mell?
Did it come from the valley, that shout?
Urien is thereabout.
Was it up the mountain, a cry of fear?
Urien's weight is behind the spear.
Or the cry of a wound, this side of the hill?
Urien's sword drinks its fill.
If the shrill
Pitch of his anger cried, and they run,
Neither pass nor defile, road nor ravine
Shall let them out:
His battle-rage will run its course
And trace the heart's blood to its source.

Because of its little ways,
His spear is known as the death child:

It wears a long blue ribbon about its neck,
And nobody goes hungry who takes pot luck
With that young lord.
When I am old,
May I not die with a smile
If my tongue is not still busy with the praise
Of Urien –
The bread-winner, the open hand
Of this whole land.

Here, too, we may imagine the bard passing the hat round, the assembled gentry not yet having pelted him with beef-bones.

The precise location of Rheged is in doubt, but it was certainly not in any part of what is now Wales. It is easy to see how such a transference of setting would take place. Generations later, perhaps even centuries, after recounting some battle or other episode of the heroic age, a bard or scribe might well be asked where the battle had taken place, where the *gwledig* Arthur's castle had stood? The supposed authority on the matter would tell the enquirer, as he had been told himself by word of mouth or as his manuscript told him, that all these things had taken place, and that Taliesin had celebrated them, in territory which had once belonged to the Cymry, but from which, alas, they had later been driven. Well, that might have been almost anywhere beyond the Wye, beyond Offa's dyke. It might have been in regretted Somerset, *Gwlad yr Haf*, the Land of Summer. It might have been further, across the Severn estuary, perhaps even as far as Cornwall.

That is perhaps why the Vortigern of the Welsh sources flourished not at Ramsgate but on the Wye, at Rhayader. *His* Hengist and Horsa would be Saxons already established in Herefordshire. Perhaps they were. That account is less nonsensical than the one based on English sources which still occurs in school history-books. Most of us may have doubted, even at school, whether those two shaggy gentlemen, accompanied by three boatloads of Angles, Saxons and Jutes, presumably one boatload of each, landing at Ebbsfleet or on the shores of Pegwell Bay, can really have done quite all they were credited with. Certainly, if they were our first Angles, Saxons and Jutes, they must have landed more than two hundred years before the date either Bede or Nennius gives them. The Romans had long known our east and south-east as 'the Saxon shore', and the latest archeological discoveries are clear as to settled communities of 'English' two centuries before the legions finally departed, leaving behind them a very mixed population indeed.

Yet most people still believe that, the Romans having departed in about A.D. 400, a 'wave' of Angles, Saxons and Jutes in due course appeared on our east and south-east coasts and drove all the degenerate 'Britons' into Wales and, to some extent, Cornwall. This is pure mythology. In terms of the populations of those days, the idea of waves of invaders pushing waves of inhabitants westward simply won't do. Agricultural populations just don't down tools *en masse* and move. If they did, they would all starve to death, and so would the agriculturally unskilled and otherwise occupied invading armies. The important consequence of the 'wave' theory is that it gives us a hopelessly false ethnological picture of ourselves. However massive and total an invasion, settlers need women to breed from, so that, in the first generation of their descendants, the old 'blood' will be at least as profuse as the new. The chiefs and their cavalry may have got on their horses and ridden off, and some of the more humble native population (as well as some of the invaders) may have been killed. But, by and large, the natives stay put and learn the new language and, with more or less resentment, try to be helpful. Among the earliest Anglo-Saxon documents are legal codes which formulate the rights of *Wealas* in conquered territory.

It is not only the ethnology we get wrong. We get the linguistics wrong, too. For instance, it is assumed that the Britons spoke or had spoken, uniformly, a language related to modern Welsh. There are no more than two pieces of evidence to support this. The evidence of place-names is surprisingly (surprisingly, that is to say, from the point of view of those who make the assumption) inconclusive, but, in quite late Anglo-Saxon times, St Guthlac, in the Cambridgeshire fens, is on record as having been tormented by demons who spoke to him 'in the British tongue', and until very recent times the shepherds in the Yorkshire dales counted their sheep in decayed forms of what were recognisably Welsh numerals. It is slender evidence for the assumption as a whole, but one does so hate to think of languages wholly vanishing without trace. A further assumption is that, when Cymric chieftains and their armies from Lothian or from what became England moved into Wales and established their rule, the populations over whom they established it also spoke a kind of *Ur*-Welsh already. In fact, later Welsh itself provides us with evidence against this further assumption.

This is a very tangled bit of linguistics, and I shall not ask my readers to consider it. I am not, in any case, competent to lay it before them in all its detail. They may, however, have heard of a supposed 'Iberian' strain in Wales (if they are Welsh, they will). The point really is that Welsh as we know it appears to be a language of 'Indo-European' vocabulary imposed on a 'non-Indo-European' grammatical (or sub-grammatical) sub-structure. The language spoken by the Silures *et al.* may have been related to that other anomalously 'non-Indo-European' language, Basque. Perhaps we should call it 'Siluric', at any rate for South Wales. The present-day relevance of this is as follows. A population of short, dark, plump people once had imposed on it the language of a tall, fair, lean Cymric military caste. The Cymry having either been killed off by Anglo-Normans in the male line or having slain each other in family feuds, their women then becoming the female founders of the great English families, the small, dark slave-classes bred copiously among themselves. They are now the characteristic Welsh (though, of course, a minority of tall, fair, slender Welsh and some huge rugger forwards from mountain regions may still be found). That they should patriotically and aggressively assert the language of their earlier against their later masters is historically amusing.

Initially through the enthusiasm of Matthew Arnold, that language is now academically enshrined as a principal representative of 'the Celtic languages', a curious misnomer. Neither in Welsh nor in Gaelic is there any word 'Celt' or any word cognate with it or any word to suggest that the ancient Welsh and Irish entertained notions of any ethnological or linguistic bond between them. To the Greeks, the *Keltoi* were all the fair-haired tribes north of the Alps, but the only people on record as 'in their own tongue *Celtae*' were the Gauls of central France in Julius Caesar's time. Caesar did not suggest that the Britons also were Celts, nor did anyone else at the time. The idea that the Welsh (let alone the Irish and highland Scots) were themselves Celts and their language a form of *Celtick* was evolved by eighteenth-century antiquarians, arguing from the erroneous premise that Breton was a survival of Gaulish and therefore the aboriginal language of the *Celtae*, whereas it is now understood that Breton was first introduced into the Armorican peninsula from this island, whence the peninsula's later name and that of its language and inhabitants.

The two language-groups, on the one hand Welsh with Old Cornish and Breton and, on the other, the various forms of Gaelic, seem to have rather less in common than Latin and Greek. There is no reason, certainly, why the two groups should not be studied in single departments at our universities or why the same teachers should not also be curators of the five recorded words of Pictish and what little can be established about Gaulish. It is, however, time that those departments ceased to describe themselves as devoted to 'Celtic Studies' and that the term 'the Celtic languages' was dropped. The work done by 'Celtic' scholars is often valuable and fine, but the mere designation leads them into historical fantasy and obstinately pre-determined linguistic speculation. It is rather as though, because of some known or suspected further affinity, Greek and Latin were to be known as the Illyrian languages.

But that is perhaps enough on linguistics within the context of this book. I return to my own *curriculum vitae*. In 1950, I was a good deal in Wales. In the spring, I stayed briefly in Cardiff, then outside Llanelly, then at Tenby, Pembroke Dock and St David's. In the summer, I attended the national *eisteddfod*, that year held at Caerphilly, then stayed for some days in Abergavenny and finally at the house of my wife's parents in Newport (Mon.). Early the following year, I adjudicated at a drama festival in Abertridwr, where (and in Senghenydd nearby) members of my wife's family lived.

The family connection itself makes some interest in that territory understandable. In terms of her immediate ante-

112

cedents, my wife is half-Welsh (but has always thought of herself as Welsh). My children are thus fully a quarter Welsh. I have sometimes felt that there must be some sense of the idea of nationality[1] in which this fact makes me at least one eighth Welsh. However, my 1950 trips to Wales were provided with specific purposes, the summer one, as I have said, to attend an *eisteddfod*, the spring one to conduct topographical and other research into the career of Giraldus Cambrensis, a lively and attractive figure of the twelfth and early thirteenth centuries. This was for a radio play, which in due course went out as *The Battle for St David's*, with music by Dylan Thomas's boyhood friend Daniel Jones.

Giraldus Cambrensis, son of William de Barri (he was in fact three parts Norman), was brought up at the castle of Manorbier, just outside Tenby. That is why I stayed in Tenby. In his *Itinerary*, Giraldus describes the castle, the fishpond, the dovecote, signs of all of which were still to be seen, and concludes that Manorbier is the pleasantest spot in Wales. I found it, certainly, pleasant. St David's is at the extreme tip of Pembrokeshire, almost as far west as Land's End. Although a cathedral city, there is not even a railway line to St David's, and in 1950 its tourist amenities were minimal, so that I had to stay at a temperance hotel. The admirable cathedral was built in a hollow, so that it should be out of sight of sea-rovers, who nevertheless burned and looted it several times. Its roofing is not turquoise but dazzling white, and from the narrow roadway one descends to it by thirty-nine steps, facetiously known to the clergy as the thirty-nine articles. The rearing pale-granite cape shows visibly to what height the ice-sheet rose many thousands of years ago, but in May the headlands below are like planted rockeries, bee-loud in sunlight, occasionally sea-loud, rarely, I imagine, even to-day, disturbed by transistor sets or voices more raucous than those of wandering sheep. Certainly, there will be no motor-cars out there.

My brief stay in Cardigan had to do rather with a story back

[1] Two Welsh thinkers, the biologist H. J. Fleure and the linguist and historian A. W. Wade-Evans, have argued that both race and nationality must be regarded not as an *origo a qua* but as a *terminus ad quem*. The ideas of race and of nation are both slippery in the extreme.

in Giraldus's family history, concerning his Welsh grand-mother, Princess Nest, 'the Helen of Wales', and the dreadful eye-gouging feud between Owain ap Cadwgan and Madog ap Rhiryd ap Bleddyn. This involved me in visiting the castle of Cilgerran, from which Owain abducted Nest. It is an appalling story, and I was contemplating a play or perhaps a historical novel on it, to be called *The Glens of Desolation*, which I aban-doned. From the history of those two princely families, extinct in the male line, their womenfolk married off elsewhere, we may typically see how little of that 'Celtic' blood remains in Wales and how much is to be found in the longest-ennobled English families. The Fitzgeralds and the FitzStephens who conquered Ireland were also relations of Giraldus Cambrensis, through Nest, whose exertions on behalf of the human stud-book were prodigious.

But I must finish with this trip. At St Dogmael's, I talked, in the afternoon heat, with an intelligent Ministry of Works fore-man. At Cenarth, for a small fee, a nice man called Mr Llewellyn allowed me to paddle his tarred-canvas coracle below the falls on the Teifi. I went back to London. I saw an Italian film called *Bitter Rice*, *The Bells* in Camden Town with Frederick Valk and an extraordinarily silly play called *The Cocktail Party*, by T. S. Eliot. I had a holiday on the Suffolk coast, and then I went to the *eisteddfod* at Caerphilly.

The fancy-dress side of *eisteddfodau* is, I suppose, familiar to most people through cinema, television and so on. It is, of course, all quite exquisitely ridiculous, but conducted with so much diffidence and good humour that, really, one cannot object. That year, there was some element of grimness about the language question, a new all-Welsh rule having been im-posed. This was criticised by the Lord Mayor of Cardiff and by the local M.P., Mr Ness Edwards, who was Postmaster-Gen-eral in the Attlee government. Controversy still raged in *The Western Mail* and elsewhere later in the month, while I was at Newport. During *eisteddfod* week, two young men of the ex-treme republican wing of the nationalist party had, it seemed, also hauled down a Union Jack (flying over Caerphilly castle among the far more numerous green-and-white flags with red dragons) and had set fire to it and re-hoisted it in flames. They

114

were fined £25 and £15 respectively, for malicious destruction of property, and *The Western Mail* pointed out to them how light this punishment was and what they might have expected had they performed a similar act in some other countries.

I had picked up a very little Welsh, which I have since forgotten. In the main, this was a pure display of one-upmanship, since my wife spoke no Welsh. At the breakfast table and on retiring at night, I was thus able to exchange some remarks in a language she did not understand with her father, whose first language it was. Among the stalls round the field in which stood the *eisteddfod* pavilion had been one at which you could buy badges proclaiming that you spoke Welsh. My wife's suggestion was that I should buy one of these and pin beside it a square of white card on which a capital 'L' was printed in red. My father-in-law was a man I was very fond of. He was the very noblest type of provincial worthy, a huge, handsome man, fair in colouring, a voice of mercy on the Newport magistrates' bench.

During *eisteddfod* week, the P.E.N. had been holding its international conference in Edinburgh. There had been, I gathered, many interventions by Scottish nationalist poets, who had appeared in the kilts they normally reserve for their visits to London. 'Hugh MacDiarmid' had made one of his well-known stormy exits, protesting, however, or so it appeared, rather against American action in Korea than against the iron heel of the English in Scotland. Towards the end of August, there was a Celtic Congress in Truro. A Mr Liam Cogan of the National Museum of Ireland was reported in *The Western Mail* as making imperialistic speeches on behalf of a united Celtic *Herrenvolk*. The Welsh and Scottish nationalists, he said, should not be depressed by their failure in British general elections. The one in February had been 'a panic election, encouraging the idea that the English economy may have reached the stage reached by the Roman economy in the fourth century – one of near-dissolution'. In this situation, Mr Cogan evidently went on to explain, lay the opportunity of 'the Celtic nation' which, occupying the Atlantic seaboard, 'could, properly organised and developed, become the foremost power in Europe, stretching out a friendly hand to the great republics beyond'. At the same time, a Captain Cowan in Eire was reported to be gathering recruits for a private army to invade Ulster.

The Scottish nationalists in particular have often seemed disposed to make common cause with the Irish. The difficulty there is that the basic myths are opposite. The Irish agitation has long been against Partition. An island, they feel, is a sacred, womblike entity, which ought not to be divided. The Scots, on the other hand (and the separatist Welsh), are only too anxious to carve up an island. At least it was so in 1950, at which time also yet further fracture was desired by those who lived in the islands to the north of Scotland. A friend from those parts sent me copies of a little paper called *The New Shetlander*, whose editorial view was that Shetland is as distinct from Scotland as Scotland is from England and that the distinctness ought to receive political expression. A writer complained:

> We are now dependent on Scotland for our administration, our bread and cheese and beef, and permission to fish in our own waters and build a house on our own land. It would be disastrous to add to these dependence in the essential things of the mind and spirit.

The same writer complained that Shetland words were printed in the so-far-published volumes of *The Scottish National Dictionary* as Scottish words and that, in a series of twenty-four dramatised wireless programmes which, under the title 'The Guid Scots Tongue', had been broadcast from Edinburgh at weekly intervals all through that spring and summer, Orkney and Shetland were taken together as a Scottish dialectal area on a par with Buchan, Aberdeen or the Lothians. The Shetlanders have a Lallans of their own, called Norn.

It all seems very quaint now, but it was vicious. During the recent years of affluence, there has been little display of separatist tendencies or even of Irish to-do about the six counties. It will all start up again next time we feel the pinch, as perhaps we are beginning to do at the moment. When, on returning to London from that first Edinburgh trip, I described my impressions to an influential colleague, his summing-up had been that it was all a clamour of rats anxious to leave the sinking ship. I am not happy with such metaphors, but that one did not altogether lack aptness to the mood I had found. There was, on the one hand, the resentment of those Scottish intellectuals and professional men whose ambitions had once been checked in London. It was a resentment not directed wholly against 'the English', but sometimes more explicitly against other Scots who had not failed, who (in an expression I remember from a literary review) were 'belly-pushing to success in London'. But, at a more popular level, beneath all the historical and other trimmings, it was, I fancy, the food-shortage thing that was essential.

In any internationally awkward situation, the great problem in these islands is feeding London, whose population (I mean what is known as 'Greater London', of course) is twice that of Scotland, twice that of Ulster and Eire together, between four and five times that of Wales. During the war, Eire had done nicely out of her neutrality, guaranteed only by our sinking ships and burning cities. Draw an economic frontier across this island and, it was clearly felt in Edinburgh, those north of it could feast, while those further south went hungry, including the millions of Scots, half-Scots and quarter-Scots in London. For London is not simply an English city. Its vast population has been created by centuries of the southward and eastward drift of Dick Whittingtons, a preponderance of them Scottish, though 'Jones' has long been known as one of the three commonest names in England.

I do not think I exaggerate the meanness of the calculations that were made at that time. Certainly, none of the arguments then advanced made any suggestion that separation would be to the advantage of other people, including the English. Perhaps it was part of the Calvinist legacy, which is also strong in Wales. The Scots (I never caught this sense among the Welsh) were the elect who must be saved, not (in my quotation from 'Hugh MacDiarmid') 'dragged down in England's well-deserved and unavoidable ruin', the 'unavoidable' being more Calvinist than the 'well-deserved', which was perhaps a concession to Lutheranism.

What kind of moral ailment may result from Calvinist doctrine, it had not long before been possible to discover from a reprint of that truly great novel of Edinburgh, James Hogg's

Confessions of a Justified Sinner. That nationalism itself is, in the modern world, a moral disease had, not long before, been suggested to us by Nazi Germany. Four years after a war supposedly fought against that variety of extreme nationalism, it had been a bit depressing to meet pub-Nazis plotting at the Abbotsford and the Café Royal. The underlying, never-expressed quibble was that, while nationalism is a disease in a powerful nation, in 'small' or 'emergent' nations it should be encouraged. This notion is still with us.

At that moment in 1949-50, the mood in London was no pleasanter than anywhere else. At the time of the February election, I could not myself have voted anything but Labour. Yet I know that I thought and said at the time that it might be best if we now had a change of government, if only to bring the middle class to its senses. The Government had become a mere scapegoat. Those who pinned their hopes on a Conservative government needed a practical demonstration of just what differences it could make. If they had a government of their own, business men and their wives might even discover that tax-dodges and black marketeering did not in themselves constitute a superior way of life. For *their* agitations, too, constituted a kind of separatist movement.

The moral collapse of the nation was pitiable. The prevailing mood was a blend of self-pity and callousness. The hypochondria showed physically in London. Five years after the war, almost no attempt had been made to repair the bomb damage, let alone rebuild. It was positively stimulating when, that Christmas, a group of priggish undergraduates from Glasgow stole the coronation stone from Westminster Abbey. I admired their enterprise. The priggishness lay in pretending to feel deeply about this object and its obscure history. Most English people had never till then heard of the coronation stone, and certainly they did not care about it. Before the war, 'Hugh MacDiarmid' was said to have tried to steal it. Appparently, a lady called Wendy Wood had got up a fund. 'Chris' and his companions were (it appears) to be seen drinking away this fund in Charlotte Street, having found the stone too heavy for them.

XVIII

IN 1951, we had the Festival of Britain and a change of government. I reached the age of forty and moved to a top floor in Notting Hill Gate. There has been a Conservative government ever since, and I am still in the same flat, while for most of us forty is a traumatic age. In my own life, therefore, as in the life of the country as a whole, there were changes which increasingly began to look permanent. Among other men of letters, there was much talk of consolidation. But a new decade had begun, and there was also much decade talk among the younger literary journalists, with whom the 'Twenties (and the 'Nineties of the last century) were rather popular and the 'Thirties very unpopular. No doubt the attitude was quite sincere, though it was conspicuous that those 'men of the 'Thirties' so much attacked were just the ones who stood in the way of their juniors' advancement.

Later to be known as the race-riot area, Notting Hill Gate was at that time still the murder belt. I found that I much preferred the neighbourhood to Hampstead. Our bit of it remained genteel. Until we took up our abode in what had once been the servants' bedrooms of two houses, all the names on the In-and-Out indicator in the hallway had been either hyphenated or preceded by a military rank not lower than Major. A board affixed to railings prohibited street-cries, and the terms of our lease forbade us to keep any dog, cat, parrot or other noisy or offensive fowl or beast. The young men in Campden Hill and Church Street wore bowler hats, planted squarely on their heads like those of Guards officers out of uniform, carried rolled umbrellas and, as their British warms wore out, adopted overcoats with velvet collars. They had, it appeared, also taken to going to church on Sunday mornings, to set the working classes an example. The working-class young were more intrigued by the velvet collars, which they presently adopted, together with the narrower trousers of this revived Edwardian style.

I thought the Festival of Britain an admirable affair. It ought perhaps to have been made permanent, the individual attractions being replaced or modified annually. It was, however, treated politically. The swan-song of the Attlee government, it was systematically panned by the Conservative newspapers, who succeeded to no small extent in damping the whole thing down. Two years later, a Conservative government was to have its own Festival of Britain, the Coronation.

At the time of first visiting Edinburgh the year before, I had sold off, at a ridiculously small price, large numbers of French books, upon which, during the preceding years, I had spent a great deal in having them bound. A notion I had was that, by too much reading (and a fair amount of talking) in a foreign language, a writer might lose the mastery of his own, which was his strong rock. I was, I felt, beginning to think in French. I now find the notion absurd and am inclined to take the opposite view, *viz.*, that only through constant rubbing against a foreign language can a writer achieve mastery of his own. I am further inclined to say that the principal foreign language against which an English writer rubs must be French.

It may be that, since, as a writer, I was unhappy and unproductive, I had found a scapegoat in the foreign language and was cooking up an alibi for myself. How grotesque, for instance, to reject France and all French writing for such reasons and then at once to start learning Welsh. Yet the total syndrome had its rational side. Eccentricity implies a centre. But my preoccupations during the past year or more had been not so much eccentric as centrifugal. The centre was London.

I should inevitably regret selling those books, but not yet. I had kept all I had by Jouhandeau, and, out of a kind of retrospective piety, I had kept Léon Bloy. This was fortunate, since, at the beginning of 1951, I found myself committed to writing a monograph on Bloy. In late April, I again went to Paris, but, apart from a visit to the aged Fernand Gregh in that village within Paris, the Hameau de Boulainvilliers, the trip did not involve me with any living writer. Indeed, though I was to be frequently in Paris, during the next eight or nine years I had nothing whatever to do with writers there. I had to do mostly with actors.

That April, my purpose was to record three French actors and actresses reading poems by Baudelaire, Nerval, Rimbaud and Mallarmé. It was to be the first of many such trips, during which, among others, I should record Edwige Feuillère, Madeleine Renaud, Suzanne Flon, Gérard Philipe, Jean Vilar and Daniel Gélin, as well as (more recently) Jean Cocteau and Jacques Prévert. The first group of readers, in 1951, consisted of Madeleine Renaud, Roger Blin and Jean Yonnel, an enormously dignified older member of the Comédie Française. The selection of poems had been made by Raymond Mortimer. He would have made further selections, but later in the year fell very ill, so that I got into the way of making the selections, and introducing them, myself. Translations of all the poems were specially made. For that first group of programmes, and frequently thereafter, they were made by translators of whom Mr Mortimer was aware as *New Statesman* competition winners, two of them Frances Cornford and L. E. Jones.

In a general way, I am not much in favour of the reading aloud of poems. The need for it progressively disappeared with the spread of literacy, which is no doubt why its popularity has increased since the war. When poets tell you that all verse is meant to be heard, what they mean is that they would like a nice fee from the BBC or a gramophone company. Upon completing a poem, their first impulse is always to get it into print, and, although with practice they have improved in recent years, what I found during the five or six first post-war years was that, if you asked a poet to read a poem aloud to you or even to help you to explain to an actor how it should be done, he hadn't the slightest idea. For at least a hundred years past, the appeal of most poems has been to the mind's ear, which is capable of far greater subtlety than the physical ear of all but a very few people. With poems in foreign languages, it is different. With them, the mind's ear cannot do its job properly unaided, but needs stimulus through the physical ear. And so I have always found a particular satisfaction in doing those bilingual programmes devoted to French (occasionally, Italian) verse, quite apart from the incidental delights. I knew just what I was doing and why I was doing it. I also quickly discovered for what audience I was doing it and that they were surprisingly numerous.

The trips involved have, as I say, had little or nothing to do with my interest, as a writer, in French writers. From 1949 until, say, 1954, I was not in fact much interested in, at any rate, contemporary French writing. I was not very interested in any contemporary writing in the late 'Forties or early 'Fifties. I found the literary scene unattractive, and in retrospect I can see that it was a peculiarly flat, uninteresting landscape. In fiction, for instance, there was not much sign of life between Angus Wilson's two volumes of stories and the appearance of *Lucky Jim*. During those years, there was also a notable absence of literary magazines. *Horizon* and *New Writing* had vanished. So had *John o' London's Weekly* and *World Review*. *Encounter* and *London Magazine* had not appeared. But I dare say that, even if the literary scene had been lively, I should have stayed off it. Perhaps other writers were feeling the same, and that is why it was not lively. I have no *Zeitgeist* explanation to offer. In my own case, the abstention was voluntary. Apart from its intrinsic fascinations and apart from the demands it made on my time and energy, my work in broadcasting made me in other people's eyes an extra-literary figure, and in a somewhat perverse and defiant way I too-heartily concurred in this view.

In 1951, I was in fact writing the monograph on Léon Bloy, but that turned out to be largely a work of rejection. I had begun to find many varieties of Christian thought repulsive. Until March, I had been living in Hampstead, in a flat once occupied by the Anglo-Catholic poet, novelist, critic and amateur playwright Charles Williams. I had read his books, and in Oxford on PQ conferences (the last time was 1951) I had been made aware of that ambience of cider-drinking with holy jokes at the Eagle and Child, which, with its other churchy accoutrements, struck me as pure ecclesiastical foppery, rather homosexual in tone, though learned ladies and spiritual girls were allowed, and some marriages took place and parturition ensued, presumably not parthenogenetical, since it was never claimed to be so.

Also in 1951 appeared Graham Greene's *The End of the Affair*.

Three years before, there had been *The Heart of the Matter*, set, it will be remembered, in Africa, the story concerned with a man ensuring his own eternal damnation by going to communion without previously confessing his recurrent adultery. That, too, was foppery. Like birth-control, the question whether unconfessed Saturday-night fornication followed by Sunday-morning communion was or was not a mortal sin had been a favourite talking point among the young Catholic set in London before the war. Until *The Heart of the Matter*, I had greatly admired pretty well everything Graham Greene did.

A good deal of wavering in matters of faith, perceptible in 1951, had been set up by the recently promulgated dogma of the Bodily Assumption (of the B.V.M. into Heaven). It was rather like what we should see five years later among Communists at the time of the suppression of the Hungarian rising. In neither case did, I think, many believers finally lapse. After all, it would have been to strain at a midge after swallowing a camel. There may even have been a special kind of (perhaps faintly masochistic) pleasure in assenting to anything so patently absurd as the new doctrine, which the Vatican had perhaps even devised consciously as a wanton test of faith, *i.e.*, of persistent credulousness. Once you have (like the heroine of *The End of the Affair*) 'caught belief like a disease', no doubt it must run its course, and certainly it may, like a vaccination, be prophylactic against other ailments. It was, I felt in 1951, still possible to envy a believer his belief, though, in the case of intellectual converts, very difficult to believe in it. I should have described myself as a fanatical agnostic, a more difficult position, but, I thought, nobler.

What I particularly did not like was agnosticism parading as, and perhaps believing itself to be, belief. There was and is a great deal of this. The Christian literature published every year would sink a battleship, and yet there are those who complain of irreligion. Religion is a very big industry. The point of all those books is, one supposes, to confirm people in their uneasy attitudes. I do not imagine that I should have made any study of them, but a fair number have come my way for review. In 1950, there had been one by Reinhold Niebuhr, an important figure in the Protestant world, working in New York at the Union Theological Seminary. I had met him briefly, and been impressed, when in 1936 he came to lecture at Middleton Murry's Adelphi Centre. His new book represented a threefold revision of lectures given successively at Yale, in Scotland and at Uppsala. It was very much an example of the most respectable kind of such book. And yet I did not see how Dr Niebuhr could disbelieve more and continue to hold down even a Protestant appointment.

We must not, he said, with St Augustine, 'exempt the church from the ambiguities and contradictions of history more absolutely than the prophets of Israel exempted their own nation'. We must not indulge in that false rationalising whereby 'the Jesus of history who becomes the Christ by faith is interpreted as an inhuman and incredible personality with alleged powers of omniscience'. The Resurrection ('an alteration in the story'), the Virgin Birth ('this type of miracle is in opposition to true faith') and the immortality of the soul ('a transcendental version of the old sin of trying too desperately to live') were all written off. Elsewhere, Dr Niebuhr denounced both Unitarian deism and the view of Christ as the great exemplar, but if one of the quotations above ('the Jesus of history who becomes the Christ by faith') was not exemplarism, it was surely adoptionist. Which of the Christian stage-properties had we been left with? I could find none except 'a symbolic historical event such as the "fall" of man' and sacraments 'to symbolise the having and not having the final virtue and truth'. I could not see what 'the "Mercy" of God' (Dr Niebuhr's inverted commas) portended upon the bare boards of a stage like that. It meant perhaps that we ought to try to regard the play as less intolerable than we privately thought it.

Even so much attempt at self-consolation might have seemed too much to Simone Weil, and perhaps her view of the metaphysical world was not so very different from Dr Niebuhr's. And yet when her *Waiting on God* came out in the early autumn of 1951, I found it extremely attractive. In part, this was for wholly personal reasons. In essence, her grounds for refusing baptism had been those which kept me out of the Church in 1936. But also there was in the very quality of her writing and the texture of her thought (I in fact read her first and, for the most part, have continued to read her in translation) something so entirely scrupulous and fine that one hardly ever demurred. Certainly, there have been, in the modern world, only three Christian or near-Christian thinkers by whom I was attracted for long, first (in the order in which I read them) Léon Bloy, then Kierkegaard, then Simone Weil.

I had first heard of her from Sir Richard Rees, when I was staying with him in Edinburgh two years before. I had made no attempt to read her at that time, though no doubt volumes of hers in French had lain around that flat in Douglas Crescent. And now I find myself wondering if in fact it can have been in English that I first read Simone Weil. For it was while I was in Paris again in early October 1951 that I went round to Plon's to get for Richard three back-numbers of *La Table Ronde* which contained essays by Simone Weil, and one of the essays was certainly on the fallacy in Emmanuel Mounier's Personalism (it is the general and not the personal in people to which you must pay regard, or you create injustice). I must, I fancy, have read this at the time. Perhaps not. Perhaps I took the three volumes back to London uncut, then almost at once read *Waiting on God*.

XIX

FOR about six months before, and
during the first year of, Hitler's war, my usual public house
was the Marlborough, in Abbey Road, at the corner of Blenheim Terrace, St John's Wood. It was well-placed for drinking
out of doors in fine weather, the pavements both in the main
road and in Blenheim Terrace being wide, and the landlord
being a man with a highly developed sense of amenity. I was
sitting, with a pint of bitter ale, at a small, square teak table
on the Abbey Road side of the Marlborough, at about noon on
a sunny day in, I fancy, the spring of 1940, though it may have
been the previous autumn or even in the late summer, just
before the declaration of war.

Not only were there no other customers, but there seemed
to be not a soul (and no traffic) from one end to the other of
Abbey Road (which is long and broad and an important,
though not a congested, thoroughfare) except, I suddenly
noticed, that policemen had appeared at all the street corners.
Just then two open motor-cars came in sight. Sitting in the
back of the second car was a man in air-force uniform (I dare
say other occupants of the two cars wore air-force uniform,
too). As the cars passed, I was, as it happens, just raising the
glass tankard to my lips. The man sitting in the back of the
second car saluted me. It was, I realised as he speeded by, H.M.
King George VI. No doubt he had taken the raising of my glass
as a loyal salute.

Possibly the most interesting thing about the story is that it
did not seem interesting at the time. No doubt I chuckled inwardly, but I said nothing about the incident even to the
publican, even to my wife. Not until twelve years later did I
think it a story worth telling. It was not that I suffered from a
conspicuous or eccentric lack of interest in royal personages.
The cult which was to develop in the early 'Fifties simply did
not exist before or during the early days of the war, at any rate

among educated people. If I *had* told the story at the time, nobody else would have found it interesting. I first told it on 6th February 1952, or very shortly thereafter. It then went down well. I told it with a genuine wistfulness.

I first read the news of the King's death on a handwritten placard displayed by a newsvendor just below the Polytechnic in Upper Regent Street. I was still no royalist, but I found the news upsetting. I felt that an important safeguard had been removed. There was, so to speak, only Churchill left now. I was no great Churchill fan either, but I did see him as a bulwark against the more disreputable type of Conservatism which had gathered about him, representing the commercial interest exclusively. Once he was dead or retired, the racketeers would go uncurbed. In the meantime, with a malleable young woman on the throne, they could (I thought) begin to run the institution of monarchy their own way.

The main argument against constitutional monarchy lies precisely in its symbolic nature. Children, savages and neurotics habitually take symbols for realities, but a modern nation should not be encouraged to do so. It is a sign of infantilism, and we live in a world in which some maturity of imagination would not come amiss. It is true that, in the affairs of the world to-day, the surviving monarchies do not in general behave either more wickedly or more foolishly than the republics, but none of the other surviving monarchies is quite so exposed to the major contemporary stresses as we are. Several of them are quiet little enclaves, with small populations. None is so urgently faced as we are with a need for intellectual energy, for willingness to change our established customs and, in the first place, for a truer, more accurate picture of who and what we are and of what possibilities are open to us and what closed.

There are, I suppose, very few republicans in the country. There used to be more. In the 'Twenties and 'Thirties, all socialists were republicans. At any rate in the West Riding, any socialist, trapped in a theatre or concert hall by the strains of 'God Save the King', would put on his hat and sit firmly in his place. In 1945, though one had found the spectacle faintly disturbing, one had seen well enough that Mr Attlee and his colleagues might, at first, think it advisable to hire morning coats and top hats or even knee breeches and black silk stockings from Moss Bros. and present themselves at Buckingham Palace in traditional guise. But they were still doing it in 1950, and, though by then in opposition, in 1952 they fell over backward with loyal protestations. With one notable exception, a Welshman who represented a Scottish rural constituency, they were clearly willing to do it indefinitely.

My own worst fears in 1952 have turned out to be unfounded. Despite the excesses of that year and the next, British monarchy remains pretty well as it was. The present reign seems likely to be a long one, and only a fanatical purist would now urge that it should be abrupted.[1] As to the next reign, that is another matter. A mild republicanism might well take the view that, while the present reign must run its course, it should be the last. It would have been kindest to explain such a position to the young Prince of Wales some few years ago. He could then have been differently educated. When he was sent to Gordonstoun, *The New Statesman* did criticise the choice of a school, but only on the basis of the assumption that one day the boy would be King and that Gordonstoun would not equip him to play the part as *The New Statesman* thought it should be played. However, if even now the idea requires some little while to take root, it seems probable that the young man will have forty years or so in which to grow used to it. I don't know what the bulk of my readers feel, if they have contemplated it, about the alternative idea, which is that, in the early years of the third millennium A.D., a man in his fifties, married to goodness knows whom, should accede as Charles III of a Commonwealth whose bounds at that time none of us can reasonably predict. However, a majority of us won't be around at the time.

I had grown up in a world before the war in which royalty was little esteemed, except by charwomen and the proprietresses of riding schools. In early 1952, I was so little aware of the new mood that I remember being surprised when people appeared wearing black ties. As a result of clothes rationing, mourning had largely been given up even for one's nearest and dearest. I could understand that, for instance, very senior

[1] The remainder of it might perhaps with advantage be conducted from Canada. There is so much to make room for on this tiny island.

BBC figures might be expected to indulge in some manifestation of the kind, but I thought it odd when I saw Norman Cameron in a black tie. Professionally, he was in advertising. He had been in advertising when I first met him. He was, I fancy, the first of the many poets and men of letters who have been in advertising. He was a very good poet. He was, I would say, the best of the now-little-known, comparatively unproductive, *New Verse* poets of the 'Thirties. In his odd, abrupt way, he was also a man of great personal charm and distinction and what I can only describe as brave in his private involvements. I had first met him, in 1934, through Innes Stewart, with whom he had been at school in Edinburgh. At his studio flat in Chiswick, on my first visit one Saturday to luncheon, I had also first met Stephen Spender. Later, Dylan Thomas had been staying with him. I had not seen him for years.

What brought us together in 1952 were verse translations of Alfred de Musset's four *Nuits*, which he was to make in connection with Paris recordings I was to do at the end of March and in early April. Those translations must have been Cameron's last serious literary labour, for he was not to see the year out. He had been gravely ill, with what complaint I have never discovered, and in early 1952 he went to one of the remote Spanish islands to recuperate. I was surprised to see him in a black tie. I had not thought him a conventional man. The poetry of settled forms had begun, however, to enfold him. He had recently married an Austrian Catholic girl and had been, or was just about to be, received into the Church, mainly, or so he said, in order to please her family.

I do not know how quickly other organs of opinion discovered that, as the new Queen's name was Elizabeth, we now lived in what could be described as a second Elizabethan age. *The News Chronicle* had worked it out by 11th February. The King lay in state, with mile-long queues round Westminster Abbey. The royal women, a mute, black-draped Greek chorus, were to be seen in newspaper photographs grieving on railway platforms. Most broadcasting had been stopped, but the BBC occasionally broke silence to play *Nimrod* from the 'Enigma' variations. In Scotland, the nationalists calculated that, as the first Elizabeth had not reigned over Scotland, her successor could not there be properly designated Elizabeth II. Since two Williams, two Edwards and a second James had been allowed to accede without comment, to make a fuss about this seemed a bit mean. However, when recast pillar-boxes appeared with an E II R monogram, the quibble provided an excuse for the pastime of blowing them up. I could see that the pastime itself must have been quite enjoyable. I remembered how, on Mischief Night, which meant the evening of 4th November, in Huddersfield, I had been accustomed to put lighted thunder-flashes in dustbins and quickly ram on the lid. It would sometimes rise to roof-top height.

With the aid of their journalist friends, business men had by now got it worked out that, in the new Elizabethan age, they themselves were merchant venturers. This made them seem more respectable. They were now to reap their reward for six years' devoted sabotage of the measures of the preceding government. I had imagined that, once in power, a Conservative government would set itself to the task of creating large-scale unemployment, so that the employers might beat down wages. As now began to appear, that was not the plan. Just as the Attlee government had lacked the courage to risk an all-out battle against the commercial and the landed interests, so now the Tories dared not quite run into headlong collision with the working-class organisations. They did not even crack down very hard on the provisions of what had come to be known as the Welfare State, that is to say, on the National Health Service, free milk in schools, free secondary and subsidised university education or, at first, on controlled rents. Instead, they proposed to reward their supporters by superimposing on what already existed a Business Man's Welfare State, whereby private speculation might be conducted without risk and indirectly or even directly subsidised.

There was an autumn Budget in 1952. The most significant of its provisions was for taxation relief on what was described as 'ploughing the profits back into the business'. I do not know whether the Chancellor of the Exchequer (then Mr R. A. Butler) quite saw what would be the most appalling single consequence of his manoeuvre. To suppose that he did not would be to suppose him remarkably unintelligent. On the other hand, to suppose that he did would be to convict him in one's mind of a combined Machiavellianism and lack of imagination which might be thought more unintelligent still. At any rate, in the next breath (on the wireless, it was strictly the next breath), he announced that most types of motor-car were to be no longer restricted to the export market, but could be bought at once, without the delay which since the war had been attendant upon all applications to buy a new car. In other words, through his firm, every biz gent could have a new car at half price, the loss to the Exchequer through profits tax unpaid being made up by the community as a whole.

During the next twelve months, the community must have paid three hundred million pounds in this way to subsidise business men's cars, for a million new cars were bought, of which only one in seventeen was bought by a private individual. This continues. Most people don't seem to realise even now how few new cars are bought or even run by the individuals who so lord it in them. The flood of cheap, fairly new, second-hand cars which *are* bought by agricultural labourers and schoolboys are there on the market only because the community as a whole continues to pay for the racket whereby commercial enterprises avoid paying tax on their profits by annual replacement of the new cars we all pay to be deafened, gassed and sooner or later probably crippled or killed by.

A very large number of people are, one finds, more or less radically offended by what they describe as 'the modern world'. What there is no general agreement about is just when this disastrous 'modern world' may be thought to have begun. Some people date it from the First World War. Others trace it back to the nineteenth century and the Industrial Revolution. Catholic publicists may go back as far as the Reformation. I date it from Butler's autumn Budget of 1952. Till then, this country was fit to live in. I mean, as a physical environment. The moral environment may have been bad, but at least when you were in the country there was something resembling the traditional rural peace. Mr Butler destroyed it all in two breaths.

To do them justice, our little friends were not slow in taking his point. Within a matter of days, quiet streets like the one

I lived in were crowded with little shining juggernauts. Luckily, I lived on a fourth floor. Light was excluded from all the basement windows by cars 'belonging to' persons who lived at Ruislip, Uxbridge or Pinner. Here, for the benefit of younger readers or those with short memories, I had better say that before Hitler's war motor-cars were not parked in the streets, even before one's own house. If a car-driver had no private garage, he took his car to the nearest public garage, even if he would be wanting it again in an hour or two. The streets were streets, not car parks.

That year's (1952's) cars had curious, grilled bonnets which, as certainly *The News Chronicle*'s cartoonists saw, gave them a kind of facial expression reminiscent of that which, in war-time cartoons, had been attributed to sadistically grinning Japanese. As, however, one quickly realised when one had seen and heard them in action on the main road, the chief difference between the new cars and the old was the unprecedently loud horns of the new ones. These seemed designed not to warn but rather to freeze the intended victim in his tracks. As they were all tuned to the same note, it was clear that there would be many collisions at street corners on approaching which at an angle of forty-five degrees to each other the two motorists pressed the buttons of their identically pitched horns at the same moment.

Something of the kind happened frequently at the corner on which I live. Luckily or unluckily, from all but one (at a lower level than the rest) of our many windows, parapets prevent us seeing down into the street (unless we stand on a chair and open and crane out through the windows, which are small and square and breast-high, with broad ledges, under which runs a gutter). However, from about ten o' clock each Friday evening, one used to wait for the screaming brakes and the impact, then the murmur of passers-by assembling. Some individual from Ruislip, Uxbridge or Pinner had stayed drinking with his associates and, wishing to convince his wife that he had at least not stayed till closing time and knowing his short cuts, had met at our corner a local resident driving home, perhaps, from a party in Chelsea. One felt comparatively sorry for the local resident, but reminded oneself hopefully that he who takes the sword shall perish by the sword. In a general way, that motorists sometimes killed or crippled each other might even be a consolation for what oneself had to put up with in the street, which one entered with the sensations of an infantryman about to engage tanks, without sticky bombs and forbidden even the use of small arms.

I concluded I had better stay in as much as possible, though indeed from our flat (with so many windows and, from those at the back, a view on a clear day of Richmond and hills beyond) going out felt like going in. To enlarge the scope of my indoor activities and perhaps also, in some obscure way, to compete with all the new cars, I went down to Harrods' vast show-room and paid the deposit on a piano, by far the most expensive piece of goods I had ever gone in for. It was a reconditioned baby grand by Moore and Moore, of an attractive russet colour and elegant proportions.

A properly constituted team of pianoforte-removers consists of four men, three of them large and florid, the fourth pale and small, like the sickly pigling in a litter. He is the one who provides the motive force, the others being there mainly to re-assure spectators. The large members of a Harrods team wear splendid green uniforms. The undersized one has to wear his own clothes, pianoforte-removers' uniforms being made only in large sizes. This I discovered between three and four o' clock one November afternoon, when a team so composed appeared with the Moore and Moore.

Our largest room is at a level below the rest of our premises. Even so, the piano had to come up eighty steps (in eight short flights) and down one. From the end window of that room, one looks westward or, more exactly, west-south-westward down Ladbroke Road to the police station in Ladbroke Grove. As I looked out, a policeman was pulling at the wrist of a man who clung to the railings of a house. Another policeman ran unhurriedly up, and together they marched the man, who was bald and wore an old raincoat, off to the station.

When the removal men were sitting on the landing just below, I asked them how they were getting on.
I said:
'I thought I saw two policemen marching one of you off.'

'Not us, guv'nor,' they said.

One of them added:

'They could have had this job, too, if they'd liked.'

'What was it?' I said.

'Oh, a drunk, wa'n' it, George?'

The main part of the piano they elevated in gusts. Having gently raised it, they would run up a short flight, loudly and concertedly gabbling their advices to each other, then lower it with a great sigh on to the cradle roped to it for the purpose.

While they fetched up the legs, the lid and the pedal mechanism, I made tea.

'It's a nice piano,' they said when they had set it up.

Yet in fact Moore and Moore brought little pleasure into our lives. At first it was simply the sustaining pedal which creaked. It creaked not from tightness but because the brass rod had too much play. It lacked spring. That evening, there came to dinner a friend whom we had not seen for some years. He must have wondered what strange despondency was gnawing at our hearts. My wife dreamed that night that Moore and Moore stood in a public house and that there were beer-mugs all over its polished surface.

Then notes stuck. Two of them rang tinnily. One of these yielded to tuning, but the strings of the other had to be haled out. I decided that I did not like the piano. The bass was cold and wooden, the treble dead, the middle excessively sweet. Worst of all, the whole thing swayed. If you played at all loudly or rapidly or used the pedal much, it began to buck like a horse and would almost throw you. The chief technician came. The pedal was tightened up until it hardly engaged the dampers at all. The legs were taken away, and the piano top was left resting on trestles covered with a great sheet of billiard cloth. When the legs came back, it was just the same. Harrods' chief buyer and I corresponded acrimoniously about the said legs.

'We mustn't', said my wife, 'let it get on top of us.'

But it did. For almost six weeks, Moore and Moore stayed on top of us. Then happiness was restored by Collard and Collard.

The auspices were not good. It was the Saturday morning on which that new kind of fog called 'smog' started (it was

134

less impenetrable than the pre-war pea-soupers) that my wife and I went again to Harrods' salerooms. Mr Harris, the salesman, described the Collard and Collard as 'brilliant'. I thought of it rather as 'clean'. It was like the Festival Hall by comparison with the Albert Hall. There was no buzz of delayed sonorities to disguise confusion. A wrong note was unmistakably a wrong note. The treble had a ker-plunkety, xylophone-like limpidity all its own. The bass was strong and decisive. In the middle lay all those subtle shades which not even the most expert toning could needle out of the felt. There was general hand-shaking. Rubicund and immaculate in his black coat and trousers, a clean white handkerchief peeping from his breast-pocket, the chief buyer, Mr Murdoch, towered above us and assured me jovially that he would not hear a word against the Moore and Moore.

It was just before Christmas when a different team of three large men in green uniforms and one small one in his shirt sleeves arrived with Collard and Collard and took Moore and Moore away.

As they were moving out with Moore and Moore, the ladies who live below us came to their door.

'We hope,' they said, 'that you won't knock our wall.'

'Madam,' said the enormously dignified foreman (who would not himself touch a drop but saw no reason why the others should not replace the moisture they had lost by perspiration), 'if we was to touch your wall, we should go right through it.'

The Collard and Collard dates from the early 'Twenties. Its colour is of the darkest, its legs massive and fluted. The castors lie invisibly cupped under the legs, which, at the bottom, broaden out into a heavy rim. I felt that Herbert Read would not approve of the said legs. We liked them very much, though I was occasionally reminded of the legs of a species of barnyard fowl whose legs are heavily feathered all the way down in such a way as to conceal its feet.

XX

AT the beginning of 1953, Herbert Read was knighted. He attended the same investiture as three policemen who were decorated for not running away when a youth called Craig was firing a revolver, with which he killed one of their friends. Craig was too young to be hanged, but in his place it was proposed to hang an older youth, Derek Bentley, who was nineteen. Bentley had not killed anybody. He had not been armed, when the two young illiterates were surprised by the police on a warehouse roof. The police stated, however, that, while his younger companion was firing, Bentley had said, 'Let him have it, Chris!' This ambiguous exhortation, they also insisted, clearly meant that Craig was to go on firing, not that he should give the police his revolver.

Craig was to be detained at Her Majesty's pleasure and, I believe, is now at liberty. The jury were so directed from the bench by Lord Chief Justice Goddard that they could hardly fail to bring in a verdict of guilty against the other young man. They also put in a recommendation to mercy, but this was ignored by Lord Goddard. Bentley was appointed to be hanged on 26th February, a Wednesday.

I well remember the previous weekend's Sunday papers. There was a good deal of cant on both sides. The popular papers were for a reprieve, and a petition had gone round collecting signatures. The quality papers begged us rather to sympathise with poor old Maxwell-Fyfe, the Home Secretary, 'alone with his conscience' (any reprieve, that is to say, would have to come from him). That was cant. One imagined fat-bottomed lawyers deliberating in comfort over their port. I was for a reprieve, but I was equally repelled by the popular cant. One of the cheap and nasty Sunday papers devoted its front-page photographs to Bentley's family and pets. Evidently, he had several dogs at home, and the main reason for his reprieve was that, since his arrest, these dogs had been off their food.

A reprieve was, I fancied, to be expected. Whatever the legal position, the young man was clearly not a proper murderer and had not killed the policeman, while there had been the jury's recommendation to mercy, and popular feeling was all on Bentley's side. It could not, one felt, be utterly scouted. There was, however, a new authoritarian spirit abroad. For months past, the correspondence columns of the newspapers had been full of letters on the subject of flogging, which the more illiberal sections of the middle class were manifestly anxious to see restored for crimes of robbery with violence, these being in general perpetrated by young men of the lower class. The merchant venturers and their wives clearly felt that it was time for their government to put its foot down. It was all part of the resurgent Tory spirit, like the tendency of young men in Kensington to wear bowler hats, carry rolled umbrellas and attend church services on a Sunday morning. The public schools were also coming back into favour. Before the war, they had become a joke.

On Monday morning, the newsvendors' placards announced that there was to be no reprieve. I felt extremely angry. I was not and am not particularly opposed to all capital or, indeed, corporal punishment. I was even inclined to suggest that any motorist who killed a pedestrian should automatically be put on a capital charge and that any who, with any show of fault, merely injured a pedestrian should be flogged. But the zealots for both capital and corporal punishment envisaged these as punishments to be inflicted only upon the lower orders, who for their part showed a surprising readiness to accept as part of the natural course of things the knocking down by cars of their nearest and dearest (I have often wondered why, near the scene of a fatal accident, you did not almost inevitably see the body of a motorist hanging from the nearest lamp-post). Certainly, during any period of two months in which, say, two old ladies and a night watchman had been knocked on the head by young thugs, three hundred people would have been killed, and three thousand permanently injured, by motorists in London alone. That young Bentley should be hanged I

137

thought monstrous. It was the new class of killers (and their wives) who wanted his execution and who had to be appeased because they had voted the new government in.

This episode in the class war was consummated two days later. Bentley was hanged *as an example*. It was almost a political assassination. There was more than the usual crowd outside the prison, and more of it was there to protest and not out of the usual morbid curiosity. I read about it on the top of a 'bus. When I got off the 'bus in Notting Hill Gate, there were signs of a small crowd dispersing from the scene of 'an accident'. No wonder. I have never seen our little friends tearing back to their suburbs with so much elation. At last, they seemed to be saying, our government has spoken. Thumb on horn, foot on accelerator, these merchant venturers charged the pedestrian crossings like Drake sailing into Cadiz.

There might, I fancy, have been a serious popular outcry about Bentley. At the time, I went so far as to imagine that it might even topple the government. That weekend, however, a ship with many well-known people aboard went down on the Stranraer-Larne crossing. Immediately after that and as a result of the same high seas, large parts of our east coast were flooded. It became impossible to raise one's voice about one death among so many, even if these were acts of God and that one young man had been put down by a human calculation. At any rate, the year of the Coronation had got off to a good start.

On Monday, the day the floods started, I went to Paris to do more poetry-recording. The boat had some difficulty in putting into the harbour at Boulogne. As, turning, it came sideways on to the swell, I thought it would turn over. The French, too, were much concerned at the time with a question of guilt and responsibility. At Oradour in 1943, the Germans had perpetrated a retributive massacre on a scale not much inferior to the one at Lidice the summer before. Those charged with complicity in the affair had only just been brought to trial. Thirteen of them were Alsatians, *incorporés de force* in the German Army. Alsace demanded their release under a general amnesty. Limoges insisted upon their punishment. What they had done was not pretty (there had been women and children locked in a burning church). They were released.

138

Stalin died. Queen Mary died. On the morning of her funeral, the last day of March, John Reginald Halliday Christie was picked up by a policeman on Putney embankment. They brought him to our local police station. Our caretaker had friends among the local police. She told me, just before ten o'clock, that they would be bringing the celebrated multiple murderer and necrophile any time now. As I looked down the road from the end window of the downstairs room, the first two press photographers came in sight. It was a day of alternating rain and sunlight. Willesden gasworks stood out upon a mistily unreal false horizon. A crowd gathered opposite the police station and remained there, periodically rained upon, until the evening.

I had recently bought a great deal of music, including, a few weeks before, from Durand in the Place de la Madeleine, the four pale-blue volumes of *Clavecinistes Français*. I played the piano most of that day. Formerly, I had played the piano quite well. I had even had two young pupils. After so many years of having no piano, my fingers were stiff. I could just about manage Couperin's *Soeur Monique*. I could manage the first of Debussy's *Two Arabesques*. 'The Golliwog's Cakewalk' from *The Children's Corner* defeated me. I had several times decided that I would take a teacher again. I have not done so. Nobody plays on Collard and Collard now, except my daughter and occasional visitors.

Christie was a proper murderer. That had been murder on the grand Victorian scale. There he sat (was perhaps lying down) in his cell, feeling no doubt unhappy and confused, but also perhaps glad of a rest, for he had been on the run for some days. Like myself, he was a Yorkshireman who had ended up in North Kensington. But, really, what could one possibly do with a man who had got himself into such a muddle over gas taps and the sex organs of dead women? Keep him impounded as an interesting case for psychiatrists to study? Surely, best put him out of his misery.

Abolitionists mention Christie only in connection with another case, which shows British justice in a poor light, that of the mentally defective Evans, who had lived in the same house, 10 Rillington Place, and was hanged for a murder which

Christie almost certainly committed and against whom Christie had given evidence at his trial. The trouble with all campaigners is that they will so over-simplify. In the first place, they assume that capital punishment can only be either retributive or intended as a deterrent (always a false hope, as they most carefully prove). In a case like Christie's, it is to my mind more in the nature of what is known in other circumstances as a mercy killing. I am sure that 'society' had no feeling that it wanted to be 'avenged on' John Reginald Halliday Christie or, indeed, that it felt that hanging him would prevent other people from messing about with gas pipes in quite that way in connection with girls lonely in London or with their own or neighbours' wives and children. The wish to do that kind of thing is so very unusual and a persistence in gratifying the wish even more so.

In Evans's case, there was, I feel, almost certainly 'a miscarriage of justice'. That is always a bad thing. I can't honestly think it, in his case, a *very* bad thing. The abolitionists are fond of Evans because he proves for them a general point, *viz.*, that justice may miscarry in this way and that, as a result of a capital sentence being carried out, it becomes impossible to right things later. So far as I know, it has never been claimed that Evans's life was or could have been a happy one or that he would rather have been kept in prison for a long time than hanged.

I went round to look at the house in Rillington Place, a short road of tiny, paper-thin, jerry-built houses, the house in question the last or last but one on the left. I did not see how so many people could have lived at such close quarters and not have been obscurely aware of all that went on above and below. Surely, there must have been at least a frightened, half-conscious complicity, even in neighbouring houses. It seemed impossible, in such a house, that a single person had died even innocently without a large number of people knowing all about it. Evans's state of mind, at the time of making his doubtless false admissions, is quite unimaginable to me. I find it no easier to imagine the state of mind in which he might conceivably have gone on living, his wife and child dead and Christie perhaps in the next cell. At least he died, in some way, tragically. Our earnest abolitionists would rob him even of that, turning him into a general principle. A great novelist, devoting years to his theme, might have made something of all the horror at that end of Rillington Place. All that abolitionist argument makes of it is a bit of high-minded cheapness. The street has been renamed, out of consideration for the susceptibilities of its more genteel inhabitants. It might have been better to pull it down.

There was no shortage of other murders that year. Like Christie, the grim-faced poisoner Mrs Merrifield was kept waiting until the Coronation was decently over, but, even as that portentous ceremony dragged on, police were dragging the Thames at Teddington for the second of two girls who had been knifed on the embankment. That day, there was little traffic in Notting Hill Gate. Outside my local pub, however, stood a space-ship, ready to flicker all over like a pin-table as soon as it was switched on. No doubt its owner had driven into London too late to be allowed through by the police to occupy his five-guinea seat along the Coronation route. As I went in, he grunted down the four or five steps from the gentlemen's lavatory and puffed across the saloon-bar linoleum to rejoin his bottle of Worthington at the counter. He was white-haired, his complexion a dry mauve. Beautiful tailoring accommodated an almost perfect rotundity of form. I felt sure he was kind to his dependents and paid his employees well.

'Well,' he wheezed, turning affably to me, 'I see we've climbed Everest!'

As a matter of fact, I was not altogether sure that I approved of Everest being climbed. It seemed rather sad that no part of the earth's surface was any longer inaccessible. However, perhaps I was too anti-Elizabethan.

The day after the Coronation, I left my office at twenty minutes past one. My secretary returned at twenty minutes to two. During those twenty minutes, somebody went into my unmanned office and stole my brief-case from the drawer in my writing-table (as a matter of fact, I think I know who it was, and I believe him to have been and to be an actor). At the time, I was over at the Stag's Head, reading in a midday paper what bishops and such had been saying about the effects of the Coronation. We had all, it seemed, been spiritually uplifted, and Britain had regained the moral leadership of the world.

That, I suppose, was the last year during which the Americans could, with impunity, have atom-bombed the main centres of Russian and Chinese population. They had ample excuse when Russian airmen joined Chinese land forces in an attack on United Nations troops in Korea. Instead, Russian ships were invited to attend a naval review at Spithead. Riots broke out in East Berlin and were brutally suppressed by Russians in tanks. In America, the Rosenbergs awaited electrocution. And so the year went on. The deb. of the year was a girl called Fiona Campbell-Walter, now married to somebody or other. In November, Dylan Thomas drank himself to death in America. On Christmas Eve, there were fifty-three road deaths.

XXI

IN the late summer of 1954, my father-in-law died at the age of eighty-five, almost exactly twice what I then was. My daughter and I were in Jersey. That day, in a tiny boat with a French skipper, we had sailed through mountainous seas to Carteret in Normandy, a mere twenty miles away, only a fifth of the distance to Southampton. Late back for dinner at the hotel in Gorey, we almost at once had the news over the telephone from Newport, where my wife and son, whom we supposed in London, had gone down that day or the day before.

My parents and those of my wife had never met, mainly, I suppose, because of the distance between Huddersfield and Newport. And yet there had been much in common to the two family and regional backgrounds. My own little family in London now represented some kind of extreme-provincial, radical-nonconformist axis. If in due course my daughter went to St Andrews, that, so to speak, would stretch us further.

In the meantime, my daughter went to a Catholic school, a convent of the order of Our Lady of Sion, which had been founded by two Jewish convert brothers in Strasbourg. My wife worked as school secretary at the Brompton Oratory. My son, however, sang in a C. of E. choir.

Already, the previous Christmas, hearing carols decently sung outside, we had pushed up a window of the room I am writing in at present, leaned out over the fourth-floor parapet and detected himself among the group in a pool of light under a street-lamp. Towards Christmas in 1954, I all-unsuspecting went to a carol service at St George's up Campden Hill. Instead of coming out through the usual door from the vestry, the choir perambulated outside the church. The organ stopped. From the open church door behind us, there came 'Once in Royal David's . . .' in a solo, unaccompanied treble. It was *his*.

The emotional effect on me was considerable, as, dear reader, you will readily imagine.

The idea had been twofold. The boy having a voice and a musical ear, I wanted him to sing, and that was the obvious place for him to do it, since the church was in some way attached to his elementary school round the corner. I had also thought that, instead of being dependent on the L.C.C. and the results of his eleven-plus examination, he might get a choir scholarship to Magdalen or elsewhere. As it turned out, it was a good thing he didn't, since his voice broke early.

The calculation was in any case perhaps reprehensible, for I didn't much care for the C. of E. A national church must always be something of a monstrosity, for it is, surely, of the essence of religion, at any rate of the Christian religion, to cut across other divisions of power. It is true that in times of war Catholicism has tended to behave in each country as though it were a national religion, but the notion of universality persists. This is true even of Calvinism, which at least reaches from Switzerland through France to Scotland and Wales, and the Lutheran churches, which link Germany with Holland and the Scandinavian countries and which have their counterpart in Methodism here, while both Calvinism and Lutheranism thrive in America and the Dominions. But the C. of E. exists solely for the English. Indeed, it exists solely for the maintenance of a squirearchy in the forelock-pulling counties south of the Trent and for the development in towns of the urban equivalent of a squirearchy. It is not a uniting but a dividing force. It does not unite even the English. Clearly it does not unite all the people of these islands or even of this one island, not even with the help of its small and unpopular episcopal counterparts in Scotland, Wales and Ireland. But even the northern and western counties go massively unrepresented by it.

The West Riding is or, at any rate, was almost solidly Methodist, Monmouthshire largely Congregationalist, and it was not that either of these areas broke away from a Church of England once more widely established. They had never been C. of E. Many present-day nonconformist bodies can trace their own histories back earlier than 1688, which is when the

C. of E. as we know it began, the Elizabethan and the Laudian establishments having been quite obliterated. But what is perhaps even more remarkable is that none of the predominantly nonconformist larger areas in these islands was first evangelised from Rome by way of Canterbury. England south to the Humber was evangelised from Iona by way of Lindisfarne. All these areas long maintained the 'Celtic' usage. Later, they were the areas which maintained their loyalty to Rome into Elizabethan times.

The C. of E. is a regional church and a class church. It maintains its hold on public institutions in part because these are centred upon the metropolis and in part because they enshrine the interests of a class. On the public schools and on Oxford and Cambridge, the hold is a stranglehold. Inevitably, its administration is simoniacal, the polite fiction being that all benefice is vested in the Queen, who, among the many other parts for which she is cast, is head of that church. Not that, if the pretence had any reality, the administration would then be less simoniacal. A queen as the head of even a simple diocese would have seemed to the medieval Popes to be necessarily productive of simony. Clearly, it is not a Catholic church. But neither is it Protestant in any other sense than that it rejects the authority of the Pope, except in so far as some of its thirty-nine Articles appear to be confusedly Calvinistic, for which reason they were rejected by John Wesley, a firm Lutheran. The Catechism is more directly concerned with keeping the lower orders in their places.

I must, I fear, here also mention a third characteristic of institutions dominated by the C. of E. The ways of curates with choir-boys are part of our folklore. It is also well-known that at public and other boarding schools boys get up to antics of which, in general, working-class and lower-middle-class boys are innocent. In this country, most boarding (other than co-educational, progressive) schools are dominated by the C. of E. From talking to old boys of both, I gather that less homosexuality is evident at Catholic than at the usual public schools. Outside this educational and the immediately ecclesiastical context, the centres of homosexual practice are commonly understood to be the theatre, the Navy and the Boy Scouts. The theatre is no doubt a natural meeting-place for queers, as to some extent is the metropolis itself. The other organisations are, in this country, essentially C. of E. institutions, the Merchant Navy by contrast being recruited mainly in non-conformist areas.

It happens that I am not at all strongly prejudiced against homosexual practices 'between' (as they say) 'consenting adults'. I ought not therefore to regard it as prejudicial to the religious claims of the Church of England that it so encourages homosexuality. On the other hand, it is an odd phenomenon, and essentially a religion has no more business getting itself mixed up with a variety of sexual experience than it has in getting itself mixed up with the social and political interests of a nation, region or class. At any rate, in 1954, it seemed to me not unfair to describe the C. of E. as standing for simony, snobbery, sodomy and thirty-six other Articles of dubious merit.

I could see no reason for its continued existence. As an adjunct of royalty, it had recently performed its two principal functions for what the most devout royalist might hope would be the last time for half a century. In any case, the organisation needed to crown and bury sovereigns might well consist of a mere handful of clergy, resident perhaps in one of the smaller royal palaces (or they might be allowed to keep Lambeth). There was no need for thousands of them, and the Catholics might be willing to take over even those ceremonial occasions, as well as gratifying the whims of mothers and daughters who continued to insist on white weddings. In a nation which had almost uniformly adopted the practice of funerary cremation, there was no need for parsons to read the burial service (a recording could be used at the request of the bereaved). But the Church of England would have to be not merely disbanded but expropriated. It is, as we all know, the largest of our landowners, even if we do not count the rich Oxford and Cambridge colleges as bits of the Church of England. As to what would become of all those pretty country churches, there are perhaps fewer than we like to imagine. The rest could be pulled down without loss to the community. The pretty ones, since they were all built by and for Catholics, are in any case disaffected. Perhaps the Catholics would like to buy them back and could then pull down so many of the architectural mistakes in which they worship at present. Perhaps one or two might be preserved purely as historical monuments under the Ministry of Works, who could also run the more admirable cathedrals in conjunction with the Arts Council.

The R.C.s, I felt, should be allowed to continue. I had once flirted with them and then dodged the font. I had not then quite managed to share their beliefs. I was even less close to doing so in 1954. Yet I found their general *ethos* livable-with. I did not suffocate in their company, even if they were of the Downside variety. The usual notion is that R.C.s, C. of E. and nonconformists are, as it were, in denominational terms Right, Centre and Left, so that nonconformists and R.C.s are poles apart. I have not found this to be the case. It seems to me that Catholics and nonconformists can as a rule get on together, while neither can get on with the C. of E. In this country, Catholics *are* nonconformists. From the cradle, both to my wife's family and to my own, the Church of England had seemed to be at one with the political enemy, to be in essence the spiritual propaganda department of the Conservative Central Office.

Though totally lapsed as regards Congregationalist or any other denominational practice, my wife retained some elements of Christian belief. I did not mind. On the one hand, I found Christian belief more suitable to women, so that I tended to attach the term 'male Christians' to men who professed belief, especially those of the Anglo-Catholic persuasion, who seemed to me to constitute a kind of intellectual third sex. On the other hand, I was pleased rather than otherwise to have, as it were, God in the family. If my wife did a bit of believing, that let me out. Otherwise, I myself might have had to do something about it. As for me, I had just published a monograph on Léon Bloy, a great French Catholic nonconformist.

There was much talk at that time about the English tradition. What it meant was something essentially metropolitan and southern-squirearchical, royalist and Conservative, a tradition established for and maintained by people who sent their sons to one or another of half a dozen schools and then to Oxford or Cambridge and who described that as a 'conventional' education. I had been brought up otherwise. If that was the English tradition, I had no part in it and wanted none. It was not in the least that I lacked a sense of tradition. With the onset of middle age, I was myself becoming rather conservative in the general sense, only what I wanted to conserve was different. I wanted to conserve values, attitudes, ways of thought and behaviour, a general *ethos* characteristic of self-respecting families in regions as far apart as those in which my father and my father-in-law had lived out their modest but admirable lives. I had come out of and felt that I still in some way belonged to a second, a nonconformist-radical and provincial, a British rather than an English tradition.

It was a fruitful tradition. It had, for instance, produced almost every English writer I most admired, from (say) Bunyan to D. H. Lawrence. Shakespeare himself had been a poor boy from Stratford, a scandalous fact which accounted for the recurrent outbreaks of Baconianism, though in Shakespeare's time the tradition had not been divided, so that the term 'radical-nonconformist' would have meant little. Even the great Irish writers of our time had belonged to that second tradition, for until 1922 (when I was eleven) southern Ireland remained an English province in the political sense (it is still an English province in most respects). Such patriotic feelings as I had embraced the whole archipelago. I had feelings about Huddersfield and the West Riding and the North as a whole. I had feelings about the United Kingdom, with Eire its little republican appendage. I had no feelings (or none but feelings of irritation) about the entity properly known as England. Of all the large regional groups within these islands, if not indeed within the Commonwealth or, even more largely, the English-speaking world, the southern English were, by and large, those with whom I had least feeling of kinship.

And then, there was France and, more largely, Europe or a part of Europe. That also must be included in anything I could think of, with emotion, as my country. This attitude was certainly to be explained in part by my private history. It had so happened that, before I went through my Dick Whittington routine and first came to live in London in 1934, at the age of twenty-two, I had spent a good deal more time in France than in England south of the Trent. Of the two foreign languages I could pretend to know, I had spoken far more French than southern English. But the feeling was not merely private. For three hundred years, French had been the polite and admini- strative language of most of this island. For much of that time, the capital of England had been Rouen. But for the disasters of the Hundred Years War, the two countries might not have been separated. As to the French tradition, it has been notoriously twofold, at any rate since the Revolution.

This was in due course to be the argument of *The Fourfold Tradition*. It may seem a rather elaborate superstructure of thought to have erected upon the death of a Welsh father-in- law and a boat trip from Jersey to the Cotentin peninsula. That, in the early thirteenth century, the capital of England was still Rouen had been brought home to me by that study of the administrative troubles of Giraldus Cambrensis which had taken me to St David's four and a half years before. Three years before, in Picardy, the sight of signposts pointing to places like Agincourt had given rise to a good deal of meditation. During the autumn of 1954, in conversation, at an editorial party of the monthly *The Twentieth Century*, my dark murmurings against Joan of Arc led to an editorial suggestion that I should write on her as a villain of history, a suggestion I did not accept at the time, because I felt I had not read nearly enough, but which later was to give me 'That Dreadful Girl', the first chapter of *The Fourfold Tradition*, done in the first place for *The Twentieth Century*.

I had at the time no intention of writing a critical book. I toyed rather with the idea of an autobiography. It seemed to me that a set of opinions was best not paraded as though it were a pure intellectual formation, that what one thought received mean- ing only in terms of its genesis. Thought should be, and should be seen to be, derived from, and expressive of, a body of per- sonal experience, and the experience should be stated. In that sense, thought should be existential. My position had its peculiarities and might seem worth explaining in personal terms. There were also general truths which seemed at that moment in need of personal testimony, as, for instance, that there had been provincial universities long before the end of Hitler's war.

Over against the prevailing Conservatism, there had recently arisen a lively and irreverent group of younger writers, of whom the liveliest and most irreverent had just published a novel called *Lucky Jim*. The activities of this group had given rise to much talk about 'the new red-brick intellectuals'. I was a vintage red-brick intellectual, by no means of the first generation at that. I had been no more than one year old when Sir Herbert Read went up to my own university in Leeds, and even before that D. H. Lawrence had been at Nottingham. Later, in the 'Thirties, Birmingham had produced a whole crop of literary talent. As a matter of fact, 'the new red-brick intellectuals' merely *taught* at provincial universities. Like Auden, Spender, Day Lewis and MacNeice, they had been up at Oxford. Nor was it so original for young Oxford poets to *teach* at provincial universities. Louis MacNeice had been a lecturer at Birmingham for six years in the 'Thirties.

It was simply the mood which had changed. At PQ conferences, I had met younger lecturers at provincial universities, and I had been struck by their evident resentment against the hard fate which denied them a nice, fat fellowship at Oxford or Cambridge. They felt (perhaps rightly) that the younger fellows of those rich colleges, already sitting pretty, had been nepotistically put there. It was an ugly mood, and some of it had crept into *Lucky Jim*. It seemed to be new. If any members of either the English or French departments at Leeds in my time had suffered from it, they had kept the matter decently to themselves. In part, it was simply the obverse side of the new Conservatism and the deliberately revived snobberies which accompanied it. Before the war, Oxford and Cambridge had not been *so* smart or the provincial universities so despised. In the same way, the public schools and especially Eton had been newly endowed with a *chic* they had almost wholly lost before the war.

I enjoyed *Lucky Jim*. I had enjoyed John Wain's *Hurry On Down*. A poem by one of the group was the only new poem I had much liked for years. By and large, I was in sympathy with these writers. Politically, I thought them right on the ball, diffidently pro-Labour, savagely anti-Tory. I had not met any of them. I felt there were things that I could explain to them. I could have explained, for instance, that, during the 'Thirties, nobody but themselves had considered the literary scene to be dominated by the Oxford communist poets. I could have explained to them that, in those days, it was not only the sons of privilege who went abroad, that indeed, the rate of exchange being what it was, sheer poverty might drive a man to Paris. I understood their insularity. They had all read Eng. Lit., which itself is insularising, but also they had been at university towards the end of or just after the war, when European travel had been difficult or impossible, as it continued to be expensive.

They wouldn't have listened, of course. For one thing, they were happily occupied with their grievances, their private jokes and their mock battles. For another, I wasn't even one of their shadowy enemies. I had let myself drift too far out of the literary swim. Apart from a most unsuccessful novel the year before and the more recently issued Bloy monograph which had gone quite unnoticed, I had published nothing for some years. My personal life went on pleasantly, and so did my professional (*i.e.*, BBC) life, but as a writer I had reached a point of extreme demoralisation. From that point of view, *The Twentieth Century* was important to me. My old friend Bernard Wall had just become its editor, and, although its circulation was smaller than that of the two newer monthlies, *Encounter* and *The London Magazine*, it was good and lively, and its reputation with the young stood high. As it turned out, the first autobiographical piece I wrote for *The Twentieth Century* was in no way addressed to 'the new red-brick intellectuals'. It was an account of my sharing a flat with 'George Orwell' in 1935. If anything had inspired it, it was an account, in *The London Magazine*, of Christopher Hollis's relations with him at Eton. There was growing up a whole Orwell mythology, which seemed to me to bear little relation to the man I had known.

XXII

DURING the winter of 1954-5, I did a great deal of carpentry and some interior decoration. These activities had in themselves something autobiographical about them. My father had practised them with a degree of skill, and the tools I was using had been his, while, among the pieces of furniture I dismantled for their timber, two had been his handi-work, so that I became intimately aware of the merits and faults of his joints and dowelling. The oak for the bookshelves and two small tables still in this room came from furniture which, until late the previous summer, had stood in the garden room at my father-in-law's house in Somerset Road, off Caer-leon Road, Newport. What skill I had with a saw, drill, brace and countersinking bit, plane or screwdriver I had acquired directly from my father.

By Easter in 1955, the white-painted shelves in my own room, along the passage, stood against a midnight-blue dis-temper. At that time, the walls of this room, now an acid jasmine, were covered with a satin-striped wallpaper, white and silvered white with a primrose stripe. There was none of this black linoleum on the floor. There was no red linoleum in the kitchen, across the passage, directly facing me (if I could see through two walls) from where I sit writing, with my back to the windows. There was no blue linoleum, beyond one wall, in the room to my right still full of my daughter's things, or, beyond one wall to my left, black linoleum in my wife's room or, a wall further, blue in my son's. In those rooms, as here, there were, sketchily dotted with unimpressive rugs, bare floorboards stained with permanganate of potash and polished. Bands of cold air came up between the floorboards in winter.

Just after Easter, my daughter went to Paris with her school friends (the year before, they had been to Venice and Rome). Before her return, my wife, who had not travelled abroad for twenty years, set off with a mixed party from the Oratory. The Oratorian fathers paid for the trip. The coachload would stay at Innsbruck and Venice and end up with two days in Paris. My son was staying with some nuns at Broadstairs. This also had been arranged by Sister Mary Gregory at the Oratory. I received picture-postcards from all over the place. Wavy-edged, they were propped on the kitchen dresser.

On Saturday, I met my daughter at Victoria. On Monday, I saw her off to the Innes Stewarts in Oxford, then went to a studio, at the Warren Street end of Tottenham Court Road, to rehearse and record the eighth of a series of twelve Boccaccio stories dramatised from the splendid anonymous translation of 1620.

The particular story that day was *The Crane's Leg*. This story concerns a nobleman's witty cook, who has to explain away the fact that a roast crane he serves up has only one leg, the other having been eaten by the cook's girl friend, who has come into the kitchen, begged a taste, been refused, pouted and made a fuss. The cook sings:

> My Brunetta, fair and feat-a,
> Why should you say so?
> The meat of my master
> Allows you for no taster –
> Go from the kitchen, go!

I had put a tune to these words, and they were sung by the actor Charles Leno, a particularly agreeable member of his profession. It had been a minor but important satisfaction to me, during the past ten years in broadcasting, that I was often enough able to slip into programmes some musical fragment of my own composition. But, indeed, there was a peculiar satisfactoriness about everything that day.

The day also had its autobiographical reminders. The Brunetta, a recent auditionee I was trying out, knew and brought me news of the former art master at the school in Dagenham, the one man there I had been at all thick with twenty-one years before. And, during the midday break, I walked down Tottenham Court Road to see if Mortimer Market, where I had lived a few years after that, had yet been completely demolished. It hadn't. Indeed, since I last revisited those glimpses, small undertakings seemed to have been newly set up in a few of the premises which remained intact. Behind this whole scene rose a backcloth of one wall of the hospital in which Orwell had died.

It was a sunny day. The date was 18th April. I went back to the studio. Everything went by effortlessly and without hitch. The little programme itself seemed to me eminently worth doing. The small cast was amiable, intelligent and responsive. The technician beside me at the panel was pretty and enormously capable, a young woman with a faultless ear and miraculous hands and one of whom I had always been particularly fond. My secretary at that time was a girl whose blend of quick intelligence and utter conscientiousness sometimes made me weep inwardly with gratitude. She had come to me thin and nervous, inclined to talk to herself while typing, wheezing at the least upset with asthma. Now she was gay and relaxed. So, clearly, I did no harm. Perhaps, in a small way, I could even think I exercised a healing influence.

That was the mood. In the evening, I rang up a Polish upholsterer, who was making us some gorgeous curtains of dark blue corduroy for the big windows downstairs. He had been supposed to come that day and take the fittings away, but, not for the first time, had failed to appear. He now said he would come round on Wednesday morning. It must in fact have been Thursday or Friday when he came.

I did not propose to go to my office on Tuesday. I got up not too late and breakfasted at leisure. It was another sunny day. There were more wavy-edged picture postcards, of Brussels no doubt and Innsbruck. I brought my coffee in here and sat in the chair in which I am sitting now. The sun shone in at the window behind me, catching the primrose stripe in the wallpaper. The pigeons cooed delightfully on the parapet. Even the occasional motor-horn from the street far below sounded friendly, since it represented no threat to anybody with whom I was concerned. My family was scattered, in Oxford, in Broadstairs, perhaps by now in Venice. I did not envy them. I did not even miss them. Soon they would re-assemble. In the meantime, I liked being here and receiving picture-postcards. My family were my *antennae*. I was their centre. I had no need to go travelling myself.

In a volume of Yeats's autobiography, he quotes the actress, Florence Farr, as saying to him:

'If we could say to ourselves, with sincerity, "This passing moment is as good as any I shall ever know," we would die upon the instant, or be united to God.'

I did not precisely say that to myself, but I did have a sense of oceanic contentment. I could, I felt, be regarded as perfectly happy. The only thing was, I had a bit of a headache.

When my secretary rang up at a quarter past ten, I evidently told her about my headache. I said I would not, I thought, go in to-day.

The other big chair in this room is at present upholstered in a dull red material, with a faint lozenge pattern. In those days, its original upholstery was concealed by a loose cover of beige corduroy, patchily bleached by periodical washing. It is built low and very comfortable, perhaps too comfortable. The arms are very broad. I can lean forward and touch the nearer arm. At present, the hearthrug in front of that chair is of much the same beige or oatmeal colour the loose cover of the chair was in the spring of 1955. The hearthrug would then be a green one.

That Tuesday, at what must have been about noon, I was kneeling on the hearthrug, with my elbows on the nearer arm of the chair, on which perhaps I had been resting my head. My headache must have got worse, though I do not recall any pain or distress, but only the sensation of something pressing into my head at the front and a little to the *left*, over the left eye.

What I also retain is the clear visual and auditory memory of myself, seen, as it were, and heard from outside, putting the tips of the fingers of both hands to my forehead and saying:

'A tumour . . .'

It appears that my secretary telephoned again in the afternoon. I told her my headache was worse, and she thought I sounded a bit distraught. When she rang the following morning, I did not answer.

To cover the next five days, I retain only two distinct memories. The first of these may belong either to Thursday or to Saturday morning. The caretaker had been coming in to wash up and make my bed. She had rung up my usual doctor's son on Thursday. He, coming then, said I had 'flu. On Friday, it became apparent to the caretaker that I was mentally discomposed, since I would get out of bed, wander into the kitchen and ask her such absurd questions as whether my wife had gone out and, if so, where and at what time she would be back? The caretaker also took away from me a bottle of aspirin, of which she thought I had been eating too many.

All I remember is that my usual doctor's son stood in the room, presumably my room along the passage. I had not met him before. This memory is purely visual. The young man wore a well-brushed, slightly threadbare, navy-blue suit and buff waistcoat. A stethoscope hung round his neck. He seemed, I thought, at once puzzled and faintly reproving.

When, at mid-day on Saturday, my daughter returned from Oxford, it seems that, after she had repeatedly rung the bell, I answered the door to her. I then walked past her and went straight back to bed. She, after taking my temperature, rang up the doctor's house. She was told that he was out and would not be able to call until the evening. As it transpired, the caretaker had sent for him a second time that morning. My usual doctor's son had then diagnosed either polio or meningitis. My reception at the isolation hospital was already arranged.

For a moment presumably late that afternoon, memory clears again. My surroundings were unfamiliar. A very charming, rather young, rather small, very shy Irishman, in a coat not quite Persil-white, had apparently just said he must send for my wife, for I was begging him not to. This, I said, was the poor girl's first foreign trip since the war, and, if it was interrupted, she would miss her two concluding days in Paris. The reason why memory clears so distinctly for that moment must, I feel ruefully certain, have something to do with the splendid light it shows me in. There, as I know very well I felt at the time, was I, unmistakably in trouble of some kind, thinking only of others.

A telegram awaited her on her arrival in Paris. She could not get a seat on an aeroplane and had to return by boat. When she appeared, presumably on Sunday evening, I was rude and disagreeable to her. I don't think I remember that first visit.

I think the memory is of a later visit, during the early part of the week which followed. I am sure I was rude and disagreeable on that occasion, too. I felt rude and disagreeable. I thought my wife very ugly, which she is not. Before she went away and, in memory, while she was away, I had never thought her more beautiful. But I distinctly remember her face as it appeared to me on that visit. I especially disliked the shape of her nose. The objective fact of the matter probably was that she was looking worried, and a worried expression has never become her. And so perhaps she *was comparatively* ugly, but, during those days, I seem to have been conspicuously affected by people's facial expressions, as the next distinct memory suggests.

On arrival in hospital, I had been given a lumbar puncture. The spinal fluid drawn off had been found heavily mixed with blood. I had therefore had a sub-arachnoid haemorrhage. This means that an artery, no doubt part of the carotid system, has burst between the second and third skins of your brain. There is no real treatment. All they can do is try to keep your head down on the pillow for three weeks, in the hope of avoiding a 'recurrence'. If you have a 'recurrence', you certainly croak. It is a bit of a wonder you did not croak the first time.

I took to walking at night. It seems I walked several times, but I recall only one of these occasions. In a long hospital shirt, I was padding along the corridor, with a number of people hanging on to me. Holding my right wrist was a strongly built, handsome Scottish nurse.

'For goodness' sake,' I said, 'stop pulling me about!'

I explained to the others that all I wanted was a bit of a change. I was tired of the room I had been lying in, and I only wanted to find some other room and sit down in a chair for a while, after which I would go back to bed as they wished. Later, the Scottish nurse told me that on this occasion I had struck her, though only on the arm, which, she said, as I almost fell out of bed with apologies, didn't really count as striking a woman, quite apart from the disordered state of mind I was in. It was certainly against her that all my animosity had been directed, and this was because hers was the only face I could see clearly and because she looked, as I considered, unduly tense.

In the morning, the senior consultant, another Scot, remonstrated with me over my medinocturnal perambulations. He wagged his finger at me as I lay in bed.

'Mr Heppenstall,' he said, 'if you do this, you will die!'

I do not suppose that in any objective sense I laughed in his face, but inwardly that is what I was doing, perhaps because I knew that I had no intention of dying at the moment or perhaps because it did not seem to me, as it apparently did to him, a matter of consequence. He went on to ask me rhetorically what I supposed would then happen to my wife and children? My inner response to that was wholly egocentric.

'Oh, blow *them*!' I thought. '*I'm* the one who's in trouble!'

That night, by all accounts, I got up again, but a male orderly had been posted outside my door.

The woman doctor who made out certificates was reported by my wife as saying to her:

'The things he's done, Mrs Heppenstall! With a sub-arachnoid! He must have a constitution of iron!'

This pleased me enormously. By now, I was fairly lucid in the daytime, though I still forgot a good deal. My *right* eyelid had dropped, so that I leered horribly. I complained of the light in my eyes, and black-out material was pinned over the window of my room. This photophobia may have been one of the reasons why my usual doctor soon had suspected meningitis.

From my daughter's and the caretaker's accounts, my wife had pieced together a fairly coherent picture of the course of events during the previous week. Only much later did we learn with certainty that I had also answered the door to the Polish upholsterer. My wife asked him whether my manner had struck him as odd, and he said, 'Yes, perhaps a little,' but in the tones of a man to whom the behaviour of English people is odd at the best of times. Reconstructing a period of lost or intermittent memory has all the fascination of a thriller. One might, after all, have committed a murder. Or witnessed one. When my wife came home, the old curtains in the room downstairs had lain in unaccountable disorder about the floor.

I was in that hospital for just over four weeks, and then I was moved to the central hospital. There had appeared upon the scene a new and menacing figure. He was still quite young, and the nurses said he was brilliant. He was the neurologist from the central hospital, and he spoke with a Belfast accent. He wanted to move me, X-ray me and tie knots in the veins and arteries of my head.

He turned out to be a rational being and rather nice, but I did not trust brilliant doctors whose eyes (it seemed to me) gleamed with suppressed excitement at the thought of performing difficult operations *on me*. So I at once started trying to play off against each other the Ulsterman and the Irish Catholic. The Scot, naturally, was hand-in-glove with his fellow-Calvinist. From one and the other, I wormed out bits of statistics. I set my wife pursuing her medical friends. It was not, I told myself, fear. I *am* a physical coward. Until 1955, I had no medical history to speak of, and to this day the thought of a simple appendectomy fills me with suicidal panic. I have never felt quite the same about my head, but I would not (I told myself) be left with a scar on my neck by an Ulsterman, without whose intervention, moreover, I should have been up and going home next week.

In the end, I agreed to an X-ray, if I could have it promptly. The point was that only if the rupture occurred at certain points can you get at the artery and make your beastly ligature. If my friend from Belfast found that he could not get at it, that would set everyone's mind at rest.

Nurses at the central hospital apparently had to do occasional stints at the isolation hospital. That weekend, the pretty Irish nurse had gone, and in her place there was an even prettier Yorkshire girl. It turned out that she came from the village of Heptonstall, in the hills above Hebden Bridge, near Halifax. That is the village from which, it appears, my surname comes in a variety of spellings. I have never been there. Apart from that extremely attractive nurse, I have never met anybody who either came from the village or spoke of even so much as driving through it. It sounded very pleasant, and, since I had said I should like to go and stay there, the nurse later sent me the name of an inn with rooms. I have lost her letter and forgotten the name of the inn.

On Monday afternoon, I was wheeled out to an ambulance. There sat beside me a tall, gangling black nurse from Jamaica, with whom I had sometimes been on good and sometimes on bad terms. Rolled off another trolley, I found myself in all the din and horror of a large, crowded public ward. Late in the evening, screens were put around my bed, and a nice-looking young woman doctor came and pricked me all over lightly with a pin. This was delightful. She also played with my toes and fingers, making me guess which way she was moving them. I enjoyed that, too (and scored, I believe, full marks), but I liked the pin even better. This delectable love-play is, I suppose, neurological routine. Three hundred years ago, it was a test for witches, an area of insensibility being held to prove collusion with the devil. No doubt the pin was then sometimes jabbed right in, and the spectators would laugh as some poor old woman or unpopular girl yelped.

My wife arranged for a private room after the X-ray. This required an anaesthetic, and a young man came round and tested my heart and blood-pressure and suggested I should try to stop smoking until it was over. I was wheeled away again, jagged, told to count, heard my own voice faltering at twenty-four and came to in a narrow cell, a bandage about my throat. The man from Belfast had given up all thought of tying my neck in knots.

On Friday, a firm of contractors began to drive new hot-water pipes through the hospital walls. They stopped on Saturday afternoon and began again on Monday. This was no place for me. I demanded to be let out. I discharged myself, as they say in hospital circles.

I was encouraged to sit in a chair for a quarter of an hour. I reminded myself that not long ago I had been toying with the idea of writing an autobiography. Indeed, I seemed to remember that in the winter I had written two pieces about my acquaintance with 'George Orwell' and that one of them had been printed just before all the present nonsense started. Yes, that was it. My irreverent manner had shocked various Orwell fans. It was all very well to feel sorry for witches. They had been handy with pins themselves. A number of Orwell fans must have made a wax image of me and stuck pins in the head. I must be careful not to provoke anybody to a further *envoûtement*.

My neck was a thread, and my leaden head was huge. When

I moved, it began to roll on my shoulders. As nobody came, I crawled gratefully back into bed.

Next day, the ambulance men made a cradle of their arms and carried me, in pyjamas and dressing gown, up the ninety-two steps from street level to the landing outside the door of the room in which I am writing at the moment. That door is shut just now because the weather is cold. The woman who then lived on the second floor was coming downstairs.

'See,' she sang out, 'the conquering hero come!'

She was quite a nice woman, but prone to observations of that kind.

'*We*'re the conquering 'eroes, mum,' panted one of the ambulance men.

I was settled in the midnight-blue room, with flowers, new curtains, my books, nice things to eat, my family to say good night and good morning to. My usual doctor's son, in the same blue suit and buff waistcoat, looked a bit crestfallen and apologised for sending me to the wrong hospital. I rallied him and pointed out how great an advantage it had been to me to have a room to myself for a month on the National Health.

His father, back from a holiday, came to see me. There was, he said, no explanation. The weakness must be hereditary. I was to regard myself as having had an accident, it was as if I had fallen downstairs. I ought to be up and about in a week or two. My blood-pressure was, if anything, low, but it might be as well to avoid anger and high altitudes. I took this to mean flying over the Andes, not living on a fourth floor. As to anger, I must clearly avoid both feeling it and arousing it in others.

XXIII

I HAD not really disliked lying at death's door. Indeed, certain little medical and sub-medical episodes that autumn, consequent upon the major disorder, made me wonder if, having successfully reached that neighbour-hood, I ought not (if only to spare myself the trouble of finding the place again at some time in the future and perhaps by a more arduous route) to have stretched up a hand and given the door a push. By the following spring, however, physically I was in prime condition, and my nervous tone was exemplary. All through 1956, I hadn't (as I put it) felt so well for years. Moreover, I wrote extensively, though not at top level.

I suddenly found myself well in with various papers, so that much of what I wrote was mere criticism and such. I briefly returned to verse, though again only by way of translation. The French verse recorded in Paris that spring had consisted of the personal choices of Edwige Feuillère, Jean Vilar, Daniel Gélin and an actress somewhat less well-known, Sylvia Montfort, then appearing in a French version of Schiller's *Mary Stuart*. Among the poems picked by her had been four which particularly delighted me, and those four I translated myself, instead of, as with all the rest, farming them out. They needed, I felt, a kind of false simplicity, which I thought myself able to supply.

The first of them was a *rondeau* attributed to the fifteenth-century woman poet, Clothilde de Surville, whose real exist-ence has been doubted. If her extensive works are indeed nine-teenth-century forgeries, the forger was, I would say, as good a poet as Chatterton or Macpherson and a very much better *pasticheur* than either. The fifteenth century was, in France, a great age of women poets, the best known of them being Chris-tine de Pisan, about whose authenticity no doubts are raised.

RONDEAU

Since the day I lost my king,
A veil of night is on everything;

Time goes by on a broken wing
Since the day I lost my king.

I cannot go, I cannot stay,
While my lord's so far away:
Since the day I lost my king,
A veil of night is on everything.

The other three poems are anonymous ballads, such as we do
not much associate with the French poetic tradition. The first
has an obvious affinity with Dante Gabriel Rossetti's 'King
John'. A tune to it is known.

KING RENAUD

King Renaud from war returned
With his guts into his hand.
His mother from the battlement high
Called to her son where he went by:

'*Renaud, Renaud, rejoice and sing,
Your wife is brought to bed of a king.*'
'*Neither of wife nor of son,*' quoth he,
'*Can I rejoice or merry be.*

'*Go, mother, go before me,*' he said,
'*And bid them make up a fair white bed.
Little time shall I lie there:
I die at midnight, upon the hour.*

'*But let them bring down my cot,
That a woman in labour hear me not.*'
And when the hour of midnight tolled,
King Renaud yielded up his soul.

Before the day began to break
The varlets all wept for his sake;
It had not come to breakfast-time,
The maidservants wept at his name.

'*Tell me, tell me, mother my dear,
Why are the servants weeping here?*'
'*Daughter, down by the ford they found
The best of all our horses drowned.*'

'*And why, why, mother my dear,
Weep for a horse so loud and drear?*

When King Renaud comes again,
He'll bring better horses home.

'Tell me, tell me, mother my dear,
What is the knocking that I hear?'
'Daughter, I bade carpenters come
To mend the floorboards in that room.'

Now when she rose up from her bed
And that she would to mass be led
And when a week was past and gone,
She wanted to put on her gown.

'Tell me, tell me, mother my dear,
What gown to-day shall I wear?'
'Take the green, take the grey,
Take the black to wear this day.'

'Tell me, tell me, mother mine,
Why should I wear a black gown?'
'Women who get up from childbed
Wear black to be well-suited.'

When she came in the church to stand
She took a candle in her hand;
When she came in the church to kneel
Fresh-dug earth lay at her heel.

'Tell me, tell me, mother my dear,
Why is the earth so fresh in here?'
'Daughter, I cannot lie to you:
Renaud is dead and lies below.'

'Since Renaud is dead, whom I loved best,
Here are the keys of my treasure chest;
Take my rings, take my jewels,
Feed well my son Renaud.

'Open the earth, wide gaping,
That I may go with Renaud my king.'
Earth opened, earth gaped wide
And swallowed up King Renaud's bride.

THE FAIR CORSE

Under the white rose-tree
The girl walks at her ease,

White as snow,
Fair as the day;
Three captains go by, all three
Would have their way.

The youngest of the three
Took her by the hand:
'*Fair maid, get you up
And on my grey horse ride,
To Paris you shall go
In great state to abide.*'

To Paris when they came
The mistress of that place
Says, '*Are you here by choice,*
'*Or have they forced you in?*'
Lo, they were captains three
Came here along with me.

Supper was soon laid;
The girl had no appetite.
'*Sup well, sup well, fair maid,
And smile for all to see,
For you shall spend this night
Among your captains three.*'

When supper was half done
She lay dead on the floor.
'*Now let the trumpet sound
And the drum beat;
My heart is sore
Since my love died.*'

Where shall her burial be?
In her father's garden
Under the white lily,
This lady all gentleness;
And pray God
That her soul find bliss.

After three days,
Her father is walking by.
'*Father, father, come
Dig me up from my grave:
Three days have I feigned death
My honour for to save.*'

There must be many variants of the third of these ballads. There is one, in Provençal, in Mistral's *Mirèio*, of which, in Gounod's opera, *Mireille*, a French version is sung as a duet.

METAMORPHOSES

If you still follow me,
Being so fond,
I'll turn into a carp
Within a pond,
So never shall you hold
My heart in your hand.

— Turn you into a carp
Within a pond,
I will a fisherman be,
Fisherman fond,
And I will catch that carp
Within a pond.

And I a fisherman see
Tying his knot,
I'll turn into a rose
In a green plot,
And never there shall be
My friendship got.

— Turn you into a rose
In a green plot,
The form I'll take then
Will be the gardener's
And pluck there as it grows
The cruel rose.

If you're a gardener,
I'll not stay by
But turn into a star
Up in the sky,
So never shall my heart
To yours reply.

— Turn you into a star
Up in the sky
A cloud is what I'll be,
A white cloud

Following that star
Up in the sky.

When you're a cloud,
A white cloud
Still wanting my heart,
I'd not say no,
For once we've reached the sky
Where else could I go?

And that is the last versification I have done to date, unless we accept Mallarmé's view that, wherever there is effort made upon style, there is versification.

It seems likely that, in some way, my accident had been intellectually tonic. It may also have been good for my character. John Middleton Murry thought it had, though he was not well-informed on the matter. At our penultimate meeting in August, I told him about the experience. Afterwards, he recorded in his diary:

Aug. 15, 1956
On Monday we drove to a very pleasant farmhouse near Debenham, to see Margaret and Rayner Heppenstall who are spending a holiday there. I liked Rayner much better than I have been used to for some years. He seemed mellowed. There were no signs of the intellectual conceit and aggressiveness which used to offend me; so that I just enjoyed the meeting . . . In the Easter of 1955, he told me, he had been seriously ill for three months with a sub-arachnoid haemorrhage – apparently between the outer and inner membranes of the brain – which in 50% of cases is fatal. Perhaps this grim experience has made the change in him which I welcome.

The fact was that Murry had seen me only once during the past seventeen years, and I should have said that, at our previous meeting, six years before, all the awkwardness and constraint had been on his side. By that time, I should have said, I had been mellow for years, the intellectual conceit and aggressiveness he recalled having belonged to a period, several years before the war, when he and I had been much involved with each other over his *communitas* at Langham. Still, it is certainly the case that in the summer of 1956 I felt extremely well-disposed towards Murry, whose *Unprofessional Essays* I had reviewed in the spring and whom I was to see only once more, in November.

XXIV

THE view from inside is a view of things outside, even if they have been put there only by time. At this moment, all I can see of myself is my right hand writing. The piece of oak under my exercise book is the raised right arm (it will let down) of a chair I have owned a little over a quarter of a century. It was a wedding present, and it is described in *Four Absentees* (where it is referred to as 'the coffin') because of a night I remember when 'George Orwell' slept in it (the back also lets down, and the seat folds out). It has been twice re-covered since then. At present, its upholstery is light brown with a white flower pattern, and the shelves at both sides are largely occupied by Balzac in fifty small volumes.

Light falls on my exercise book from a window behind me. It is one of two windows in this room, one of six similar windows on this side of the house, facing east-north-east. In the whole flat, there are twenty-one windows and a skylight. Three pairs of small casement windows and the skylight are in the attic overhead. A very large, much divided (casement-opening) and four smaller sash windows are on the level twelve steps down, the big window and the least insignificant of the others in the largest room which contains the piano, the remainder lighting a landing, a lavatory and a cubby-hole, from which a door or hatchway also opens on to the rubbish lift. Most of our rooms are on the same level as this one, which is usually called the dining room, though it is more often worked in by me than dined in by anyone else. Of the thirteen windows on this floor, eleven are identical in size and have sashes, the tiny, gauzed larder window and the scullery window being casements. Four of the six windows on this side (which is the front) of the house contain sixty-four small, almost square panes of clear glass and thirty surrounding strips of knobbly, pale-green glass each, with this qualification, that the sixteen uppermost panes of clear glass are disturbed as to shape by a four-times-repeated tulip pattern in glass of a slightly darker and bluer green. No other windows in the flat or in the house are leaded.

If one stands at any of the six windows on this side of the house in our flat, a ledge, fist-to-elbow breadth, separates the window frame from the lower part of one's breast (if one is a man five feet nine inches tall). The ledge is wider before the north-north-west-facing window of identical size on the landing. Elsewhere, there is no appreciable ledge. The ledges are screwed down. Beneath them runs a gutter, square in section and lined with zinc or lead. At the back of the house and outside the tiny larder window, the equivalent gutter lies exposed and beyond the glass. A low parapet runs outside the gutter. To a window-cleaner, the front of the house is thus more dangerous than the back, where he can walk along the gutter and inside the parapet, except at one point where a buttress projects.

On this side of the house, there are, as I have already explained four rooms in our flat. As I sit writing with my back to the window, I have to my right, beyond a flimsy wall, a small room, with one, unleaded window. That is my daughter's room. To my left, beyond a far solider wall, lies my wife's room, identical with this one. Beyond that lies another small room, my son's. At the back of the house, from left to right as I sit here, are the bathroom, my room, the kitchen and scullery, then a window which is only theoretically breast-high, since it stands over the internal staircase and must be attained by way of a fixed ladder. Beyond it lies a piece of square roof over the room containing the piano.

From those back windows, there is, marvellously, a view on a clear day of Richmond and of hills in Surrey beyond. Willesden gasworks marks a central point on the horizon. That is west-south-west. Richmond lies a little way over to the left. An important new block of flats does not seriously affect the view. The land slopes away on that side. The white trails the aeroplanes leave are, you would swear, at a level below your feet. Even with the door of this room open, I cannot see any of those windows, but light from two of them (a cold north light from the landing window and, from the window over the well of the staircase, a light which from mid-day will grow steadily warmer and more intense until, at any rate in summer, the evening light falls warmly through the landing window itself, which, after all, faces not due north but north-north-west) converges on the old green linoleum of the landing, which also receives a diffused light through the open door of the kitchen. The larder door lies more or less in shadow according to whether the door of my daughter's room (to my right) is open.

On this side are roof-tops and some trees. As it is February, the biggest tree does not conceal the Walls' house, which it did till November. I can also see the Mercury, a little to the left, and even the ridge of the Kensington Temple roof, over which in two or three months I shall no longer be able to see the top of the no-longer-quite-new buildings opposite Paddington Station. Our own newer buildings stand over to the right, along the main road. The tallest is eighteen stories high, but only so near the winter solstice does it shut out an hour of morning sun (presently, the sun will rise further over to the left and ride over it by ten o' clock). The backs of the two nearer buildings are not unpleasant, despite some blue glass. Those are flats on two floors above shops which face the main road and project at the rear, thus providing for the people who live above them a long stretch of flat roof of which even in summer they make little use, no doubt because it is sunless.

About us, but more especially to this side, lies London, the vast car park I inhabit. The bit of it immediately below is better sign-posted now, and there are fewer accidents at our corner. It was not, as it happened, on a Friday but on a Sunday evening when that particular accident occurred. That mashed beetroot had been the face of a recent bride, who had come from the provinces to live in Ladbroke Square a few weeks before. Municipal sand was spread over the mixture of blood and petrol, and not long afterwards a sign was set up declaring Ladbroke Road a major road, at which sensible motorists would halt. And so, on Friday evenings, from about quarter to ten, we no longer find ourselves listening for the scream of brakes and the impact.

Before the war, I commonly went to the Mercury on Sunday evenings, when there were Ballet Club performances on its

tiny stage. *The Ascent of F 6* and (apart from a cathedral performance) *Murder in the Cathedral* were also first put on at the
Mercury. Several verse plays were done there after the war,
and ballet performances were revived for a while after we
moved into the neighbourhood. There were also verse-readings
on Sunday, one of which (of English and Scottish popular
ballads) I arranged. Then all that stopped. The auditorium was
cleared of its seating and became a room for classes and rehearsals. In the print-room and bar, a wine club was started.

Ashley Dukes, who owned the Mercury and a fair amount
of other property in the neighbourhood, had made his name
and a great deal of money in the 'Twenties with a play called
The Man with a Load of Mischief. He was a portly man, with a
florid complexion and a stately gait, frequently to be seen
walking about the Ladbrokes, his broad, bespectacled face
tilted back, carrying and sometimes twirling a stick, the Squire,
one felt, looking round his estate. He was a great walker.
Occasionally, he would take a morning train out to Southend
or (I think he told me) Shoeburyness and spend the day on cliff
paths, making his lunch of shellfish and jellied eels bought
somewhere along the route. The Mercury bar had always had
on display a wonderful collection of old ballet prints, one of
which I had long ago reproduced in *Apology for Dancing*. It
further contained a certain amount of antique furniture and a
grand piano, since removed. Ashley was knowledgeable about
wine, and he spent much of his time at wine auctions. Among
the *clientèle* were serious musicians, who sometimes performed
for the club members present. Ashley himself looked in at
least once every evening. His conversation also was somewhat
portly, though many of his stories were quite first-rate and one
always hoped that he would some day come out with an autobiography.

The Dionysus club still exists, but I rarely go there nowadays.
That central figure gave it a distinction which it has lost. Ashley
Dukes died on 4th May 1959, at the age of seventy-three. This
I know from the *Times* obituary which I pasted into a press-
cutting book. I remember him mainly, then, as a man in his
late sixties and early seventies, but knew him already when he
was not quite as old as I am now. At this height, with sky all

171

round and so many windows, I take my bearings both in space and in time. It is almost eighteen years since Hitler's war ended, seventeen and a half since Hiroshima, eight since I had my sub-arachnoid haemorrhage. We have occupied this flat for twelve years. When we first came here, my daughter was rising eleven, my son was six. My son is now eighteen, my daughter twenty-two. I was still under forty. I am fifty-one. The year we came here was the year of the Festival of Britain. Early next year, the King died. In June the year after that, the Queen was crowned. Between those two events occurred Butler's autumn budget, whence the continuing traffic difficulties and much of the squalor of our economic life.

It is seven years ago since our forces abandoned the Suez canal zone to the Egyptians. A few months later, they briefly reoccupied it, in concert with French and Israeli forces. At the time, a Russian army with tanks was butchering civilians in Budapest. This operation was carried through with the utmost ruthlessness. The Suez invasion was called off within little more than twenty-four hours, apparently because the Americans, in the person of John Foster Dulles, had objected and because Sir Anthony Eden was convinced that public opinion in this country was on the whole against what he had ordered. In this, so far as I can judge, he was wrong. The American indignation was, I thought, purely formal. American public opinion would clearly have been delighted to see the British and the French behaving in a traditionally wicked and independent manner after so many years of boring subservience. In the face of any conceivable interference from the Russians, the operation had been beautifully timed.

At first, the suppression of the Hungarian rising caused more indignation. Many fellow-travellers were understood to have been disabused by it. It was even said that one or two actual members had left the Party. A fair number *pretended* to have left it. But presently, on the Left and among those who regarded themselves as simply and uncommittedly 'liberal,' the impression was created that 'the Suez adventure' (after a while referred to merely as 'Suez') had somehow been *worse* than the Russian massacre in Budapest and the subsequent imprisonments and hangings. There formed, in fact, in the aftermath of the Suez *fiasco*, both a New Left and a 'liberal' orthodoxy, whose principal shibboleth was 'Suez' itself, the word being spoken in a distinctive manner. As the year-old game of U and non-U dragged on, the two things became associated in one's mind. Now you said not only 'kinsmen' and 'chimney-piece' but 'Suez'. It is perhaps of some interest to recall here that the original '*shibboleth*' in *Judges* xii had also had to do with a battle across a waterway, not far from where Ferdinand de Lesseps much later created the Suez canal.

I had been as surprised as anyone by the sudden dropping of British parachute troops in that area. I hardly knew what to think about it. In a sense, it was a relief. For one thing, it had seemed, the day before, from *The Evening Standard*, as though we might be on the point of declaring war on Israel, to whom it appeared an ultimatum had been sent. That, to my mind, would have been frightful. Then it turned out to be only the Egyptians, and I had never heard a good word said for *them*. I was pleased to find myself in alliance with the French (and officially disapproved of by the Americans). I was delighted to find what a first-rate army Israel now had. I was rather sentimental about that new country (I was still a bit sentimental about India, but that sentiment was not to survive the destruction of Goa). I still think it very wicked that her allies then should still be party to the fact that Israel is denied access to the Suez canal. Indeed, it seems to me (one only has to look at a map) that Israeli territory should come up to the canal and that the canal itself should now be under joint Israeli-Egyptian control. Our rapid withdrawal had left Israel more than ever vulnerable and would certainly increase French difficulties further west in North Africa.

In early 1957, John Middleton Murry died. In the autumn, Third Programme was savagely cut back. I seem nevertheless to have done a great many programmes that year and to have written a fair number of *Times Literary Supplement* 'middles' and other pieces of a critical nature, most of them (programmes, too) calculatedly within the sphere of interest of *The Fourfold Tradition*, which thus made some progress. My one Paris trip had to do with a Baudelaire centenary.

In May 1958, the government of M. Pflimlin collapsed and

with it the Fourth Republic. General de Gaulle was brought out of retirement. The Left and 'liberal' journalists here at once started squeaking about the Fascist danger and described the General as a dictator. He and France needed help. They got none from us. In June, we had a 'bus strike in London. It was judged a failure, even by the 'busmen. In the result, there have simply been fewer 'buses in London ever since. This failure was not to prevent the strike's organiser, Mr Frank Cousins, from presently emerging as a *prima donna* among trade union leaders, so that his smooth, ill-natured, self-righteous features would soon become painfully familiar to us all.

Six months before, I had been elected to the P.E.N. committee. I even went to some literary parties. Five years ago the shops along this side of the main road stood empty. They were being actively demolished when General de Gaulle was called to power. The demolition of those shops brought a lot of extra dust into this house, even up here. By August, the site was clear. In Cyprus, the gunmen went on firing. They killed the two sons of a family then living in this house.

North of here, mainly around Westbourne Grove, during recent years an astonishing number of negroes from the West Indies had settled into streets not in themselves very attractive. In the end, one foresaw, that whole area would become a kind of Harlem. Fair enough. Once it was firmly established, I didn't mind a Harlem just north of here. I didn't think it would reach even as far south as Ladbroke Square. Its natural expansion would be around Paddington and up into Kilburn. It could be made a separate police district. One would then live on the genteel fringes of a well-contained Harlem, to whose night spots one might even take one's friends, for, clearly, the corporate behaviour of West Indian negroes would develop its picturesque side. Already, one could buy yams, green bananas, occras and salt cod in shops up that way.

But the Harlem was not yet firmly established. A lot of poor whites lived up there, and they had already had much to put up with from the Irish. In the end, everything would be fine. It was not fine in August 1958. Elderly couples, who had always lived on good terms with their neighbours and who hoped to spend their declining years in tranquillity where they were,

174

suddenly found the house being bought over their heads and jolly, rampageous black men everywhere, in some cases no doubt quite nice ones, but there were also decidedly unpleasant types, who might well be running a night club downstairs, with brothel facilities overhead. The sons, visiting their parents, had their own grumbles about black men in and outside public houses and smart West Indian operators dealing in houses and cars and buying up girls.

What became known as 'the Notting Hill race riots' lasted three nights, from 30th August to 1st September, in 1958. They were not pretty, that is certain. I never witnessed one, though I heard the police vans milling around quite late. Still, as riots go, they were very mild. Nobody was killed. That amount of anti-white rioting in an African town would hardly have got into the newspapers. The most unpleasant incident, because it was so utterly cold-blooded and unprovoked, was one, during the days which followed, in which nine youths from outside the neighbourhood drove round its outskirts, beating up negroes who were inoffensively walking alone in the street, their most battered victim being a small, highly educated man.

The following Saturday evening, worse trouble was expected. Things had been organised, houses (it was said) marked and the scenes of major incidents decided. The weather took a hand (it was early September). I was sitting in the Mercury bar. A man with a van came to deliver a load of folding chairs. He had driven by way of Westbourne Grove. He told us that a crowd there had started baying. Suddenly, down came what the newspapers later said must have been the heaviest cloudburst of the century. The crowd ran for shelter. The rain stopped. A bit later, the manageress's husband went out. He rang up from a telephone kiosk. On the cleared site, where the tallest of the new buildings now stands, a Fascist speaker had gathered a new crowd and was stirring the boys up. Over the telephone, one suddenly heard rain beating down on the roof of the kiosk. That crowd also dispersed. When the rain stopped again, it was already too late to re-organise.

The nine youths were given four-year sentences. We gasped, but thought that perhaps it had been necessary. In retrospect,

I am not so sure. Unspeakably vicious as the behaviour of those youths had been, the sentences were, like the hanging of Bentley, *exemplary*, and that is the last thing a sentence should ever be, except perhaps occasionally in war-time. I suppose that the sentences did have some effect. They must have made the new pastime seem less attractive. I don't think moral indignation and high-mindedness helped at all. Middle-class disapproval was clearly a thing which yobboes enjoyed, perhaps even hungrily sought, an integral part of the excitement with which their hollow young days were to be filled. What put an end to the organised negro-baiting round these parts was the rain that Saturday evening. To the intending participants, it must have seemed most retributive and satisfactory. To the high-minded, it was all a great disappointment. A bit later, a black man *was* killed in the street not far from here. It was never established who did it or for what reason, but the moral indignationists wanted a martyr and made the most of this one. A long procession of holy Willies followed him to his grave. Then, as there were no more incidents, they took up nuclear disarmament and boycotting South African goods.

XXV

IN October, my daughter went duly to St Andrews and wore a red gown. On the building site, mechanical pile-drivers were set up. They were said to be sinking a thousand concrete pillars. Every few seconds during the day, a pile-driver descended. The house jumped, shuddered, settled down. Cracks opened in the corners of rooms, but no compensation was to be expected.

At the end of the month, the Royal Court in Chelsea put on Samuel Beckett's *Endgame* and the new *Krapp's Last Tape*, a duet between one actor and his recorded voice. Beckett did not appear at his first night, but he was in London and spent a good deal of time at rehearsals. There he sat in the darkened auditorium, saying very little but ready to do all he could when appealed to. If it was a question of meaning or intention, he would consider the point as though it arose in a work by somebody else, about which he possessed only the most general information. If he ventured to make a point of his own, it would be of a technical nature, the direction, for instance, in which an actor should turn while moving from a table to a door. The cast insisted that he had been most helpful. They manifestly viewed him with affection.

At mid-day, he sat in the pub next door, not precisely holding court but somewhat frequented. He smoked French cigarettes and drank stout. He was thin, brown-faced, beaky, the pale-blue eyes not deep-set but well lodged under frontal bone, a wide mouth stretched across his teeth, the hint of a dimple in the left cheek. His hair was not wholly grey and must have started fair. The voice was light in pitch and not without edge, the accent still recognisably Irish. He could be described as ascetic-looking. When he stood up, he was fairly tall, quick and neat in his movements. All that naturalness, ease and charm of manner had conceivably required practice at one time.

It had been said that he did not give interviews and that he would not be photographed. Neither statement turned out to be true. His own view of the matter was that he would talk about anything else, but not his work. Even that was not quite true. I suppose him to have meant that he would not discuss meanings and intentions. He did not mind telling you where, for instance, or when such and such a thing had been written. I don't know when or where the photographs were taken, but no fewer than four illustrate my *Observer* profile, which appeared on 9th November, four years and three months ago. The press-cutting book lies open on the oak 'refectory' table, beside my typewriter. There is Samuel Beckett, looking sad, frightened, stern and, with face averted, drawing with thoughtful adhesion upon a cigarette presumably French. He wears a roll-collared sweater darker in tone than his jacket, into the breast pocket of which a fountain or a ball-point pen is clipped.

A sartorial matter occupied me also in December, when the Oratorian fathers gave a party. I wondered who designed the *biretta*? Obviously, you took a cardboard box, about five inches square and three deep, and knocked the bottom out. You crushed it a little to make its shape rhomboidal, then braced what were to become the front and back corners by means of an eight-inch fin with its corners trimmed and a snip in the middle. You covered the structure you then had with black silk, gluing it down wherever a cardboard surface permitted. You bored a hole just below the point of the snip in the bracing fin, and through this you tied a bit of black cord. The result was extremely fetching, as were the little silk collars peeping over the high-necked cassocks. The general effect was theatrical. It might have been a backstage party after the first night of a new play by Henry de Montherlant. As one had come late and not seen the play, one wondered to what dreadful spiritual and personal ordeal the tall, sardonic juvenile lead with the long cigarette-holder had been subjected on-stage. He moved about, glass in hand, with an air of quiet satisfaction in his performance, not much talking to the lesser brethren. These were experienced character-actors, pinkly made up. One of them, looking very old and saintly, had clearly played an important part, wrestling no doubt with the young priest. Some of the others had removed the headgear. Some wore it over one ear.

At that time, my head stood in an exhibition of sculptured heads in Conduit Street. It had been coated with bronze paint and unaccountably given pointed ears. The only other head my head knew in the exhibition was that of the playwright and author of nature notes, Ronald Duncan. He was turquoise and smooth. From under lowered lids, he looked at me searchingly from a distance. I ignored him, but was obviously aware of what he was thinking and likely to break down under the strain. It was a relief when that exhibition was over. Till then, my head could not relax its attempt to preserve a rugged and indifferent dignity.

There was plenty of musical life. Jon Vickers was in excellent voice. Beecham had come back. Klemperer was at his finest. There was a positive outcry against Hindemith's Beethoven. Stravinsky was in London conducting his own works (I had not heard *Agon*). On the building site, the tall, elegant, red or yellow German cranes were set up, to be much admired, in the spring of 1959, from the window at present behind me, against the evening sky, by Sir Herbert Read, shortly after the death of Ashley Dukes. In June, a printers' strike started. It cost me two hundred pounds. The reprint of a paperback *Blaze of Noon*, just then due, had, when the strike was settled, gone again to the back of the queue. In the end, it never appeared.

That year, I did not go to France at all. It was to be the first of three years during which I did not go to France. My children were there a good deal, my daughter for three months, *au pairing* it with an American family in Paris and fitting this in with courses at the Sorbonne, my son (aged fourteen) put up, with a school friend of his, by a bachelor who had once been in love with the other boy's mother. One evening, from the street outside that lower-middle-class Parisian flat, revolver shots sounded. It was five Algerians shooting down another. The five were no doubt pursuing what *The New Statesman* would have described as their legitimate aspirations. The aspirations of the dead man had, no doubt, been illegitimate. The number of Arabs shot in the streets of Paris by other Arabs was remarkable. One marvelled at the patience of the Parisians, who cannot really have enjoyed the pastime, in many cases dangerous to themselves.

By and large, it must have been a good summer. The 1959 wines were copious. In July and August, I had no luck with the sun. While it blazed in Devonshire, my wife and I were being drenched in Suffolk. While it blazed in Suffolk, I was briefly drenched in Devonshire. We had intended to stay there, but almost at once paid up and fled back to London, where at least some interior decorating could usefully be done. My room was at last to have a proper carpet. The walls were to be re-distempered a pale blue, the surrounding boards to be stained black and a new arrangement of bookshelves to be built. The new ('shadow blue') distemper was of the kind known as emulsion paint, an ICI product, very pleasant-smelling. At one point, just after the return from Devonshire, it was all on the floor, I, a moment earlier standing on a chair, having taken a header across another chair and the tall stool on which the bucket stood. Bravely postponing consideration of my bruises, I mopped up the emulsion paint with large cloths and slopped it on the walls, my wife following me round to even it out with a brush. It is quick-drying stuff, but we got the walls covered.

That part of the floor which lies under the carpet is still blue. The carpet arrived just as, a day or two later, I had finished staining the surrounding part black, an hour or two before I was due to set off to rejoin my wife at a hotel on the south coast. I left the carpet rolled on the landing. Also on the landing stood two planks of twelve-inch pine and an acreage of plywood. I caught up with the sun and, by 2nd September, had acquired the right, salty, *terra cotta* face, with thin white lines horizontal from the eye corners. I was writing, for Bernard Wall at the *Twentieth Century*, one of those relaxedly self-indulgent essays under the heading of 'The Month'. That is how, as for the previous December, I come to have note of so many *trivia* of the time.

I wrote at a green basketwork table, upon which a few ants scurried. I sat in a green basketwork chair set against the wall of a conservatory given over to ping-pong. I might have sat in a deck-chair reading P. G. Wodehouse, but all the deck-chairs had been bagged. They were set up on the pebbles below the fifty yards of sea-wall belonging to the hotel. P. G. Wodehouse was an author whom I had passed-up till that year. What really put me on to him was a radio script on Bertie Wooster, in a series of 'Favourite Characters', which I got from Richard Usborne, author of *Clubland Heroes*, who was then writing a book on Wodehouse (it came out three years later, at the time of Wodehouse's eightieth birthday). All comedy, Usborne contended, was innocent and based on innocence, hence the undying charm of Bertie Wooster. Although Jeeves had had to extricate Bertie from involvements with no fewer than fifteen girls, it was obvious that Bertie was still a virgin. Yet he was impelled by two moral imperatives, always to help a pal and never to reject a woman's proffered love. In the Wooster cycle, all the complications of plot arose from strict obedience to this dual code. At all costs, marriage had to be avoided. Jeeves would not like to work for a married man.

Not long before, there had appeared a Jungian book on *No Orchids for Miss Blandish* and, during the previous winter, a ridiculous Christian-Jungian study of Evelyn Waugh. It seemed surprising that no Jungian had yet published a volume on Jeeves and Bertie Wooster. There was no lack of animas, animuses, archetypes, actings-out and doubles in Wodehouse. For several hundred pages in *The Mating Season*, Bertie and the newt-fancying Gussie Fink-Nottle exchanged identities. Bertie had aunts, good and bad fairy-godmothers, but he was apparently fatherless, the source of 'the Wooster millions' magical. In other respects, Bertie was clearly a Faust figure, Jeeves his 'shimmering' Mephistopheles. And so on. No doubt similar profundities could be discovered in the Blandings pig cycle. As there were no deck-chairs, however, I should have to read Wodehouse in the hotel lounge after dinner or on my bed in the afternoon. In the morning, I wrote at a green basketwork table, scurried over by a few ants.

There was a parched lawn, then concrete, then the invisible pebbles, then the sea, in which a few heads bobbed. Three or four ships progressed slowly along the skyline. A bit to the right, that was the Isle of Wight. From time to time, white and pink sails appeared in front of it, as though expensive pleasures were afoot at Cowes. Across the lawn came and went mothers and daughters, business men in shorts, poodles, children. There were rather too many children, not all of them enchanting. A slim, brown daughter played jokari with the nicest of the mothers. A riding school was attached to the hotel, and sometimes the slim, brown daughter was to be seen about the lounge or at the entrance in jodhpurs and black velvet cap. France was seventy-five miles away and invisible. That would be Normandy, source of English kingship and of so much of our language and laws. Two hundred miles away (about as far as Manchester) lay Paris, where my daughter still was. The American wife nagged, it seemed. The husband was a distinguished historian, doing a year's research in Paris.

People went out before breakfast to bag the deck-chairs. There were even some who left belongings on them overnight. Others, of forceful corporate personality, having occupied a certain number of chairs against a particular bit of sea-wall the day before, felt (and communicated to timid would-be interlopers) that their position was established in perpetuity and that no amount of before-breakfast bagging could dislodge them. An epitome, I thought (and noted), of the development of human society, which is created less by the aggressive than by the abnormally timid, who are always there to put ideas into the heads of their intellectual and moral inferiors, the people without nervous systems. The days went by. A further development took place. Two north-country (Lancashire, I hoped) mothers, deprived of male protection but supplied with a portable wireless, a German girl and three children of whom two were particularly engaging and the third innocuous, had established an enviable beach-head near the steps, with four deck-chairs. From this position they had repelled a succession of discomfited newcomers. Then, one morning, a person or persons unknown having, with singular resolution, carried through his before-breakfast manoeuvres, the lawn was progressively stripped even of green basketwork chairs and tables, most of which stood below the sea-wall on the pebbles. Revolution was in the air. Stands were being made.

I tried Chichester and liked it. That evening, there appeared five unsmart Italian males. They went to bed early and were out of the hotel before breakfast. They were Ferrari mechanics. They spent all day at Goodwood, where on Saturday ace drivers were to keep it up for six hours, round and round. There appeared journalists and enthusiastic amateurs in red and sky-blue sports cars of their own. In the hotel yard, they sat in these curious little vehicles, revving them up, surrounded by groups of admiring biz gents in dark blazers with elaborate badges, put on as a form of dressing for dinner. In the cocktail-bar, knowledgeable shop was talked. An enthusiastic amateur in a sky-blue Berkeley, apparently collapsible, talked of Saturday's do at Goodwood as 'a needle race'. A journalist bought rounds of what he called 'haggis water'. He seriously offended an American correspondent by criticising his choice of vodka and tonic as a drink.

Back in London, the new buildings had risen to various heights. The nearest and lowest was almost finished, though some kind of superstructure seemed to be going on top, an incinerator perhaps or a water tank. The tallest building still had a long way to go before it reached its scheduled eighteen stories. Meanwhile, the new pavement and part of the road were being laid behind temporary walls. Suddenly, the road would be many yards wider, and crossing it would be a real adventure. I laid my carpet and started work on the book-shelves. I noted:

> Eisenhower is playing golf with Macmillan. They snub General de Gaulle in the most gentlemanly manner. This is hate-France year in world affairs. France is the Joneses we have not merely kept up with but ditched. They have no H-bomb. They do not hob-nob with our Russian and American fine friends.

A general election loomed again. I did not know how to vote or if I should vote. I noted:

> Politics has never been my subject, but I have a vote, pay taxes and am sometimes livid with political anger. I belong, I suppose, to the professional class. My salary is unambiguously salary, and so I pay my taxes in full. I thus help to subsidise the various tax-dodging arrangements by which persons in commerce

disguise their income. During the past year, for instance, I have contributed towards the cost of a million new motor-cars bought by and for tradesmen, commercial travellers, directors, executives and all kinds of other miscellaneous riff-raff. I also help to support the business lunches, the expense-account housemaids and chauffeurs, the farms, the trips to America. So do you, dear reader, especially if you are a teacher or do some other work directly useful to the community and are not able to recoup by participating in the racket yourself.

By upbringing, I am near enough a cradle-socialist. Atavistically, I *could* not vote Conservative if I tried (the pencil point would break or the pen splutter as I began to make a cross). Unless a third candidate appears, my only alternative to voting Labour is to stay away from the polling booth. This I have done at the last two elections. It seems to me that, on the one hand, the Labour Party is no longer socialist and, on the other, that no party in this country now represents the only interests much worth representing. In 1945, a Labour government instituted its Welfare State, whose principal beneficiaries (and it was then a good thing) were unskilled or half-skilled workmen. In 1952, a Conservative government craftily and silently converted it into a Business Man's Welfare State, without, however, too openly practising against the labouring interest. The Conservative Party is a business man's party. The Labour Party is the party of un-skilled labour. No party represents that twofold *élite* of highly skilled craftsmen and disinterested public functionaries, who do not even realise that they share a common interest. The one part of it sees itself as working-class and supposes its interest to lie with that of unskilled labour. The other sees itself as middle-class and goes on supposing the middle class to be made up of itself and business men. This *élite* of honest men could be very power-ful. Between them, its members alone possess the gifts and display the attitudes without which biz gents and navvies would not even have a human society to prosecute their silly warfare in.

The Liberal Party *could* represent this interest, but doesn't. Like the other parties, it is caught up in historical paradox, which partly bemuses it and which it partly exploits. Like all the old ladies in Kensington, it doesn't yet see that the Whigs of to-day are those who call themselves Tories, still pretending to stand for tradition and the landed interest, whereas the commercial interest alone is what they rest on. However, it does not look, in any case, as though I should have the opportunity of voting for a Liberal candidate. The only third force in my constituency is

Sir Oswald Mosley. It is a terrible thought that he alone now stands for the community of Europe. And so, once again, I shall have to abstain.

Luckily, as I say, politics has never been my subject. I touch on it only because I am writing an *air du mois* piece for a month which has a General Election in it. I sometimes feel, nevertheless, that I should have liked to live in a world in which all respectable grown men had their political duties to perform. Too many of us are left in a political vacuum, murmuring to ourselves lines like Yeats's:

> The best lack all conviction, while the worst
> Are full of passionate intensity.

The only duty we clearly and unmistakably recognise is that of combating ignorant or deliberate untruth in our immediate vicinity. If we are writers and if anybody is still willing to publish us, we do it, to some extent, publicly, but never without a feeling that it is hopeless and that our self-respect will be the only beneficiary.

I toyed with the idea of voting for Sir Oswald Mosley, but on the way to the polling booth saw the faces of two of his supporters in a Jaguar car. A Liberal candidate having at last appeared, in the end I voted Liberal. It seemed a rather silly thing to do.

XXVI

THAT autumn and early winter, I was on sick leave for three months. I had coughed blood, and X-ray photographs showed a patch on the lung. I was bronchoscoped for a possible cancer, then treated for pulmonary tuberculosis. I don't know to this day whether I once had TB. The main argument against my having had it seems to be that I recovered so quickly. This may have been due to the prayers of a handful of nuns and several hundred schoolgirls[1] at the Oratory, or it may have been due to the fact that I washed down my B-pas. powders with gin, it being characteristic of alcohol to make other drugs work faster.

If it was the prayers that did the trick, that organised praying was a mistake from the Catholic point of view. The fact was that, as I lay there in bed, I had been toying with the idea of doing a conversion after all, especially as under the circumstances I could no doubt go through the whole routine in my own home. 'The Devil was sick, the Devil a saint would be . . .' Once I got up, there was no further question of me becoming a Catholic, and so by the very effectiveness of its prayers the Church may have lost a convert.

There was a twofold reversion. The prospect of a long illness, conceivably fatal, induces relaxation of the mind and a carelessness for practical considerations. In that condition, I also thought of taking up verse again. Luckily, this also came to nothing.

The BBC lent me a television set. It came in December and was taken away in March, by which time I had been back at work for almost two months. I was relieved when the thing went. I had enjoyed a number of programmes, notably, I recall, a half-hour of Georgian dancers, the gliding women all modesty and soft charm, the men, with their uniform black moustaches,

[1] One knows what *they* can do, individually, in the way of producing *Poltergeist* phenomena.

incredibly athletic and bellicose, leaping (it did not seem possible) high in the air and landing *on both knees* or slashing at each other with sword strokes you would not have thought could invariably be countered. But the better the programmes the worse, I felt, would be the problem and threat presented by a television set, for the more time would one's family and oneself spend gaping at that small, bulging, hypnotic rectangle.

Luckily, the young seemed to be giving up television, which they had come to regard as belonging essentially to their demented elders. Still, one never knew when or in what direction the fashion would change again. Meanwhile, millions of older persons sat in front of those screens, neglecting their household duties, making no conversation with each other and gradually losing all sense of reality.

For that, I thought, must happen. It might well be that most people had never had much sense of reality, whether specifically 'in our time' or at any period in the world's history. From the medley of televisual images by which his waking and dreaming life was invaded, it might be that each viewer constructed a personal reality or unreality, though for every viewer the images were much the same and were not related to each other by any objectively significant order or sequence.

As in dreams, even the mere chronometrical sense was suspended. In my own case, I find that I retain many televisual images. They include railwaymen and trade union leaders discussing a strike, Tshombe of Katanga striding loose-limbed and smiling among people in a large room, Pierre Lagaillarde striding thin, conceited and bearded among other French paratroops in a barricaded Algerian street, a short, dark man called, it seemed, George Brown snapping at some journalist or interviewer at the beginning of a Labour Party conference. Because I had a television set in this flat (briefly in my room along the passage, then in the downstairs room) only during the winter of 1959-60, I have tended to think of the threatened railway strike, those troubles in the Congo, the Algerian revolt and the Labour Party conference as all taking place at that time. It has needed research to establish that the railway strike was averted and that the Congo troubles began much later in 1960, so that I must have seen Tshombe on somebody else's television set, probably that at the 'very pleasant farmhouse near Debenham' which Middleton Murry had visited four years before. Labour Party conferences take place in early autumn.

Just estimates of public figures and of the causes they represented or the disreputable games they were caught up in must, I thought, also be falsified not only by their general 'telegenicity' or 'telegeneticity' (the word could only mean that they had been begotten at a distance) but also by the accidents of the moment at which they had been screened. I think that I had good reason to favour Tshombe in the Congo, but I am sure that I was predisposed to do so by the fact that, alone among all those black politicians, he struck me, on television, as a man of engaging personality. I think equally that, during the past twelve years, I have had sound reasons for distrusting Labour Party and trade union leaders, but certainly the feeling hardened three years ago because on television their features and movements failed to engage either liking or respect.

In certain cases, the inbred stupidity of the face and the indurated smugness of its expression struck me as radically unamiable. Such-and-such a man was, I felt, one whom I should find insufferable in any context. It was not quite like that with the late Hugh Gaitskell. He might, I thought, be very tolerable in private life. But he would never be Prime Minister. People might want a Labour government. They might even want a non-socialist Labour government such as he would have headed. Though it was never said, what would prevent there ever being a Labour government headed by him was the fact that, obscurely, everyone knew that that face could not appear at international occasions as the face representing this country. The face of Harold Macmillan was full of caricaturable silliness, but somehow it would do, and Gaitskell's would not have done. I rather fancy that Mr Butler's would never do. I shall avoid saying what I feel about Mr Wilson's. There is a lot against him, but he is a Huddersfield man. During his childhood, my father worked in Milnsbridge and must have sold Mrs Wilson little Harold's first pairs of trousers.

Perhaps it is not a bad thing that some physiognomical reaction should enter into politics. It must have been so in ancient Greece. Perhaps the handsome Alcibiades looked a bit like Mr

Duncan Sandys. Certainly, by early 1960, one of my purely physiognomical responses had been proved to be not without substance. In the *Twentieth Century* 'Month' for December 1958, I had described Jacques Soustelle as having 'the kind of French face which means trouble anywhere in France'. But I fancy I had not seen Soustelle on television, only in newspaper stills. In any case, a few lucky deductions from a face are no consolation for the fact that people's dreams everywhere are disordered and robbed of personal meaning by a crowd of visual images imprinted on the retina under hypnotic conditions in what are supposed to be their waking hours.

XXVII

IN April, I went to Scotland with my
wife, who till then had never been north of Preston. First we
stayed for some days in St Andrews, then picked up a midget
tape recorder in Edinburgh, took a train to Glasgow and there
caught one of MacBrayne's 'buses by Loch Lomond and round
Loch Fyne to Lochgilphead, where we were met by 'George
Orwell's' sister and driven by her across the peninsula to stay
with herself, her husband and Orwell's adopted son at the
farm they had on the shores of Loch Craignish. Even there, alas,
there was television, but I remember those five days as the
pleasantest of my life since the war, with the exception of
certain days in Strasbourg twelve years earlier. The weather,
in the first place, was perfect. Our wholly delightful, wholly
non-suffocating hosts had a boat in which we chugged over a
glassy sea to Jura and picnicked in a small bay below the house
in which Orwell had spent much of his last three years.

There were puffins, oyster-catchers, guillemots. Seals lay
about on the rocks like giant slugs. The gulls were laying their
first eggs, which we collected on islets in Loch Craignish. I
was recording Avril's youthful reminiscences of her brother
and her account and her Scottish husband's account of those
last years on Jura for a composite 'radio portrait' of Orwell.
My own *Four Absentees* had already gone to the printer, and
later, in page-proof, I was able only to add or modify a few
details from all the new Orwell material I collected that year.
I dare say I should not have added much. *Four Absentees* was
meant to contain only 'what I alone could personally vouch
for' (about Orwell and about Dylan Thomas, John Middleton
Murry and Eric Gill). The bulk of what Avril herself recorded
I was later able to arrange from a transcript and print in *The
Twentieth Century*, where no doubt American scholars will
locate it. An audible copy of the eventual programme was also
made for the Orwell archive at University College, London,

together, I believe, with some of the material which had to be excluded. It seems, all the same, a pity that somewhere all that material is not in print and between boards.

This book is no place for it. This book is about my less interesting self. That self did not, in 1960, go round to the extreme north of Jura where the dreadful whirlpool episode took place. Still, I saw part of the island and, from the outside, the house itself (occupied then by a shepherd whom the Dunns did not know). I was able to exert such imagination as I possess on detailed accounts of that episode and others, notably a dreadful drive, with Orwell very ill, over muddy, pot-holed tracks to the port where he could be embarked for Glasgow. But life goes on, and there, for instance, was the adopted son Richard, whom I remembered only as a child not yet able to walk, who, two years later, but for a random grab of Orwell's hand, would have gone down into the depths of Corrievreckan and whom I last saw, a big, quiet-mannered youth rising sixteen, speaking with a slight Scottish accent, going back in a kilt (the tartan that of the Argyll and Sutherland Highlanders, his second stepfather's regiment) to a well-known public school near Edinburgh. For, despite the surname, those Blairs had never thought of themselves as Scottish, and 'George Orwell' had never visited any part of Scotland until he was in his forties and had earlier adopted a pseudonym partly, I feel certain, because at Eton and elsewhere he had been told that 'Blair' was a Scottish name, so that he associated it with grouse-shooting, adopting 'Orwell' because all his feeling of regional loyalty was to East Anglia.

To my Scottish friends, this may seem an ungracious thing to insist on. That very year, however, I had seen Orwell described in *The New Statesman* (by a Scot) as 'essentially' a Scottish writer, while earlier, in the same paper, a more eminent critic, V. S. Pritchett, had characterised him as the literary equivalent of 'a Scotchman on the make', a human type about which Orwell himself had been amusing. Only a fortnight or so before, between St Andrews and Tayport, I had mentioned to Douglas Young that I had noticed a tendency to describe Orwell as a Scottish writer, and Young had said, 'Well, of *course* he was a Scottish writer' (had said no more when I reminded him that I had known Orwell pretty well and that he had never visited Scotland until he was past forty). When *Four Absentees* came out, a reviewer of Scottish Christian name and Welsh surname was even to place Orwell, by non-fact, as 'Scots-born, English adopted', whereas (this, surely, is known) he was born in India of (as I firmly established that spring) a family whose only recognised non-English strain had been provided by a *French* grandfather, himself Anglo-Indianised, a teak-grower. I noted a similar display of non-fact in one of the Fridays only the other day.

It was on the last day of April, a Saturday, that my wife and I left Argyllshire. This I establish from the date on reviews of *The Greater Infortune*. I bought *The Daily Telegraph* and *The Spectator* in Oban, *The Times Literary Supplement* in Edinburgh. *The Observer* awaited us in London the following morning, the 1st of May. The *Telegraph* review was unfavourable, the *Spectator* one not bad, those in the *TLS* and *The Observer* gratifying in the extreme. A week later, *The New Statesman* and *The Sunday Times* printed heart-warming reviews.

The Greater Infortune was only half-new. The main part of it consisted of a revised version of *Saturnine*, which had appeared in its small edition seventeen years before. To this had been added a chapter from the early part of *The Lesser Infortune*, which had come out in Coronation year. It had been very unfavourably reviewed, and I myself was discontented with it. At the time of turning *Saturnine* into *The Greater Infortune*, I had also cut some fifty pages out of a copy of *The Lesser Infortune* and revised the rest in such a way as to bring it into line with *The Greater Infortune*, in which, for instance, the names of some of the characters had been changed, including that of the narrator-protagonist. I should have liked to publish the two *Infortunes* together, but unfortunately what I had come to regard as an obsolete version of *The Lesser Infortune* was still technically in print with another publisher.

Apart from the little monograph on Bloy and *The Lesser Infortune*, no new book wholly by me had appeared since 1947. There had been volumes I had merely edited, and there had been American and British paperbacks of my first novel, *The Blaze of Noon*, but otherwise nothing. I had begun to find this a bit depressing, and so, although it was not wholly a new book, the appearance of *The Greater Infortune* and the reception it got were important to me. The *New Statesman* reviewer had expressed the hope that it would stimulate Mr H. 'to a new bout of creation'. And so it was to turn out. *Four Absentees* was already at the printers. A critical book, *The Fourfold Tradition*, was advancing towards completion. Within the next eighteen months I was to write two novels. All this has been very good for *morale*. At the same time, it has exposed me with uncomfortable frequency to the ordeal by reviewer.

XXVIII

IT is difficult for a reviewer to be *really* nasty about a novel. He can say it is a bad novel, and he may even go so far as to say that the central figure is an unpleasant character and at the same time to imply that he is a *persona* for the author. That is nothing to what can be done when the author speaks *in propria persona* with some candour. In *Four Absentees*, I was sticking my neck out and could expect to be rabbit-punched. The same is true of the present work.

Four Absentees came out at the beginning of September 1960. It was reviewed almost everywhere at great length, in most cases very pleasantly, in one or two with a degree of severity. Dylan Thomas, 'George Orwell', Eric Gill and even J. Middleton Murry were cult figures, and my simple factuality seemed irreverent, though I had not said one finally derogatory word about any of the four men. *The Observer* and *The Guardian* were a bit shocked (*their* great man was Orwell). So was a Dominican priest in *The Tablet* (*his* man was Eric Gill). The real viciousness was displayed in *Peace News* and *Tribune*. The vileness of those two reviews was barely credible. I took no action. I do not much care for our libel law, which seems to me to have been designed mainly to prevent the denunciation of rogues in high places. In any case, I dare say neither paper could have paid much in the way of damages.

A book may also produce a crop of letters. Two that I had about *Four Absentees* brought to my notice facts which, had I known them before, would have caused me to modify certain passages. In Malcolm Brinnin's *Dylan Thomas in America*, Dylan is described as appearing with a horribly bloodshot eye and accounting for it by saying that he had scratched the eye-ball on a rose-thorn, in 1953, on his last and fatal visit to America. I had seen Dylan Thomas with an eye in that condition some years before, and he had accounted for it in the same way. This had led me to doubt Brinnin's chronology. After reading *Four*

Absentees, the chief pharmacist of a London hospital wrote to me to say that the condition of Dylan's eye might in fact have been due to an attack of iridocyclitis, 'a capriciously recurrent condition of possibly tubercular background. In short there may well have been more than one occasion when the horribly bloodshot eye was manifest.' The other really helpful letter came from Lewes and concerned Eric Gill. It enclosed a cutting from *The Brighton Herald* which showed a tablet, affixed by the Regency Society, at about the time *Four Absentees* came out, to the house in which Gill had been born.

It appeared that the address of that house had been wrongly given in Gill's autobiography. It should have been 32, not 3, Hamilton Road, Brighton. The tablet had been carved by Joseph Cribb, who was Gill's first apprentice in Ditchling. These facts do not directly affect *Four Absentees*, in which I had not mentioned Eric Gill's birthplace. I had, however, said that Gill's father was 'curate' at the Countess of Huntingdon's chapel when Gill was born. I quote my correspondent:

> He did not go there until 1887, five years after Eric's birth. When Eric was born he was teaching at the 'Western College' and on Eric's birth certificate he is described as 'Tutor'. It took a good deal of 'digging' to discover when he went to the C. of H. chapel – that it was not until 1887 appears quite clearly from the Trustees' minutes. Evan Gill, Eric's brother, still has the desk presented to their father by the pupils of Western College on his marriage in 1880. He had evidently resigned from the Congregational ministry in 1878 before coming as a schoolmaster to Brighton.

The newspaper cutting (its contents themselves the fruit of my correspondent's researches) contained a good deal of further information about Gill's family background and early acquaintance.

Were there to be a new edition of *Four Absentees*, the appropriate passages would be modified in it. As there may never be a new edition, those details will have to stand here as emendations to the earlier book. I may as well also correct two errors that were brought to my notice in conversation and one possible error noted by a reviewer. It appears that Max Plowman, one-time editor of *The Adelphi*, was brought up not as a Quaker but as a Plymouth Brother. The line from a poem by

Stephen Spender which I describe Dylan Thomas as quoting in war-time is apparently wrong (it doesn't follow that Dylan had got it right, but the fault may certainly lie with my memory). And the Dominican priest who reviewed my book in *The Tablet* said he 'could hardly believe that Fr D'Arcy used incense in his Low Mass on a Saturday'. The fact is, I nowhere say that it *was* a Saturday, and I cannot see by what clues my learned critic had decided it was. I do say that the vestments that day were white. As I understand this matter, it can only therefore have been the Feast of the Presentation of the B.V.M., 21st November, which that year fell on a Thursday. However, I find that I am not sure about the incense. My clearly remembered state of nauseous suffocation was such as incense would have been likely to help induce, but perhaps I have falsely reasoned back from the state to the provoking agent. No incense occurs in a poem I wrote very shortly after the occasion.

In the autumn of 1960, the memory was already twenty-five years old. Later that autumn, *Lady Chatterley's Lover* was brought into court. This was a book I had first read thirty years before. I had just read it again, in the American paperback edition. Ostensibly a review of that edition, a *TLS* 'middle' I had written was already in proof, but the matter came *sub judice* here before it could be printed. Barely modified, the article was eventually printed on the Friday two days after the legal decision. The effect was amusing. The previous day, *The Times* itself had carried a leader denouncing the jury's decision. But I quote Francis William's comment in *The New Statesman* the following week.

> The Archbishop of Canterbury is not the only one to be having trouble with his Bishops. Lady Chatterley has brought schism to Printing House Square as well. 'Ours,' said *The Times* sombrely, in a leading article that bore every mark of being written by the Editor himself, 'Ours is still supposed to be a Christian country . . . A great shift in what is permissible legally has been made. But not morally. Yesterday's verdict is a challenge to society to resist the changes in its manners and conduct that may flow from it. It should not be taken as an invitation to succumb . . . There is no appeal against the jury's verdict. But on the grounds of

decency and taste and even morals, it is still possible to express dissent.'

Along the corridor in the offices of the *Times Literary Supplement*, as in Woolwich,[1] other ideas were stirring. Even as the *Times* leader was being written, the worms had got to work at the *TLS*. 'As for the passages which have been so much debated,' said the *Literary Supplement*, kicking its senior sharply in the shins, 'the worst thing to be said about them is that they sometimes make one laugh. It is difficult to see how any young person could get a wrong idea from them, though no doubt it is unwise to scamper around in the rain gathering forget-me-nots.' And, turning the knife, it concluded calmly: 'The actual "description of the whole act" is done with great sweetness, with, moreover, many of the pitfalls clearly and helpfully indicated. Young persons of either sex are the last out of whose hands anybody should think of keeping this book.'

There has been much discussion of the trial since, and with some of what has been said, not directly against the verdict but against the choice of defence witnesses and what they were led to say, I am afraid I found myself in agreement. *Lady Chatterley's Lover* had become another 'liberal' cause.[2] Still, I suppose that even Mr Leavis and Kingsley Amis would have preferred the verdict to go as it did than otherwise. And so would I. In the controversy started later by the Warden of All Souls, *a tergo sed non per rectum* would have been my conclusion.

---

[1] The Bishop of Woolwich had given evidence for the defence.

[2] I understand that, in novels which I have not read, two novelists of exemplary high-mindedness, Iris Murdoch and Angus Wilson, have both since used the commonest of the celebrated four-letter words. I do not know whether either understands the meaning of the term, except in the most purely general way, but no doubt both felt that they were striking a blow for liberty.

XXIX

BUT I was not at that moment particularly interested in D. H. Lawrence. I was more interested in the French *nouveau roman* and especially in Alain Robbe-Grillet, on whom, by the time my Lawrence 'middle' appeared, I was doing a further *TLS* 'middle', as a year before I had done one on Nathalie Sarraute. I had therefore read all that these two had published to date, both in the original and in translation. By Michael Butor I had only looked at *La Modification* (and in consequence was to under-rate him in *The Fourfold Tradition*). I had read Claude Simon's *La Route des Flandres*, then very recent. The occasion for the Robbe-Grillet article was the publication here of an American translation of *La Jalousie*.

A translation of M. Robbe-Grillet's previous novel, *Le Voyeur*, had appeared here the year before. It had been concertedly attacked by an influential group of novelists who, in favour of consolidation, had decreed that there should be no more 'experimental' writing, had determined, as one of them elegantly phrased it, 'to run experimental writing out of town'. The translation of Mme Sarraute's earliest novel, as *Portrait of a Man Unknown*, had been received more kindly, later in the year. The term 'anti-novel' had established itself. The idea was not generally approved of, but it was there, and the fact was helpful. If, for instance, a publisher expressed to an author the opinion that what the author had given him would not do, because according to the standards of the day it was not properly a novel at all, the author could smile and agree and explain to the publisher that it was an anti-novel. To a minor extent, consolidation had had its day. A period of excessive conformity might soon begin to draw peacefully to its close, though at moments the invalid would still show signs of bad temper.

I greatly admired *La Jalousie*. I hadn't liked anything quite so much for years. Earlier, I said that, had that kind of thing been acceptable here, I should have wanted to write like Jouhandeau. To some extent, that still goes. I should still like to write easily, from day to day, without any preliminary scheme. I may yet find that it is a possible thing to do. But, especially to a lapsed poet, the new thing was very attractive, with its tightly formal structure, its spaced repetition of certain themes as in music, more especially in serial music, its classical regard for one or another set of unities. The high deliberation of M. Robbe-Grillet's art was something we had not tasted in the novel for years, unless perhaps in Miss Compton-Burnett. Henry Green seemed to have given up writing.

In the February of 1961, both Mme Sarraute and M. Robbe-Grillet were in England, with Marguerite Duras, herself a novelist of some originality. I had not previously met any of them, though I had had some correspondence with Mme Sarraute, who had written to me very flatteringly about *The Greater Infortune*. Mme Sarraute speaks English well. By descent, she is Russian-Jewish, though, despite the fact that her family did not leave Russia until she was eight, she had lived in Paris between the ages of two and five and so may well regard French as her first language. M. Robbe-Grillet, though a Breton, is 'very French'. The extent to which he does not know English is remarkable. I vividly recall how, in February 1961, after a luncheon party and a long and arduous recording, both of which had largely gone over his head because for the most part they were conducted in English, we entered a bar, and his eyes lighted up at a familiar notice. He read out: 'Guinness Is Good For You.' I tried to teach him: 'Guinness Makes Loose Women Tight,' but that takes a lot of explaining in French.

All the *nouveaux romanciers* seem to be Leftish in their political views and, that winter, to have signed a really seditious document against the Algerian war, as a result of which they were barred from all forms of government recognition, such as university teaching or appearing on radio and television in France. The French Institute here, after ringing up Paris, were allowed to give a party, so long as it was very small and discreet. M. Robbe-Grillet must then have been thirty-eight, all black hair and moustache, rather tall and, really, very good-looking. His fair, very *petite*, no-nonsense wife says, '*Il a trop de cheveux.*' When he becomes animated in discussion, the hair, which is wavy, tumbles down over his face. Being so *petite*, Mme Robbe-Grillet cannot always keep an eye on her husband at a party, so that the taller people with whom she is talking may have to report on how he is doing.

I missed some of the junketings, because I had engaged to speak on what thus turned out to have been an ill-chosen date to a combination of two undergraduate societies in Leeds and to spend the previous week-end at a country house near Huddersfield. By the time I got back to London, the French writers were themselves touring the provincial universities. So I did not, on that visit, see either Mme Duras or M. Robbe-Grillet again. I did see Mme Sarraute, who stayed in London several days longer. From the inscription in one of her books it was on 14th February that she dined here, but that is impossible. I was in Leeds on the 14th, which must have been earlier in the same week, if not the week before.

The first thing I noticed was that the nymphs had gone. The whole central area of City Square looked newly dug. The equestrian statue of the Black Prince still stood, chain mail over his ears. I did not remember that it was the Black Prince (and had to ask later). I thought it might be Robert the Bruce or Richard Lionheart. I don't know what the Black Prince had to do with Leeds. I asked the taxi man how long the nymphs had been gone. About a month, he said. There had been a lot of to-do. A lady who was sometimes on the Brains Trust on television had said it was a disgrace to melt them down, works of art. She'd said she'd buy them. Something had now been arranged (said the taxi man). The scrap-dealers' mouths had been watering. All that bronze.

As we approached the Parkinson Building, a huge, modern, whitish building with a square clock tower and (as the taxi man had said) a lot of steps in front, I caught a glimpse, to the left, dwarfish and insignificant, in shadow, of the old main building. There were twenty-four broad steps in front of the Parkinson Building. It was imposing. The modernity was a little modified by four classical columns. Ionian, I supposed, with those scrolls. I entered a vast, echoing, marble-floored hallway, with porters willing to take you up in lifts.

It was the English Society which had invited me in the first place. As I proposed to speak on Anglo-French literary relations, to offer in fact a preview of the argument of the forthcoming *Fourfold Tradition*, I had suggested it might be made a joint meeting of the English and the French societies. In my post-graduate year, I had been secretary of the English Society, and indeed I could almost regard myself as having founded it, twenty-seven years before. Things had improved since my time. Those reading Scheme A English now had to do only one year's Anglo-Saxon and had both Welsh and Old French as options. As between the English and French, I had ended up in a state of intellectual schizophrenia, from which it had taken me long years to recover. What I had really needed and hadn't got was, say, just one course of lectures from which I could have gathered that between the English and the French authors I was expected to study (and indeed between the two languages at every stage of their development) there had been regular interplay. I had never been allowed to discover that Gower wrote as much in French as in English or, contrariwise, that Charles d'Orléans wrote as much in English as in French, far less that the lays of Marie de France and the most important of the Arthurian matter in French had been composed in this country.

I talked along those lines. My host was a young Scottish lecturer in French. With us and the two hon. secs. at dinner in town was a man I had not seen for twenty-three years, my junior contemporary as an undergraduate, now a very senior lecturer in English, which, apart from a break in war-time, he had gone on teaching exclusively at Leeds, a man of the most perfect sweetness and distinction, kept sweet, my host supposed, by the affection of generations of his pupils.

The new Union Building was almost as grand as the Parkinson Building. As my host and I entered it the following morning, we were accosted by an Indian student who wanted us to sign a petition. It was to denounce Hammerskjoeld and the Belgians and to protest against the murder of Patrice Lumumba by the gangsters Tshombe and Mobuto. Neither of us had read the papers that morning and so did not yet know that Lumumba was dead. I'd supposed him a very great nuisance, anyway.

It was Shrove Tuesday. It was also St Valentine's Day and the Chinese New Year. We read the papers in a nice coffee-room. *The Times* compared Lumumba with the ghost in *Hamlet*. Markedly paranoid, he had been expelled from his first school for immoral conduct, so became a Catholic. There were photographs of the Queen driving a pony-cart and of Lynn Seymour dancing in a ballet called *Les Deux Pigeons*, presumably after the fable by Lafontaine which Edwige Feuillère had read on my last visit but one to Paris, almost five years before. A Russian rocket seemed well on its way to Venus. The local news was much as it would have been anywhere else. There were car-crashes, theft, fires. Twelve decrees *nisi* had been granted, for desertion, for adultery, for adultery *and* desertion, for cruelty. Eight people were on trial for creating a disturbance outside the Metropole when Gaitskell was there in December. Four of them were university students and one a lecturer. There was some business about a hospital matron in Barnsley. A miner, who had crowned his wife's lover with a bottle, had been conditionally discharged. The Humber forts were to be made a tourist attraction.

To-morrow's news was being made at that moment. In Woodhouse Lane, a young man was stabbing and kicking two youngsters because they'd looked at him. In Moscow, spontaneous demonstrators were breaking all the windows in the Belgian embassy. The equivalent demonstration in London would have to wait until Sunday, as such demonstrations commonly did, however spontaneous they might be. The Polish ambassador was expected in Leeds. His non-arrival was beginning to cause anxiety. The sun and the moon were preparing a total eclipse of the former, due just before twenty to eight in the morning, the day after next.

The weather was not at all bad. I greatly enjoyed my social frequentations. I might, I thought, have liked a life in the groves of Academe, but had spoilt my chances long ago. I got back to London in the evening of the day of the eclipse. Life in the big city went on as before, and so did the international soap-opera. I bought *The Evening Standard*. Kennedy faces big Soviet clash on Congo. Seventy-three killed in air-liner crash. Ice-skating team among victims. That had been outside Brussels. Somewhere, a test crowd had been chasing the umpires. There were to be no baby cheetahs for Charles and Anne.

The skyscraper outside was rising up by stages towards the horizontal arm of the tallest crane. By night electricity, by day new curtains, began to appear in more and more of the windows. In late March, *The Fourfold Tradition* came out. My daughter went off to do her term at the university in Montpellier. In April, the generals revolted in Algeria, and there was a threat of parachute landings in metropolitan France. One tuned in to France III. General de Gaulle made the famous speech ending, '*Françaises, Français, aidez-moi!*' The conscripts listened on their transistor sets, and all was saved. It had been a bit nerve-racking, not least because I fancied Montpellier might be a likely place for a parachute landing in force.

At Whitsuntide, my wife and I went to Montpellier. I had never before been south of Grenoble. I had not seen the Mediterranean. My first glimpse did not reveal it as blue, but as turbulent and of a leaden grey. The aeroplane had been doing a lot of bucking and shuddering, and when we suddenly began to lose height it looked as though we were about to plunge into the leaden swell, but the runways of the Marignan airport come right to the water's edge, and we touched down in good order. I liked Montpellier. I liked Palavas-les-Flots and Sète, where the Mediterranean turned out to be blue after all. As to Marseilles, it was pleasant, on a mild late evening, to sit outside the pre-fabricated restaurant by the chugging small boats' entrance to (and exit from) the Old Port, but it seemed to me that the people walking up and down the Canebière were uglier even than those along Oxford Street.

XXX

IN September 1961, there appeared a
small posthumous volume by Pierre Drieu la Rochelle, *Récit
Secret*. Its obvious interest was twofold. It contained, on the
one hand, the reflections on suicide of a man who actually
committed suicide very shortly after finishing the book. It also
contained the self-justification of a Frenchman who had collaborated openly with the German authorities during the Nazi
occupation of his country. The *Récit Secret* proper had first
appeared, seven years before, in the *Nouvelle Revue Française*,
and I had read it at that time. It was followed, in the volume,
by a diary kept from October 1944 to March 1945 and by an
Exorde consisting of documents intended to be read eventually
in court, though within a day or two of a warrant being issued
for his arrest Drieu had gassed himself.

Drieu la Rochelle committed suicide in March 1945. He
had previously attempted to do so in August 1944, at the time
of the liberation of Paris. The contents of the volume had all
been either first written or completed and revised between
the two dates. For their existence it seemed that we had to
thank a gross miscalculation on Drieu's part at the first attempt.
He says:

> *Ce n'est que par hasard que je ne suis pas mort. J'avais absorbé trente
> centigrammes de luminal, ce qui est une dose tout à fait suffisante.*

There was no editorial note at this point, and neither before
nor since have I seen the question raised in the French literary
press whether thirty centigrammes of luminal do constitute
'*une dose suffisante*'. It appears that in fact they do not. Thirty
centigrammes are about five grains, which, it seems, is
a normal clinical dose of luminal and would hardly serve to do
more than procure deep sleep. It could not be a simple mis-
print. It cannot, *e.g.*, have been '*trente décigrammes*'. You could
not say that. You would have to say '*trois grammes*'. A properly

calculated fatal dose would have been more nearly that amount.

Drieu portrayed himself as having been fascinated by the idea of suicide from the age of seven. He seemed to have learnt very little about it. Statistically, for instance, he thought it rare, whereas we know that the figures do not fall much short of those for road deaths (with, no doubt, the figures for unsuccessful attempts as much greater as those for road injuries). He had evidently believed in a non-Christian, Hinduistic kind of immortality, in which the personality was much diluted. All this was fascinating and must, to most readers of the NRF seven years before, have been disturbing. I had found it so. I had also admired the courageous lucidity with which it showed a man facing the death of his choice.

I had not, as I say in an earlier chapter, previously taken much interest in Drieu la Rochelle. I had never read any of his books, though before the war I must have glanced at instalments in the NRF of Réveuse Bourgeoisie. I must have learnt at some point during the war that he was editing the NRF in occupied Paris. I had heard of his suicide, though even about that I was not well-informed. When I first heard of it, I did not know there had been previous attempts. When I first read the Récit Secret proper, I did not know that the attempt there planned had failed, but merely concluded that the suicide had taken place at a date earlier than the one I had vaguely had in mind before. I did not imagine Drieu had been a particularly attractive figure. The one photograph I have seen shows the petulant, pouting face of a spoilt child. In a diary entry for as long ago as 1927, André Gide had commented on him thus:

Met on the boulevard Drieu la Rochelle. Since he announces to me that he is going to get married in five days, I consider it proper to invite him into a bar for a glass of port.

'Yes,' he tells me; 'it is an experiment I want to make. I want to know whether or not I shall keep at it. Up to now I have never been able to maintain a friendship or a love-affair more than six months.'

All these young men are frightfully concerned with themselves. They never know how to get away from themselves. Barrès was their very bad master; his teaching leads to despair, to boredom. It is to get away from this that many among them hurl themselves headlong into Catholicism, as *he* threw himself into politics. All this will be very severely judged twenty years from now.

First noting that passage in 1949, when the second volume of Gide's journals came out in English translation, I had merely been impressed by Gide's prescience. In a little under twenty years, Drieu had indeed been very severely judged.

Five years later, first reading the *Récit Secret* proper, I had simply felt that the time had perhaps come to be indulgent to the memory of those who had collaborated with the Germans. It did not occur to me that there could have been any case for collaboration as against resistance. We ourselves, at the time at which the question arose for Frenchmen, had been engaged in a desperate struggle with Hitler's Germany. A Frenchman who collaborated had been *ipso facto* an enemy of ours. It had seemed impossible to represent him even as a patriotic French-man. It could, one had felt, safely be assumed that his motives were of the basest. I had gone on largely accepting that myth for twenty years. I had accepted the war as in some way in-evitable. I had assumed that it must take much the form it in fact took. After reading the diary and the *Exorde* in the *Récit Secret*, I began to see the matter rather as I have presented it in an earlier chapter.

Sixteen years after the end of that war, we lived in a Europe dominated by the fear of Russia. There had been those who clearly foresaw that a defeat of Germany could only have this result. I looked up Jacques Doriot in newspaper files. His car had been shot up by an American aircraft in southern Germany towards the end of the war. Earlier, he had organised a French legion to serve on the Russian front, where indeed he had served himself for a while. He had been Pierre Laval's chief rival for leadership under Pétain. The two had been very different. As to Drieu, he had never been anti-British. Part of his diary had been written in English, and he had understood what divided loyalties kept Britain (as they keep her to-day) from belonging wholly to Europe. There had been no question of 'appeasement'. Drieu wanted a strong and equal Franco-British alliance, negotiating from strength. The new Germany had to expand in some direction.

Ou nous devions lui donner des colonies ou la rejeter sur la Russie.
Nous aurions été libres d'intervenir dans le conflit en temps utile.

That was how things ought to have gone and how they might well have gone. The Germans might have been standing guard to-day on the Chinese frontier, and we should have remained with strength unimpaired. There would have been no American bases in Europe.

It seemed clear to me that Drieu la Rochelle had been no meanly calculating opportunist. He was not in collaboration for the money, and I have never heard it said by his most severe detractors that he did any of those things for which the baser collaborators were justly hated, that he ever 'denounced' another writer or that he used his position to effect any private revenge. Indeed, there appear to be good grounds for supposing that not only Jean Paulhan, his eventual successor on the *NRF*,[1] recently elected to the Académie, but also M. Sartre owed their liberties and perhaps lives to his intervention with Otto Abetz, himself, it would seem, not a particularly unpleasant fellow. Even when things had gone as far and as badly as they had by the summer of 1940, when, that is to say, German armies were in Paris instead of Moscow, it was still consistent with his previously declared views to accept editorship of the *Nouvelle Revue Française* and try to turn it towards a European war against Russia. It must have been a bitter experience. Few of the better French writers went along with him. The Germans behaved increasingly like fools and madmen, alienating all the best of the French and driving many of them into fanatical resistance. Yet Drieu would still have claimed to be at once a French patriot and a good European. By the autumn of 1961, it had become less easy to deny him these titles.

Nous avons perdu, nous avons été déclarés traîtres : cela est juste.
Vous étiez les traîtres, si votre cause était battue . . . Plus tard, on se
penchera curieusement sur nous pour entendre un autre son que le son
commun. Et ce son faible s'amplifiera.

[1] Himself no collaborator, but, in the years immediately after the war, generously disposed to the rehabilitation of mild collaborators, when other people were after their blood.

Two years ago I found that feeble sound already much amplified. Drieu la Rochelle had been a man tripped up by history, which continues to play dirty tricks on us all.

I was in Paris the following month. I saw the Robbe-Grillet film, *L'Année Dernière à Marienbad*. I met Mme Sarraute's family. I met the third of the principal exponents of the *nouveau roman*, Michael Butor (and was able to improve the acquaintance a few weeks later in London). I also met Jean Cocteau, productive of epigrams but far more natural and friendly in his manner than I had expected him to be, and jolly, bumbling, sentimental Jacques Prévert. I was in Paris to record these two and M. Butor and a group of younger actors and actresses, who included the enchanting Suzanne Flon. I had seen her at the time of her *début*, fourteen years before, in Audiberti's *Le Mal Court* at the Théâtre de Poche.

No plastic bombs exploded near me. I found the Parisians gentle and sad, the taxi-drivers, for instance, apologetic and almost reluctant to take your fare. There was a half-day electricity strike, which immobilised the *métro* and one's lift to a fourth floor. Only the police were excitable. A curfew had been imposed on Muslims. Vast numbers of them formed a procession to protest against this, and the police went into action with what struck everybody as excessive vehemence. I played *boules* at Maisons-Laffitte. In the Tuileries, I tried to imagine just how things had looked, seventeen years earlier, a little before the liberation of Paris, to Pierre Drieu la Rochelle on the last walk he describes himself as taking on the day of that first suicide attempt.

XXXI

NO writing got done that winter. I had finished *The Connecting Door* in spring and *The Woodshed* in September. The latter could not come out before the following September, and there seemed little point in writing books faster than the publisher could get them out. I had started a further novel, but I put it aside, where it still is.

The Connecting Door appeared towards the end of January last year. While writing it and on taking it in to the publisher, I had more than once referred to it jocularly as my anti-novel. The term was used on the wrapper and elsewhere. I was not sure of the advisability of this, but thought that perhaps one publicity gimmick was as good as another. Inevitably, reviewers would seize on the term. They did. In some cases, they used it to knock the book. In others, it was good for a bit of extra space. I was compared with M. Robbe-Grillet, it being commonly added that the master would have found his disciple's work impure in its exemplification of the doctrine. By and large, the publicity was good. It was certainly extensive, and that is perhaps the only thing that counts.

On this point, the still youthful master and his ageing disciple were in agreement. In February, M. Robbe-Grillet was over here for the London *première* of *L'Année Dernière à Marienbad*. As we sat together under the lights in a television studio, he asked me how *The Connecting Door* had done. I explained it to him in terms of square inches of review, and he thought that most satisfactory. His own career, he said, had been based entirely upon the acreage of insulting comment to which his work had been subject.

I told him that the reviewers had said I was influenced by him. He asked me if they were right. The truth was, I simply hadn't thought about it. After some hesitation, I said that perhaps a little influence had crept in towards the end not of the book itself but of the process of writing the book. I don't now think that even that will quite do. As I indicated earlier, one thing the practitioners of the *nouveau roman* and their critics had done was to widen the area of public responsiveness, if only by establishing the 'anti-novel' idea. I could have told the winter-sports-tanned Frenchman sitting beside me under those terrible lights that the *nouveau roman* had given me courage, that he had provided me with a moral example, that suddenly, about a year ago, I had felt able, without misgiving, to do what I had long wanted to do.

My narrative method for *The Connecting Door* had been deviously evolved over a long period. Not without misgiving, I shall now try to explain some of the considerations involved. I am well aware that many a reader, willing to give his attention to the autobiography of a writer, may yet not care to think too closely about the inwardness of writing, especially in its more purely technical aspects. A few, however, may be interested, and I shall ask the others to bear with me if, for five or six pages, I now go into the matter like a man so lost to all shame that he regards his own work as of some importance.

If, up to the end of January last year, anybody had asked me how long it had taken me to write *The Connecting Door*, I should probably have said it took me about two months. In a sense it was so, but I could have given a very different answer. I was made particularly aware of just how different the answer might have been by one of the most flattering reviews the book got. The reviewer quoted a substantial passage as an example of Mr H.'s prose at its best. Word for word as it stood, I had written it seventeen years before, while still in the Army. I knew that the book in some way took up what I had briefly started then. I knew, too, that, while finally writing it (straight on to this typewriter, with two carbons and never a word blotted), I had sometimes had open on the table beside me the Strasbourg pages of an abortive, longer novel and that I had also consulted one or another of two radio scripts I had written after a return journey to Strasbourg in 1948, as well as a Frankfurt-am-Main script done the following year. That, during the past few years, I have published so much, and during the preceding ten years so little, does not mean that I have written more, but that I wrote with greater certainty, that things which had long been hanging about came suddenly *au point*.

In, I fancy, 1958, I had sat up till four o' clock in the morning, burning typescript. Dense wads of typescript are difficult to burn on an open fire, since you must at one and the same time, with a poker, let air in between the sheets and keep them from flying in a blaze up the chimney. I fancy I burned some two or three thousand pages (many of them in duplicate, it is true). Still, after the holocaust, there were some left, and I was able to call back a copy of the abortive earlier novel from America. In my youth, writing a book had been a matter of starting at the beginning and writing on until you had reached the end. In the case of *Saturnine*, most of which I had written actually in an Army camp, it had been a matter of sending home a few pages at a time to my wife. I am not sure I ever saw the typescript.

From *The Lesser Infortune* onward, things were quite different. That was already a book very much put together. It too had been abortively attempted in the Army, and in the published version (the putting-together done with happy speed in the summer of 1952, most of it again at Newport, on the same table at the same back window overlooking the same, small, pleasant garden, with the same typewriter, not this one, as, fourteen years before, had served for *The Blaze of Noon*), there are a great many passages about which I remember the precise circumstances of their composition. For instance, Chapter Two of *The Lesser Infortune* (now Chapter Thirteen of *The Greater Infortune*) was written in billets at Campsall Hall, near Askern in Yorkshire, in the winter of 1942-3, though it minutely describes an arrival in Ireland two years previously. The ammunition-moving passage in Chapter Eight was done, in hospital, the following summer. The description of a Lincolnshire beach in Chapter Seventeen was written in a small notebook on that beach in the autumn. The description, in Chapter Eighteen, of an Army pay office in a mill near Manchester was written at the table indicated on that mill-floor in early 1944. There are other cases. The stories, for instance, of Paddy Boyle, the wild man of the woods, of the guardsman with the matchbox containing a lock of hair and of the escaping prisoner were printed as separate stories in periodicals and anthologies during the war.

The four passages closely listed have more than a merely bibliographical relevance. All four are very *chosistes*, more so than anything in *The Connecting Door*. Elaborated only a little further, they might well have been found in a volume something like Robbe-Grillet's *Instantanés*. But, indeed, an Italian critic has traced my *chosisme* even further back, to *The Blaze of Noon*. In an article which characterises me as '*il padre del* nouveau roman,' he argued that, paradoxically, what was also called the '*école du regard*' was derived from a novel recounted in the first person by a blind man. It is a flattering idea, and I should have liked to accept it, but cannot. If there was derivation, it was devious or even merely *zeitgeistig*. As *L'Embrasement de Midi*, my novel had indeed appeared in French in 1947, but I have no reason to think that M. Robbe-Grillet read it. I am confident that neither M. Butor nor Mme Sarraute read it in either English or French at the time.

A literary cue for *The Connecting Door* had been provided, in 1944, by Kierkegaard's *Repetition*. In that book, the narrator, calling himself 'Constantine Constantius,' on the one hand recounts the amorous and religious difficulties of an unnamed young man, essentially K. himself in his situation of two years before, and, on the other hand, describes a return journey he had made shortly thereafter to Berlin in search of a 'repetition' which he equates with the 'recollection' of the Greeks and glosses, in Latin, as a *redintegratio in pristinum*, a search necessarily doomed to failure. What I began to write towards the end of 1944 concerned, in so far as it was autobiographical, a certainly doomed return journey, intended to achieve some kind of *redintegratio in pristinum*, which I had made to Strasbourg eight years before (the place being much in my mind, because the European war had by then reached northern Alsace, so that Strasbourg cathedral was to be seen in newsreel flashes at the cinema). *My* 'young man', however, was not, at that stage, in any sense myself, but, quite decidedly, a fellow-undergraduate poet at Leeds who, eleven years before and in Switzerland, had developed a religious mania which divorced him both from the cousin with whom he was in love and from any secular verse-writing, a psychiatrist of my acquaintance to whom I later showed his poems and his marvellous letters then concluding that my friend was psycho-sexually impotent in just such a way as I was inclined to think the break with Regine showed Kierkegaard to have been. At the same time, my return journey had been much involved with a religious and partly amorous crisis of my own.

I did not get very far with that first attempt. At a more superficial level, what I do in *The Connecting Door* I first did briefly, four years later, in a radio programme after a subsidised return journey to Strasbourg. It was, in the first place, purely a trick of radio presentation. Two of my earlier selves had had very different associations with the town. I thought it amusing to have them played by different actors and cause them to meet my third and then-present self (a third actor) on arrival at the station, letting the three subsequently work out their misunderstandings with each other, the two earlier selves, for instance, not easily understanding that there had been a war and that buildings had been destroyed, the second earlier self having been aware that there was probably *going to be* a war, but quite uncomprehending about the form it had taken (that, for instance, the local bomb damage had been caused not by German but by British and American airmen, supposedly allies of the French). But that 'Return Journey' programme was only one of two I did after that return journey. There was also a 'Portrait of a City'. In this I used 'interior' monologue, stream of consciousness, which I thought particularly suitable to radio. An actor, playing not so much myself as a man supposed in Strasbourg for the first time, moved about the city with all its carefully noted and reconstructed sounds, seeing, consulting a guidebook, keeping a notebook, hearing the music, climbing the steps to the cathedral tower, intermittently spoken to or speaking or catching exchanges of remarks in restaurant or street. The programme opened with early-morning bells, including the great *bourdon* of the cathedral, and his first spoken words ('At whatever time I awake, bells are ringing') were to become the first words of *The Connecting Door*.

The abortive novel (called at first *The Idiot Questioner* and subsequently, after some changes, *The Alibi*) made use of further Strasbourg-notebook material. Very largely autobiographical, it was again self-divided. The narrator, a publisher, was presented as being in Strasbourg (in 1948) as part of an attempt to reconstruct the life of an author, whom the reader was encouraged to presume dead. A hint of *nouveau roman* was already contained in the fact that whether the Frobisher-Leckie figure was in fact dead was left unsaid. A fair amount of what had gone into that book was worked over, twelve years later, in *The Connecting Door*. The original framework was one I meant to use again. In the novel more recently started and put aside, the somewhat differently envisaged publisher, Atha of *The Connecting Door* and *The Woodshed*, was to recount the later (and possibly last) years of an author who was Leckie of the *Infortunes*, again penurious unexpectedly and tormented by a notion that the unintended male beneficiary of Richard St Hilda's will, being an idealist, must, if he ever understood the full implications of his position, feel bound to insist that his wife make some offer of restitution, together with a fear that abrupt revelation might prove fatal, like that in Ibsen's play *The Wild Duck*. I had a number of alternative endings in mind, but, whatever happened (or did not happen), the laugh would have been on Leckie.

In a general way, autobiographical fact was to be increasingly diverged from. But, indeed, autobiographical fact pretty well ceases to be that when it has been worked over several times. At any rate, it is quite robbed of autobiographical feeling. And here perhaps I should also say that *The Woodshed*, which I went on to write immediately I had finished *The Connecting Door*, had also had its earlier mock-up, present-tense narrative framework and all.

A further effect of much revision is to set up a new, implicit time-dimension, to create, as it were, an extra grammatical tense, not actually used on the page. Most written narrative, whether fictional or not, is conducted in the perfect or past-definite tense (in spoken narrative, the French use their past-indefinite, and working-class Londoners differ from all other English-language speakers in habitually telling their stories in the historic present). Narrative much or little worked over in a past tense has, as its implicit further tense, the real present of the author writing, which, if publication is not much delayed, will be, to all intents and purposes, the real present also of the reader (no need, I fancy, here to go into the question of the 'period sense,' itself in effect a new tense, a kind of second present, with or from which books of the past are read). *The Connecting Door* and *The Woodshed* both tell past-tense stories within a present-tense framework. The past of *The Connecting Door* is 1931 and 1936. The past of *The Woodshed* is from 1914 to 1927. The explicit present of both is 1948, with a carry-over to 1949. But both were finally written in 1961, so that their present tense was a false one. I, writing, had a further, implicit present tense.

In my own life and in respect of other people's lives, I have become increasingly preoccupied by the past within a present which moves forward constantly into a previous future, so that the past recedes at every moment (by the time I was half-way through that sentence, its opening lay already in the past and its conclusion in the future, but now it is all in the past and receding, and yet it will be at least eight months before the reader has it under his eye). It seems natural, therefore, to me to tell a past story within a present-tense narrative framework, which may be either interior monologue or the day-by-day notes of a man presumed writing. But grammar itself almost imposes the procedure in a retrospective prose narrative of some length. In connection with Mme Sarraute, I pointed out in *The Fourfold Tradition* how easily a paucity of pronouns may defeat an undertaking like hers, both in the original French and, though somewhat differently, in translation. There are also too few tenses in our verbs. The pluperfect is difficult to sustain and makes unpleasant reading when it is sustained (a difficulty with which the attentive reader may have observed me struggling some few pages back, in writing this chapter), while neither in English nor in French is there any yet remoter tense. From a narrative in the past tense, all retrospection must be in the pluperfect, and no further reaching back in time beyond that is possible without recourse to typographical tricks which are almost invariably both irritating and confusing. A present-tense narrative surface gives you an easy retrospective perfect and, behind that, a pluperfect for occasional use.

XXXII

THE biggest of the trees between here and the Mercury is still bare, so that through the crude lacework of its twigs I can see the tops of the Mercury building itself, Kensington Temple and the Walls' house. A few weeks ago, I could not, because of the snow. Some days, I still cannot, because of mist. Presently, the tree will begin to develop its 1963 crop of leaves, so that again I shall not see those buildings from these windows. On the other hand, the morning sun will by then indubitably clear the skyscraper.

The year has not yet begun to take on a shape, and so I shall stop with 1962 and the long frost which confirmed its decay. That seems to mean that I shall have to end on a political note. I would not do this by choice. Looking back, from a point of vantage in 1963, over what I wrote mostly in 1962, I am appalled by the amount of sheer opinion it contains, especially of political opinion. I should like to explain this in terms of the fact that 1962 was a very political sort of year, so that, even when I was dealing with other years, the miasma crept into what I wrote.

I am not an opinion man. I am willing to formulate and express opinions, sometimes with gusto. But I do not hold them with much tenacity. I agree with Simone Weil that opinion is a substitute for knowledge, a form of the *imagination combleuse de vides*. As she says, you cannot feed on opinion. It is without nutritional value.

Certainly, I myself cannot feed upon the opinions in this book. I would not go to the stake for any of them, least of all the political ones. One's opinions constitute a personal ideology, and, as Simone Weil would also have said, all ideologies are idolatrous. One makes idols of one's private opinions and of the opinions one shares with other people and of the institutions which embody them. Far better cultivate Keats's 'negative capability' or any scrupulous agnosticism. Those opinions which at any given moment I could be regarded as holding (holding, as often as not, in reserve) are so many attitudes which I was at one time or am now prepared to adopt under provocation.

One is always much provoked. A particular source of provocation may cease to exist, a new one appear. One may then be said to have given up or adopted an opinion. Oneself provokes, but one's most provocative views were provoked in the first place.

Take, for instance, my retrospective views on Hitler's war. They were provoked, in the first place, by pity for Drieu la Rochelle. Since they are retrospective, their only real interest is historical, and I cannot feel passionately about them. I find, however, that other people can, because they are passionately addicted to retrospective views in conflict with them. Their passionate addiction then provokes me.

Early in 1962, for instance, the parents of a young demonstrator on behalf of the Campaign for Nuclear Disarmament said to me:

'They've got to protest about something. We did.'

The parents, who are my good friends, take little interest in politics now. In the late 'Thirties, they belonged to the Left Book Club, marched in processions about Spain or Czechoslovakia and demanded that Chamberlain should go. Now they look back on all that Leftishness nostalgically. Their progressively co-educated, artistic children, they feel, should in their turn enjoy something like that happy memory of an idealistic youth. They have never realised that their late-'Thirties clamouring did harm. The resulting war had not damaged them personally.

The young demonstrator himself told me, somewhat later in the year, that he would have liked to fight in the Spanish war. It had terminated two years before he was born. He was feeding on opinions his father had once held, opinions since proved false and, in any case, effectively abandoned by the father, who no longer used them except as a theme for cynical-sentimental retrospective musing.

In such a situation, the opinions I formulated earlier on Hitler's war may usefully be deployed for purposes of deliberate conversational provocation. In 1962, I was more than once strongly provoked to adopt the Drieu point of view. As Matthew Arnold pointed out, people experience great difficulty in rising from the unclean straw of their mental habits, and sometimes a provoked opinion may help.

Sooner or later, an intelligent member of any group in which this particular variety of conversational flyting takes place will usually say:

'We weren't to know.'

And I invariably settle for that. But, indeed, in a general way, the events of the year provoked me to the adoption of a number of what I should at one time have considered to be distinctively Right-wing political attitudes. I have not enjoyed this drift to the Right. I hope it will be reversed. I do not think it was mere perversity. The outside world seemed bent on provoking it.

New pseudo-nations achieved mock-independence every few weeks. Their politicians crowded out the United Nations with their votes and drove white South Africa out of the Commonwealth, to the accompaniment of loud 'liberal' approbation here. This did not prevent the Americans from persuading the U.N., under a brown general secretary, to persevere with the feud against black Katanga, previously waged in the main by Irishmen. Algeria was self-determined in June. Apart from Spain, no European country any longer controlled any part of the southern shores of the Mediterranean, to my mind a melancholy conclusion.

At home, too, there were signs of attempted mob-rule. There were quiet CND mobs obstinately squatting, but many of the same people appear to have joined noisy mobs later, certainly the October one outside the American embassy building in Grosvenor Square at the time of the Cuba crisis, probably the July one which broke up the Mosley meeting in Trafalgar Square. This, too, was a case of sons feeding on their fathers' opinions, for, whatever one thought of his record in the 'Thirties, Sir Oswald Mosley had become a mild enough figure, best ignored. Communist-infiltrated as it was, the Cuba mob appeared to consist in the main of CND young persons, which seemed odd in view of the fact that what the Americans were insisting on at that moment was precisely the nuclear disarmament of Cuba. Possibly more important were the two permanent mobs, the mob of petty speculators and the sheep-like mob herded by trade union leaders and shop stewards. Statistically, last year was, it appears, the worst year for strikes since 1926, the year of the General Strike. Caught between one huge interest and the other, it was beginning to seem impossible for any government to govern. A Labour government had never found it easy and had been brought down without much difficulty by the commercial interest. At times, it began to look as if the life of the country were grinding to a halt.

Myself, I stirred out of London only twice, once in early June to Dieppe and places nearby, once in late August to Edinburgh. I must have settled down to this book between the two trips, putting it aside in September to translate Chateaubriand's *Atala* and *René*.

The writers' conference, which so oddly formed part of the Edinburgh Festival, was extensively written up in the papers. It was a success in that sense, as well as in the sense that the high, drum-shaped hall was full every day except one (the Scottish day). I liked the city itself better than I had liked it in the past. I liked it very much indeed, and there were incidental delights. But things had not been well-organised for the writers, and all the public sessions were rather a shambles. The French writers did not come. The proceedings were, in general, dominated by the yammering of American writers, with whose dogmatic volubility only Angus Wilson seemed able to compete effectively.

I got a word in edgewise on the last day. I quote a *Times* report as being perhaps more accurate than my seven-months-old memory.

> The discussions to-day were opened by Mr Rayner Heppenstall, . . . and he emphasised what he thought was the special difficulty for British writers at present. The 'cultural situation' here was bad, and the causes were of the same kind as were bringing political troubles over the Common Market at the moment. Britain was geographically a part of Europe but linguistically a part of the English-speaking world. He did not know what could be done, apart from having this island towed across the Atlantic.

219

I had never rooted for the Common Market. Not that I did not think it a good thing. I simply did not believe that we were likely ever to join it, and there was no point in rooting for a thing you thought unlikely to happen and could not yourself affect one way or the other. In 1945 and for some years thereafter, as the Russians and the Americans began to square up to each other, I had dreamed of a European Third Force, a United States of Europe, generally Christian socialist in flavour and strong enough to call down a plague on both their houses. I still deplored the continuing American military presence in Europe. I would cheerfully have disbanded not only N.A.T.O. but also the United Nations Organisation and all but the white Commonwealth, if not indeed all but the link with greater Australasia, for it seemed rational that Canada should one day merge with the U.S.A. In terms of any conceivable nuclear war, their interests were identical and far removed from ours. But too many interests here were rigidly opposed to the European idea, the farmers, the trade unions, much even of the intelligent and comparatively disinterested Left, apparently about half of the business community, the small part, I imagined, and that which likes to sell rubbish in a big way to a captive consumer. Among the general public, not much governed by sharp self-interest, there were the interests created by sentiment, prejudice and language, this last to me the most important of all, though it was rarely mentioned. Even middle-class anti-Americanism had been brought in alongside native insularity and distrust of those who spoke other languages, for it appeared that the man most anxious to get us into the Common Market was President Kennedy. I found it difficult to believe that the negotiations were even conducted with sincerity.

Then, with the Cuba crisis, that we should go into Europe began once more to seem not merely practicable but urgently necessary. In that crisis, I could not find fault with Kennedy's tactics. He, however, was an American, and I was not. I listened to the relay of his speech just after midnight, during what, over here, was the first hour of a new day in October, and I must have been one of a very large number who wondered, just before going to sleep, whether London or some other city would still be there at breakfast-time and whether they would be conscious of the fact.

Perhaps a fair number did not get to sleep. I got to sleep. I have never lost sleep because of the H-bomb. It is not in the least a question of bravery. It is simply that the effects of nuclear warfare, being unimaginable, are therefore also unfrightening. The Bomb, favourite alibi of the young, is, in a real sense, pure fantasy. It will certainly not kill anyone who would not otherwise die. There would be a high proportion of instantaneous, unexpected deaths, the pleasantest sort for the person who does the dying, while, as things are, a great deal of painful lingering is done which in a properly devastated area would be curtailed by lack of food and other amenities. It may very seriously be doubted whether the detonation of nuclear devices, in any quantity, on or over large centres of population, could materially affect the sum of human suffering. It would simply be concentrated in time, which indeed seems to mean that it would in the long run be diminished. This opinion may be academic, and it might usefully form the subject of a debate in the Oxford Union. As a matter of simple, brute fact, however, I, for my part, find that I have experienced almost no fear on account of the H-bomb. On the other hand, I am afraid of the traffic every day, if not on my own account then on that of members of my family who have gone out. If one of them is not home at the time expected, the thought always uppermost is that he or she has been run over. With reason, both statistically and from observation of the behaviour of motorists and van drivers in London.

But the point about those few days and nights of obvious peril in October is this. If nuclear war started, I felt certain that the first Russian attack would be on our territory and that the Americans might escape. Nobody I spoke to seemed to know just who controlled what at the American land, sea and air bases in this country. Perhaps even the Russians didn't know. Whatever else happened, the Russians would have to bomb us, however reluctantly. The Americans, being a people notoriously liable to panic, might then at once have made peace. Physically, they would have remained undamaged. We should have ceased, in their 'defence,' to exist. Defend them, in any meaningful sense, we could not. All we could do was expose ourselves as an additional, if not an alternative, target. Yet we might not even have agreed with their choice of a *casus belli* in the first place.

To say the least, such a situation was unfair. No annihilation without representation. Any missiles based here must lie unambiguously under our control. Faced with a *casus belli* between the Russians and the Americans, we must be in a position to declare ourselves neutral if we chose (or even to favour the Russians). Too long had we swallowed that American myth of an indivisible 'defence of the West'. 'The West' was at least divided by the Atlantic, a fact as important in the age of threatened atomic warfare as it had been until the development, a few years before, of long-distance, massive-freight-carrying aircraft. Nobody here seems to have understood this. General de Gaulle understood it. Two months after the Cuba crisis, his rejection of the Polaris missile and his veto on our entry into the Common Market came together. His statement that we were not ready to become Europeans followed on the demonstration, at Nassau, that not for anything would our government give up the American military alliance. That alliance, it seemed to me, could only be justified on the basis of a total co-citizenship, allowing, among other things, for a freedom of movement amounting to mass emigration from this overcrowded island to the United States.

I could, I suppose, be thought anti-American in world affairs. At this point, however, I want to argue against the anti-Americanism of other people. There exists in this country a fifty-first-state complex. Ever since Hitler's war, the feeling has been that there was a danger of the Americans taking us over and that then the whole of the United Kingdom would become an entity of no more weight than, say, Idaho or Oklahoma. But this is nonsense. The population of the United Kingdom is not much less than a third that of the present United States as a whole. In any larger United States, which could no longer be merely the United States *of America*, we should have to constitute six or seven of the most densely populated states, with Eire in addition. There would be, say, twelve states of Canada and Newfoundland, at least ten of Australasia and the Pacific

222

islands, two or more of white South Africa and Southern Rhodesia. Washington (D.C.) might well continue to be the capital, unless the new government took over the abandoned U.N. headquarters in New York, Washington then becoming one of a constellation of provincial administrative centres. The distribution of voting power would be such that we might well expect the next President to be a Queenslander, an Ulsterman, a northern or southern Englishman and so on.

No doubt others toyed with similar notions. I formulated mine in much these terms the morning after President Kennedy's speech last October, a letter from *Encounter* arriving that morning to solicit one's views on the Common Market. At that moment, the European alternative seemed possible. But it would have to mean a complete severance of any 'defensive' alliance with America, including Canada. A purely European military organisation would at once have to take the place of N.A.T.O. At that point, the CND arguments might again be listened to with patience, not only by ourselves but also on the Continent. If, however, there were to be nuclear missiles in Europe, some would indeed still have to point fixedly at Moscow and Leningrad, but others at New York and Chicago. I thought we might reasonably assume that the American high command had already studied London and Paris as targets.

The whole strategic picture has changed since, by reason of the depressing fact that in February mushroom clouds were reported in the desert regions of China. Once again, General de Gaulle had been first off the mark, with his vague overtures to Russia a few days before and his talks of a Europe from the Atlantic to the Urals. As things are, we stand, economically and *a fortiori* politically, outside the Europe which exists, to which we belong geographically and from which language separates us. The reader will not, I dare say, find it surprising that a writer should attach so much importance to language. This book will have made it apparent that I am European-minded. But I am also English-language-minded. It seems to me that any serious political integration of Europe would require us all to adopt (in our case, re-adopt) French as a common legal, administrative and, as far as possible, learned and literary language. This, too, would no doubt provoke emigration on a very large scale. There would be no objection to that. The persistently monoglot should be granted every facility.

I fancy I should stay. At a pinch, I could adopt French as my language for all but domestic purposes and with old friends and tradesmen. I could, I feel sure, let spoken English in this country revert to the position of a mere dialect and the works of Shakespeare and Jane Austen become, within a generation or two, a matter for learned study. That, I think, would have to happen, unless either English were largely obliterated in America and what had once been the Commonwealth or some at-present-unimaginable political state of things kept us out of communication with the other countries in which English was spoken and written. We could never be wholly European while most of the people who spoke and wrote our language lived elsewhere and we remained in daily touch with them, if only by way of the printed word.